LAND of DREAMS

A Reporter's Journey from Sweden to America

By Klas Bergman

Merry Christmas Mum/Farmor!

Love from Peter, Katie, Luke and Ashley

© 2013 Klas Bergman

To Marga

TABLE OF CONTENTS

FOREWORD   5

Chapter 1. DREAMS   7
Chapter 2. CALIFORNIA: THE 1960s   12
Chapter 3. I AM NOT A CROOK   37
Chapter 4. MORNING IN AMERICA   64
Chapter 5. OH, BILL...   91
Chapter 6. THE DARK YEARS   113
Chapter 7. OBAMA--FAREWELL TO THE OLD
            AMERICA   136
Chapter 8. ON THE ROAD   155
Chapter 9. THE NINE   187
Chapter 10. WAR, WAR, WAR...   212
Chapter 11. AT THE EDGE OF THE ABYSS   232
Chapter 12. WHICH AMERICA?   259

THE AUTHOR   285
BIBLIOGRAPHY   286

FOREWORD

Land of Dreams – A Reporter's Journey from Sweden to America is a personal and political retrospective on my many years in the United States, from my arrival in Los Angeles in June 1960 to today's Washington, DC, with the country's first African-American president, Barack Obama, in the White House.

This personal portrait of America draws from meetings, interviews, books, and much travel, both for work and pleasure, from the Pacific to the Atlantic, and back again.

My boyhood dream about America growing up in Stockholm, Sweden in the 1950s was impossible to resist, and when I arrived as a young immigrant and student in California, that dream became reality, and I had, in a sense, come home.

I came to Los Angeles the summer when John F. Kennedy became the presidential nominee at the Democratic Convention in that city. Those years in the first half of the 1960s, dominated by the civil rights movement and the escalation of the Vietnam War, resulted in my political awakening. Little did I know at the time what was to follow during the subsequent decades, but my dream of America mirrored these years. It faded and it strengthened, as hope and disappointment took turns, but it never vanished for good.

America is still exciting, full of hope. It constantly surprises and impresses with its openness, optimism, idealism, and energy. But there is also much that is difficult to understand and difficult to accept about America, such as the distrust, the outright hostility, towards Washington and the federal government.

And such as the poverty; the urban wastelands; the weapons culture; the super-patriotism; the almost constant wars; the deep religiosity; the importance of social issues; the ignorance of the world beyond America; or the opposition to what the rest of the Western world sees as a fundamental right: health insurance for all its citizens.

Many non-Americans think they know America and that it's like Sweden and Europe. But the United States is more difficult to know and understand than many believe. There are many Americas. Which America? Those who generalize often come to regret it. What is certain, however, is that the United States is becoming more conservative, more religious, more individualistic and more hostile towards government, and that this is a fundamental difference between America and Europe that is only increasing with the years.

Today, America is characterized by political polarization and paralysis and by increasing economic inequality. The two parties are growing further and further apart as the ideological gulf widens. The old belief in consensus and compromise has all but vanished. No major legislation gets accomplished and the problems keep piling up. Where is America heading?

Still, Americans dream. The American Dream is ever present, and we who have come from other nations are also inspired to dream, perhaps nowhere more so than in our encounters with America's grandness and beauty. There are so many different Americas, and if you look, perhaps you will find them all. That's what I have tried to do during my years in America.

Silver Spring, Maryland in September 2013.
Klas Bergman

Chapter 1.

DREAMS

> "*I pledge allegiance to the flag of the United States of America and to the Republic for which it stands ...*"

The morning was gray and cool. The clouds, which would soon disappear in the rising sun's warm rays, still hung low, like fog, over the schoolyard at Santa Monica High School in California, on the edge of the Pacific. I wore a thin, short-sleeved shirt, like hundreds of my classmates around me, and I stood with my right hand above my heart and declared allegiance to America, while the Stars and Stripes ran up the flagpole.

> "*... one nation, under God, indivisible, with liberty and justice for all.*"

Classes could begin. The month was September. The year was the 1960. I was 17 years old and my American dream had become reality.

I really do not know how or why or even exactly when I started dreaming of America. But it was early in my teens, in Stockholm, my home town, in the 1950s.

My grandfather, Otto Wilhelm, had emigrated. He went to America from Gothenburg on the Swedish American Line's "Stockholm" and arrived in New York on August 7, 1923. He was 38 years old and married, according to the official documents at the Immigration Museum on Ellis Island in the shadow of the Statue of Liberty, in the middle of the entrance to New York harbor.

He followed his brother Charles, a 29 year old bachelor, who had emigrated and arrived in New York March 14, 1910 on the Hamburg America Line's "America." My grandfather left his wife and two small children in Stockholm, one of them was my mother. The two brothers never returned to Sweden.

My grandfather's two sisters never spoke of their brother, but my mother and my grandfather exchanged letters, so he was present in our home through letters and photographs. One of the photos shows a thin and serious man, with a pipe in his mouth, formally dressed in a dark suit, tie and hat, in New York harbor. He had, by then, an American family and lived in Brooklyn, in the Scandinavian neighborhood in Bay Ridge next to Leif Ericson Square where the church services at Salem Lutheran Church at the end of the 1980s still were held in Swedish once a month for a steadily diminishing number of old immigrants for whom Sweden, by now, was far away but still remained dear to them.

I wrote to my grandfather quite often, and he always replied, often saying, why don't you come, yes, you should come west, come and study, attend university, become an American.

That was how it started, really. I would be American. In time, everything around me - music, movies, clothes, sports, books – became American or connected to America. In the 1950s in Stockholm, jazz dominated the music scene, with Louis Armstrong and Dizzy Gillespie playing at the Stockholm Concert Hall and school bands like "Black Bottom Stompers" and "Storyville Creepers" playing Dixieland music at school dances all over town or as they marched through the western suburbs on the anniversary of the closing of Storyville in New Orleans, where jazz was founded early in the century. At Swedish Radio, where my mother worked, I often sat and listened to rehearsals of jazz programs.

Short-wave radio brought the jazz hour on Voice of America in the evenings. The theme song, Duke Ellington's "Take the A-Train" kicked it off with the characteristic piano chords followed by the deep voice of Willis Conover announcing, "Time for jazz - Willis Conover from Washington, DC - with The Voice of America Jazz Hour ..."

The sound quality was often poor, full of static, but it didn't matter. This was jazz, live from America...

I spent many afternoons at the U.S. embassy's library and read newspapers, magazines and travel books. I read American literature, mostly in translation – "An American Tragedy" by Theodore Dreiser and "The Grapes of Wrath" by John Steinbeck. Or Swedish books on America, like Vilhelm Moberg's epic four books about the first Swedish immigrants in Minnesota.

A book by Mezz Mezzrow, "Really the Blues," made a big impression on me. It was an autobiography about a Jewish boy, who early in life while growing up in Chicago came in contact with black New Orleans music. It had been carried north to the big city with black migration from the South, fleeing as black fled racial oppression and looked for jobs. Mezzrow learned the clarinet and identified with the black musicians, playing their music with them, together with such white musicians, as Bix Beiderbecke, Eddie Condon, and Gene Krupa. Mezzrow eventually moved to Harlem in New York and married a black woman and died in Paris many years later. I read the book several times and my American dream grew even stronger.

The book "Mr. Jelly Roll" about New Orleans pianist and composer Jelly Roll Morton also left a deep impression on me. I took piano lessons at the time, but I was never really able to play some of his compositions.

All the films I saw were American. I probably watched every Western that was ever shown in Stockholm in those years. Then the movie "Blackboard Jungle" came along, with Glenn Ford and Sidney Poitier and its signature song "Rock Around the Clock" with "Bill Haley & His Comets." My American dream turned into America fever.

That same year, in September 1957, nine black students tried to enter and study at Central High School in Little Rock, Arkansas. The school was going to be integrated. But they were stopped at the school's entrance by the Arkansas National Guard, commandeered by Governor Orval Faubus. President Eisenhower called in federal troops, who escorted the nine into the school, allowing them to start studying there. The contrast between the screaming, hate-filled white faces and the nine serious and, I thought, utterly brave black students was like an abyss. A young, very serious, almost stoic girl in dark glasses - Elizabeth Eckford was her name, I learned much later - made an especially deep impression on me. The following week, when it was time for essay writing in school, I chose to write about Central High School. I do not remember what I wrote, but I do remember being very upset. My American dream had been tarnished.

"The Little Rock Nine" are now, of course, central characters in the history of the civil rights movement.

I saved hard for the trip I dreamed of taking across the Atlantic, although it was not a given that I would be able to go. I only knew that had to, one day. I got a crew-cut, dressed in blue jeans and a T-shirt, just like James Dean in "Rebel without a Cause." I studied hard and was top of my class in English, I became a big San Francisco Giants fan, and I knew the names of all the fifty state capitals, all of them lying out there in the vastness of America, just waiting to be discovered by me.

When I finally, in June 1960, boarded a plane to Los Angeles, California to study at Santa Monica High School for a year, I was ready. I had managed to get an immigrant visa and my mother had tears in her eyes. The agreement was that I would only be gone for a year, but she knew…Six months before departure, she had given me the Swedish edition of Jack Kerouac's book "On the Road," and in it she had written, "For my son ... before he hits the road in the States."

Yes, she knew. She had also been "over there" as a student to visit her father, my grandfather, but she had returned to Sweden after three years. It had been much earlier, in the beginning of the 30's during the Depression. Grandpa had lost his job and had run out of money, and my mother never got to complete her studies at the University of Southern California in Los Angeles. Instead, they all had gone back East and settled in Bay Ridge in Brooklyn, where my mother, to keep the family going, had started to model clothes at Macy's in Manhattan.

Times had been hard and, eventually, she had gone home to Sweden, never to see her father again. And I never met him, my grandfather. He died suddenly just a few months before I arrived in America and is now buried in the hot sun in a small cemetery in Livermore, California.

Today, half a century later, I sit in my home just outside Washington, DC and think back on my days and years in America, a much different and in many ways a much better country.

Chapter 2.

CALIFORNIA: MY 1960s

"Go West, young man, and grow up with the country."
John B. L. Soule, Terre Haute Express, Indiana, 1851.

It all began in the far west, by the Pacific Ocean. When I landed in Los Angeles after the twenty-two hour flight from Stockholm, via Winnipeg in Canada for refueling, I am sure I had never heard of John Soule's call to "go west," a phrase that was later to be popularized by the famous newspaper man Horace Greeley of the New York Tribune. But I knew I had to go there.

My arrival, I remember, was a disappointment. Los Angeles, in my mind the city of palm trees and eternal sun, was covered by clouds and morning fog, and I only got a glimpse of the swimming pools in the gardens down below during the approach to the airport. It was chilly, and not at all what I had expected or dreamed of.

But I quickly learned about the weather in Southern California, for when we headed north from the airport on the Pacific Coast Highway, Highway 1, towards Malibu and my new home with a doctor's family high above the coast road overlooking the Pacific Ocean, the morning mist lifted -- "burned off," I soon learned it was called here in Southern California – from the warmth of the rising sun.

Suddenly, the sun shone from a clear blue sky. I could hear the waves crashing against the endless beach down below all the way up here in my new home above Las Flores Canyon.

To the north, I could see the surfers sitting on their boards like little black dots in the water outside the Malibu Pier, waiting for the right wave. To the south, big, wide Santa Monica Bay dominated the view and, behind it, on the horizon, I could see the bluish, almost pink, hills of the Palos Verde Peninsula. The California of my Swedish boyhood dream was spread out before me in all its glory. Had I gone to heaven?

It is possible that I decided already on that first day that I wanted to stay in America. One year would not be enough. What would I do back home, in Sweden? Go back to my old school and the familiar rhythms of that old life, to sleet and snow, to summer rains and dark winter days? Why?

Eventually, my year at Santa Monica High School, or "Samohi," was followed by four years at Stanford University just south of San Francisco in Northern California. During those years, I visited Stockholm only once -- hitchhiking through Europe, and visiting London, Brussels, Paris, Berlin, and Copenhagen. That trip home was exciting and made California seem far away, but I still felt I belonged in California.

My recollection of my years in California is of a young Swedish boy who slowly got to know America in an unplanned, unrelentingly positive, almost naive way. The State of California – the size of Sweden – that I encountered was idyllic. The 16 million inhabitants at that time have become 37 million, with over ten million in Greater Los Angeles alone. It had yet to overtake New York as the most populous state.

During my first year in California, the governor was Edmund "Pat" Brown, a Democrat. He had, in both 1958 and 1962, defeated conservative Republicans, including Richard Nixon, who after his 1962 defeat uttered the now-famous words to the press, "well, you won't have Richard Nixon to kick around anymore."

In 1968, six years later, Nixon was elected President of the United States.

Pat Brown, who in 1966 was finally defeated, by Ronald Reagan, has been described as the last of California's governors who could rule the state as if its expansion, population growth, and optimism would never end. He built roads, found a long-term solution to water shortages, pumped money into the educational system. Both primary schools and universities were reformed. He established regional health centers, reformed prisons by granting visiting rights and helping those who completed their sentences to find jobs.

Little did I know when I arrived in California in 1960, that the state and the whole country were about to enter their most dramatic and agonizing decade since World War II. And I was there during the first five years of that decade: the Bay of Pigs invasion and then the Cuban Missile Crisis; the brave and bloody struggle of the blacks for equal rights in the South; the assassination of John F. Kennedy; the birth of America's student protest movement at the University of California at Berkeley across San Francisco Bay from Stanford University; the nomination of reactionary Barry Goldwater's as the Republican presidential candidate at the party convention in San Francisco; Cesar Chavez's entrance on the scene as the head of the United Farm Workers fighting for justice for farm workers; the murder of black Muslim leader Malcolm X; the American invasion of the Dominican Republic; the escalation of the Vietnam War; the race riots in the Watts neighborhood of Los Angeles in the summer of 1965.

But my first year in Southern California was a year of school, of new friends, sports, swimming, beaches, jazz, and books. It was all so carefree. We went out to the San Fernando Valley, where today two million people live, and picked oranges.

The car-free village of Avalon on Santa Catalina Island, just off the California coast south of Los Angeles, was the loveliest and most peaceful seaside resort imaginable. At Malibu Pier, waves rolled in, day after day, to the surfers' delight, and skiing in the deep snow at Mammoth Mountain or at Squaw Valley, where the Winter Olympics took place in 1960, was hard to beat. I fished from the pier in Santa Barbara or in a boat on Lake Sherwood. I travelled up and down the California coast, mostly on a Greyhound bus – to Oxnard, Ventura, Salinas, Gilroy, San Jose, and San Francisco. During trips back to Los Angeles, I particularly treasured the moment when the bus would leave the hot inland just south of Paso Robles and San Luis Obispo and burst through the mountains at Pismo Beach, and, suddenly, the Pacific Ocean would fill the entire horizon.

Santa Monica High School had 3,000 students. Though the majority of was white, I also encountered America's wide range of cultures and races. I had black teachers, black classmates and black sports team mates. The atmosphere was open and friendly. One day I stopped in the middle of the school yard, as a cute black girl walked past. Eventually, I invited her to the Senior Prom. We got some surprised glances, but no comments, no problems.

Yes, Santa Monica, California, was far away from the South. I was often reminded of that, not least in May 1961, when the so-called Freedom Riders were attacked with intense violence and hatred in the South. Organized by a group known as the Congress for Racial Equality (CORE), blacks and whites of all ages traveled in buses from the north down to New Orleans to push for the integration of buses and waiting rooms and toilets in bus stations in the South.

In Anniston and Birmingham and Montgomery, the Ku Klux Klan wreaked near indescribable violence on the riders. The images of the violence on television and the front-page newspaper headlines signaled the start of a deeper awareness of the lack of justice and equality in America, and a new commitment to overcoming it.

Santa Monica, with its 80 000 inhabitants, was in the early 1960s a fairly ordinary, small middle-class town, with a more elegant part in part of the town, towards San Vicente Boulevard, and a solid black middleclass neighborhood around 20th Street and Delaware Avenue. But its location by the ocean made it special. The Depression of the 1930s had hit Santa Monica hard. Corruption in the city, which Raymond Chandler called "Bay City" in his detective novels, was widespread. Eventually, the Douglas Corporation started building airplanes in Santa Monica, among them the classic DC3, which created good jobs and greater welfare for the city's residents until the plant closed in 1968. The Santa Monica Civic Auditorium, next to my school, hosted the annual Oscars during most of the 60s. The neighbor to the south, Venice, was then a rather run-down part of Greater Los Angeles.

It soon became apparent that it was not easy to get around in Los Angeles and in California without a car. I hitchhiked a lot and took the bus when I couldn't find a ride with friends who had cars -- back and forth, between my home in Malibu and Santa Monica. The last Greyhound bus north from Santa Monica left at half past twelve o'clock on Sunday morning, along the coast with the sea to the left, past Topanga Canyon to my stop at the Sea Lion restaurant, where Las Flores Canyon empties into the Pacific Ocean, and then a long walk up the steep mountain in the dark on the meandering Rambla Pacifico and home to Sumacridge Drive around half past one in the morning.

In the summer of 1961, I worked six days a week for nine dollars a day at the elegant Beach Club in Santa Monica. I served ice cream and milkshakes. I got myself a bike and started cycling to work, down the San Vicente to the Club on the Pacific Coast Highway. I cannot recall that I saw many others on bicycles. Today, Santa Monica calls itself the most bicycle-friendly city in all of California.

After three years in California, I finally got a driver's license and could afford a car and the expensive insurance. I bought a light blue 1950 Ford for 100 dollars. A whole new world opened up. The car collapsed after a year and I bought a 1955 Ford Fairlane, a black convertible, for 200 dollars. One spring, it took me through the California desert and over the snowy mountains at Flagstaff, Arizona, and east on Route 66, all the way to Norman, Oklahoma.

As a young eighteen year old, I was often in search of jazz and black culture: Langston Hughes, the poet, performed at Samohi together with West Coast flutist and saxophonist Buddy Collette; I watched films like "A Raisin in the Sun" with Sidney Poitier and Ruby Dee, and George Gershwin's "Porgy and Bess."

We often drove to North Hollywood and listened to drummer Shelly Manne at his club "The Manne-Hole" since you didn't have to be 21 years old to go there, although we had to sit in the alcohol- free section. I didn't mind…I didn't drink, but it was a little humiliating to sit in the "kids section," especially one evening a year later at the famous jazz club "The Black Hawk" at the corner of Turk and Hyde Street in San Francisco, when Miles Davis and his quintet played.

It turned out that the great Swedish jazz expert Olle Helander also had visited the club that year. He described it as a place "where the best modern jazz can be found." In his book from 1962, "I jazzens kvarter," he wrote:

"The venue is small and inconspicuous. The walls are moth-eaten with black curtains; lightning is sparse and air conditioning nonexistent. The decor is spartan: a bar, a few, very small tables scattered across a diminutive floor space and a special partition for youth."

Exactly! It was an unforgettable evening.

In the summer of 1961 in Santa Monica, we often hung out at a little place called "The Blue Horn" in Venice, where amateur musicians played, often led by my school mate Steve on his flute. Radio station KNOB in Long Beach was a constant companion, especially when it broadcast late at night from "The Lighthouse," the jazz club on Pier Avenue in Hermosa Beach, the small seaside resort just south of Los Angeles. When I finally got there one evening, thanks to a friend with a car, it was just as I had expected it to be, out there on the edge of America, where the music competed with the sound from the crashing waves.

That summer between the end of high school and the beginning of my university studies, I started to read more seriously, books like "The Naked and The Dead" by Norman Mailer, "The Quiet American" by Graham Greene, historian C. Vann Woodward's classic "The Strange Career of Jim Crow." I spent very little time reading newspapers. Los Angeles Times was then not much of a newspaper, local and reactionary, and the New York Times was not read at all in California then. It simply did not exist. It was not until October 1962, during my second year at Stanford University, that the New York Times began publishing a West Coast edition.

The paper quickly became part of my daily student life; articles by Claude Sitton and David Halberstam from the South and Saigon, respectively, became highlights of the day. I became politically aware and, in time, radicalized.

The two journalists opened my eyes to the world around me in a way no one had really done before, and although I didn't realize it at the time, their reporting came to play a crucial role in my later decision to become a journalist.

Claude Sitton came from a family with a long tradition in the South, or more specifically in South Carolina, where his grandfather had been a tax collector for the old Confederate States during the Civil War and even owned a few slaves. Sitton grew up in Georgia and often worked in the fields with blacks to bring in the cotton. After World War II, which he spent in the Navy in the Pacific, he graduated from Emory University in Atlanta, Georgia and became a journalist. After a few years in New York, he became the New York Times correspondent in the South in 1958.

Over time, Gene Roberts and Hank Klibanoff wrote in "The Race Beat," their superb book about the role and importance of the American press for the civil rights struggle -- Sitton's reporting came to occupy a unique position. All the coverage of the civil rights movement came to be measured against his dispatches. Everyone read what Sitton wrote. He was the one with whom all other reporters compared themselves.

Sitton's return to the South for the New York Times took place four years after Brown v. Board of Education, the Supreme Court's historical and unanimous decision, which banned segregation in all public schools. But despite that decision, not a single school district in Alabama, Georgia, Louisiana, Mississippi, Florida, South Carolina and Virginia had by then integrated its schools. In North Carolina and Tennessee, only three school districts in each state had accepted black students.

The South was a part of America, Roberts and Klibanoff wrote, but it had become "angry, hostile, mean, and obsessed with race."

The battle at Little Rock Central High School in 1957 had not become a new beginning for the South. On the contrary, it had become a rallying cry for reactionary forces, the segregationists, and although Arkansas Governor Orval Faubus was forced to retreat in the face of the federal troops' presence and allow nine black students' entry to the school, it turned out to be a temporary retreat. The following year, Faubus closed all the city schools rather than integrating them. Attitudes had hardened, resistance increased.

Claude Sitton was in Greensboro, North Carolina a few days after four well-dressed black students from North Carolina Agricultural and Technical College on February 1, 1960 attempted to be served a cup of coffee at the cafeteria of Woolworth's retail chain in the city. It was the first of what would become a wave of "sit-ins" to force restaurants and public facilities to treat black customers on equal terms with whites. The "sit-ins" followed the Gandhi-inspired non-violent protest methods that Martin Luther King Jr. advocated and successfully used in the bus boycott in Montgomery, Alabama in 1955 after Rosa Parks refused to give up her seat to a white passenger and move to the back of the bus.

Sitton was present at all the major events of the civil rights struggle in the South during the first half of the 60's: the Freedom Rides in 1961, the University of Mississippi's admission of its first black student, James Meredith, in 1962; the vicious dog and water cannon attacks against young black protesters in Birmingham, Alabama in 1963, the Freedom Summer in Mississippi in 1964 when hundreds of university students, especially from Stanford University and Yale University, flocked to Mississippi in spite of the brutal murders that summer in Philadelphia, Mississippi of Andrew Goodman, Michael Schwerner, and James Chaney, three young civil rights volunteers from the North; and the march from Selma to Montgomery, Alabama in the spring of 1965.

Sitton's and his journalist colleagues worked in an increasingly dangerous environment. The State of Mississippi was practically in a state of war. The personal courage of these reporters was, to me, quite extraordinary.

Unlike most other newspapers in the South, which were owned mainly by white reactionaries and segregationists, the Nashville paper, The Tennessean, was different. It closely followed the nascent civil rights movement and student "sit-ins". The paper had a young reporter at the time named David Halberstam from New York and Harvard University, who had gone to the South, first to Mississippi and then to Nashville to report on the civil rights battle. I don't know if Halberstam and Sitton knew each other, or if they ever met. While Sitton stayed in the South, Halberstam eventually went to the Congo and then to Saigon at the start of the 1960s, where his reporting about that era's biggest foreign news story -- the war in Vietnam – became as influential as Sitton's reporting in the South.

As the war escalated, Halberstam's dispatches became increasingly critical of the role of the United States and of its forces in Vietnam. His reporting eventually resulted in the acclaimed book "The Making of a Quagmire: America and Vietnam during the Kennedy Era," which won a Pulitzer Prize.

"There were many parallels between Mississippi and Vietnam," Halberstam said many years later.

For Halberstam, who died in a car crash in California in 2007, his years in the South were clearly very important, both personally and for his career, and he returned there in the 1990s, writing his splendid book "The Children" about the young black student protest movement in Nashville, Tennessee in the early 60's.

Stanford University, where I was a freshman in the autumn of 1961, was certainly a well-known university in California, but not nearly the world class institution that it is today. It was called the "best in the West" and had just started to compete seriously with the Ivy League Schools, Harvard, Yale, and Princeton. I never contemplated applying to the East Coast schools. I wanted to remain in California, I was a "west coaster," and, by the way, I was against attending a school with only men – women were still not admitted to Harvard, Yale or Princeton.

Since its founding in the 1890s, Stanford had admitted both men and women – founder Leland Stanford's wife had insisted on that. But nothing was said about racial minorities, about blacks, Asians or Hispanics. In 1961, Stanford was a "white" university. I can only recall four black classmates in my freshman class of around one thousand. In 1964, 21 black students applied to Stanford of whom 16 were admitted -- still an embarrassingly low number. It was only after the murder of Martin Luther King Jr. in 1968 that Stanford began in earnest to recruit both professors and talented students from different minority groups.

Today, the numbers are completely reversed and the white students are, in fact, in a minority. Today, over 30,000 students apply to enter Stanford every year but only 8 percent are admitted. They come from every state in the union, plus 45 foreign countries. In 2009, the student body was only 33 percent white, while 22 percent were Asians, 10 percent blacks, 8 percent Hispanics, and 3 percent American Indians. This new diversity shows how America has changed over the last decades. At elite institutions of higher education, that change is a result of "affirmative action", i.e. conscious recruitment of qualified students from minority groups. Racial diversity in the student body has become an important goal in itself.

But at Stanford in the early 60s, there was little diversity. Whites and old traditions ruled. That became clear to me when the fraternity in which I lived, refused to let a black student live there after a few seniors had refused to accept him. Deeply disappointed in my classmates and in my school, I moved out in protest in the middle of the semester.

The following year, I was told that two black students had now been accepted. But I continued to live in an apartment off campus. I liked it. The freedom was greater and the student population in town was something of a motley crew. Many were older graduate students and fellows with different specialties. And it was just nice to get away from campus a bit, to see other things, meet different people, to feel a bit like an adult.

The writer Ken Kesey first lived on Perry Lane in Menlo Park just off Stanford's campus and its golf course, and then in the small village of La Honda in the mountains that separated Stanford and Silicon Valley from the Pacific Ocean. There, in forests with their huge rain-laden redwoods, Kesey gathered with family and many others, including the rock band "The Grateful Dead." In the summer of 1964, Kesey and some friends who called themselves "The Merry Pranksters" boarded a bus they called "Further," which was painted in psychedelic colors, and they rode it all the way from La Honda to New York. Tom Wolfe described the adventure in his 1968 classic "The Electric Kool-Aid Acid Test."

Kesey had come to Stanford in the late 1950s as part of the writing program led by Professor Wallace Stegner. In 1962, Kesey published his book "One Flew over the Cuckoo's Nest" and a few years later he wrote "Sometimes a Great Notion." Both books were great successes; a new star in American fiction was born.

I never met Kesey during my Stanford years, but I did meet him much later, in the summer of 1987, on his farm in Pleasant Hill, Oregon.

As the sun was setting, throwing its last rays of the day over the valley, the light almost magic, Kesey got off his tractor and sat down on a bale of hay in the middle a yellow field. Everything was still except for some cows mooing beyond a red barn with a big yellow star on the top of its gable. Kesey took off his sunglasses and wiped the sweat from his forehead. His bushy, white whiskers stuck out under a large, wide-brimmed hat. As he smiled, his bright blue eyes sparkled, but he was serious when he said:

"I love these fields and this valley, and I love to gather in my own hay. It's special to live here with my family."

Kesey grew up here and he returned here at the end of 1968, after the wild and chaotic years in California and Mexico. He stopped writing, withdrew, and said that he would rather live a book than write one. But he never really stopped writing. "Demon Box" came out in 1986 -- "In Reagan's chilly era, we must not forget the magic summer of love in 1967." And on the twentieth anniversary of the "The Summer of Love" in San Francisco, the city's public television station, KQED, broadcast a couple of programs on about Ken Kesey -- "American Dream."

"I feel really privileged to have been part of everything that happened in the '60s," Kesey said about the program. "It was all hot stuff and I sat there in the first row. Our minds had been put in a narrow box from which we were trying to escape, using drugs, art, music, and politics. It was part of all the other things that were happening around the country and which were related to John F. Kennedy and Martin Luther King Jr. It was a new vision, trying to get away from the old. We are ready for something new like that again."

In that summer of 1987, Kesey had long since stopped traveling. He was going to start lecturing at the University of Oregon in Eugene, nearby, at his alma mater. His friends from his years in California were still in touch, people like Ken Babbs, a major figure in "The Merry Pranksters," who actually lived next door, who came over to help gathering in the hay. Kesey's farm had cows, horses, peacocks and llamas, and the old bus "Further," now with faded psychedelic colors, stood on parade in a meadow not far away. Kesey had been unable to get rid of it, even though the Smithsonian Institution in Washington had asked for it. Music by Beethoven, "The Grateful Dead," Dexter Gordon, and Paul Simon's "Graceland" could be heard from a pair of large speakers on the balcony above the main entrance. The living room had a piano, and a bass, and a great stereo system. The floors were painted in psychedelic colors. One wall was covered in Native American art.

Around the dinner table that night a dozen or so people gathered, among them Kesey's brother Chuck, who owned a dairy nearby and who participated in that great bus trip in 1964. The discussion was about books, music, sports, and just daily gossip.

Kesey said he does not like to be interviewed -- observers should not be observed. He felt it led to Hemingway's death, to Mailer's destruction, and to Salinger's isolation. Still, the next day as he sat on that bale of hay in the lovely summer evening after a long day in the fields, he talked a bit about his writing, about his latest book, "Demon Box," about what he called "the come-down" years.

A few years after our meeting on the farm in Pleasant Hill, Kesey published "Caverns," which was followed in 1992 by "Sailor Song about Alaska," and then, in 1994, together with his old friend Ken Babbs, "Last Go Round" about the big annual rodeo in Pendleton, Oregon. He never really stopped writing.

"I hope that my writing style is one of change," Kesey said when his university gave him a prize. "I don't write like everyone else. I'm not a person who can be a member of a movement. I want to keep moving forward, towards new goals.

Ken Kesey died in November 2001, 66 years old. I am glad I finally got to meet him.

My four years at Stanford were intense years, and I struggled in the beginning with my studies. I quickly discovered that many of my fellow students were smarter and better prepared than I was, and that was both scary and depressing, and not so easy to accept. I was not alone in this. Many students, who had excelled in high school, maybe even been a top student, made the same discovery at Stanford. Some couldn't dropped out. Some came back.

There was never enough money, although I worked ten hours a week in the university library and served breakfast and lunch five days a week in one of the dormitories in exchange for three free meals a day. I played varsity soccer, part of Stanford's budding soccer program, together with two Nigerians, a sprinter from Ghana's 1960 Olympic team in Rome, a Norwegian, a Dutchman, an Algerian engineering student who came practically straight from his country's freedom struggle against the French and who after independence in 1962 had become part of a large group of young Algerians who had received scholarships to study at America's finest universities. And there was also a group of Americans who had tasted soccer for the first time in their boarding schools on the American east coast, and who had become smitten. We had fun, and some success.

Summers were spent making money to pay for my studies. One summer I watered the thirsty trees on Stanford's campus; another I spent in the heat of the furnaces at Pacific States Steel Corporation in San Leandro, across the San Francisco Bay. Good money, often over three dollars an hour.

When I came to Stanford in 1961, annual tuition was 1,260.00 dollars. I managed to cover that, through work and savings and through just living cheaply. The 50 dollars a month from my parents in Sweden helped a lot.

Today, annual tuition at Stanford is around 40,000 dollars, way more than what most students can afford by themselves.

As the years went by, my interest in jazz turned to rock and pop, particularly a new wave from Detroit and Motown Records: "Smokey Robinson & the Miracles;" "Martha & the Vandellas;" "The Four Tops;" Marvin Gaye; Stevie Wonder; Diana Ross & "The Supremes;" "The Temptations;" "Gladys Knight & the Pips." They, plus Otis Redding, Sam Cooke, Etta James, John Lee Hooker became an important part of my 60's in California.

Stanford University in the early 60s pretty much earned its nickname, "The Farm." It was an idyllic campus where students were not encouraged to be politically interested or involved --quite the contrary. The constant sun and the scent of eucalyptus trees perhaps contributed to this. That wonderful scent has followed me over the years reminding me of that campus of yellow buildings and their red roofs, and of its green oak trees on straw-colored hills above the campus. To the south, the valley we now call Silicon Valley, was full of fruit trees.

When the great conflicts of the time became a part of our lives, life on the campus changed.

The student paper, the Stanford Daily, which came out every weekday, reported on so many things: the Berlin Crisis, Konrad Adenauer and Willy Brandt, Communism, right-wing extremists in the John Birch Society, "Red China" and its membership in the United Nations, the Cuban crisis, and the death of Dag Hammarskjöld, the Swedish Secretary-General of the United Nations, in a plane crash in the Congo in the autumn of 1961.

Of Hammarskjöld, the Stanford Daily wrote in its lead editorial:

"A man of his stature, his stamina, his total dedication to bringing a lasting peace to an insane world has not appeared to take his place, and it seems unlikely that one will."

Ravi Shankar, Miriam Makeba, Joan Baez, and Pete Seeger came to the campus and played and sang; Senator Strom Thurmond from South Carolina came and spoke, as did author William Shirer, New York Times journalist Harrison Salisbury, Senator Hubert Humphrey from Minnesota, U.S. Communist Party chairman Gus Hall, Supreme Court Chief Justice Earl Warren, Governor Pat Brown, and Edward Teller, the "father" of the hydrogen bomb.

Roy Wilkins, the esteemed head of the National Association for the Advancement of Colored People (NAACP) visited, as did black writer James Baldwin, whom I had read back in Sweden, and who filled the large auditorium with nearly two thousand listeners. He spoke of racism and racial discrimination as "the American way of life" and to "undo a nightmare which has taken a hundred years to create."

On that same day that Baldwin met with Stanford's students, Martin Luther King Jr. was released from a jail in Birmingham, Alabama after new demonstrations there. In a telegram to President Kennedy, Stanford students protested against the treatment of King and of Birmingham's black citizens. The civil rights struggle in the South crept steadily closer and it slowly politicized ever more students on campus. Events in Mississippi eventually came to play a key role in Stanford's increasing involvement in the civil rights struggle.

"We do not want a 'happy' university," wrote the Stanford Daily as it praised students' increased political interest and involvement. The State of Mississippi, it said, was "a lawless haven for men who not only preach but also practice disrespect for law, order and racial equality."

My first years in America were also the years of President John F. Kennedy. My host family in Malibu supported Kennedy – and the fact that he could become the country's first Catholic president was not an issue with them. They said he was younger and more exciting than Richard Nixon, President Eisenhower's vice president, and America needed someone new.

Kennedy was my president when he declared on that snowy and cold January day in 1961 in Washington during his inauguration, "Ask not what America can do for you, ask what you can do America." His Peace Corps attracted me in particular, but it accepted only U.S. citizens so I could not join. And he was my president that gray morning on November 22, 1963, when I was on my way to the student union on the Stanford campus after a lecture and a friend told me that he just heard a bad joke: Kennedy had been shot. We laughed. At the student union only minutes later, I understood that it had not been a joke. Kennedy had been shot, in Dallas, Texas. He had been gravely injured, and he died. Everything at the university stopped. Lectures were cancelled. The big football game against the University of California at Berkeley was postponed.

That Sunday we went to church, and we cried.

Student body president Bud Wedin expressed our feelings in his statement: "With Kennedy's death, it seems also to die many of his values and ideas we held with him. As students, it's more than the death of a man or a political leader, it's the death of someone who represented so much of what we value and held to be good. His inspiration and guide will always be manifest."

In the spring of 1964, a year after the great civil rights march in Washington in August 1963 and his "I have a dream" speech, Martin Luther King Jr. came to Stanford. In Washington at that time, President Lyndon Johnson had launched a final push to get the new civil rights law passed in Congress. He succeeded, and later that year, Martin Luther King Jr. was awarded the Nobel Peace Prize.

King was invited by the Stanford Student Union to its major conference of student leaders from all along the West Coast to discuss the role of students in the civil rights struggle. Dozens of Stanford students were preparing for the Mississippi "Freedom Summer" to help with voter registration of the state's black population for the presidential election that fall. Bob Moses, head of the Mississippi project and one of the leaders of the Student Non-Violent Coordinating Committee, SNCC, was there.

The school's main hall, Memorial Auditorium, which seats a few thousand, was absolutely packed. The atmosphere was electric. Cheers and applauses repeatedly interrupted King's speech and the standing ovation at the conclusion never seemed to end.

Humanity's progress, King said, never takes place by itself. There is always a right time, and that time is now. We have made great progress, but we still have a long way to go. Mississippi cannot resolve its problems by itself, it has to have outside help, and that help must mainly come from America's students.

King had no doubt that segregation in the South was on its deathbed. The question was only, he said, how expensive the funeral would be. We don't have time to slow down now, he said. The civil rights struggle was an indispensable part of the struggle for American democracy.

Dennis Sweeney was one of my classmates. He and a Stanford professor named Allard Lowenstein were among the leading activists in Stanford students' involvement in the civil rights movement, particularly in Mississippi in the summer of 1964, where Stanford had more students involved than any other American university. Lowenstein eventually became one of the great political activists of the 60s, the man behind the "Dump Johnson" campaign that led to the candidacies of Eugene McCarthy and later of Robert F. Kennedy after Lyndon Johnson dramatic and totally unexpected announcement on television in the spring of 1968 that he would not seek re-election that fall.

Lowenstein and Sweeney worked together for many years but drifted apart over the years. They did not even meet for a long time, until one day in March 1980, when Sweeney walked into Lowenstein's New York office and fired seven shots at him with his gun. Lowenstein died a few hours later. Sweeney was pronounced a paranoid schizophrenic and put in a mental hospital. He was released in 2000.

His fate and Allard Lowenstein's political career are described in detail in the book "Dreams Die Hard" by David Harris, who came to Stanford a couple of years after me and who was close to both Sweeney and Lowenstein. Eventually, Harris was elected student body president and became a leading activist in the peace movement. He married Joan Baez and served nearly two years in prison for his refusal to fight in Vietnam. He and Baez eventually divorced. To me, Harris wrote in his book, the murder of Allard Lowenstein in March 1980 was the real end of the 1960s.

Kennedy and then-President Johnson had sent ever more U.S. troops to Vietnam, half a million by the middle of the 60s. All male students, even I as an immigrant with a "green card", had a "draft card" in my wallet in my back pocket.

As full-time students, we were pretty sure of not being drafted, but we were not totally sure. Thus, the war affected every male student personally.

Meanwhile, the Vietnam debate heated up more and more. Anti-war politicians like Frank Church of Idaho and Wayne Morse from Oregon came to Stanford and spoke. A student petition in the Stanford Daily declared the Vietnam War a violation of American principles and ideals and the signatories said they refused to fight in Vietnam.

In the spring of 1965, the first so-called "teach-in" about the Vietnam War took place in in a packed Memorial Auditorium with panels of experts both against and for the war. The speakers critical of the war -- I particularly remember the Chicago Professor Hans Morgenthau – were met with cheers from the students who kept the discussions going long into the night. A few days later a similar "teach-in" at the University of California's Berkeley campus gathered 25,000 students.

That same spring, a bombing campaign against North Vietnam commenced. The war increasingly came to dominate the public debate on Stanford's and other campuses throughout America. The civil rights struggle became a victim of the war as it faded steadily into the background and Vietnam became the focal point of the public debate. We read the I.F. Stone Weekly, the most outspoken anti-war reporting in the American press, and we read Ramparts, published in nearby San Francisco.

America's students became politicized and radicalized ever faster, starting at the University of California at Berkeley, where Kennedy was welcomed during a visit in 1962 and where his Peace Corps recruited more members than at any other university.

In the fall of 1964, the American student protest movement was born. It was called the "Free Speech Movement." We crossed the San Francisco Bay from Stanford and followed events on the Berkeley campus, which was wonderfully situated on the slopes of the Bay, with San Francisco and the Golden Gate Bridge on the horizon, and beyond that, the Pacific Ocean.

The students, led by Mario Savio who had just returned from a summer in Mississippi, demanded the right to political activity on campus and the right to disseminate political information, a right that had suddenly been revoked by the university. The whole university was paralyzed. Savio came to Stanford and appealed for support, and received it in a vote, by overwhelming majority, in the Student Council. At Berkeley, thousands of students protested, teachers went on strike, Joan Baez appeared and sang Bob Dylan's "Blowin' in the Wind." Students were arrested, revolt was in the air.

Milton Viorst wrote about the connection between the civil rights movement and the student protests in his book "Fire in the Streets" apropos Savio's summer in Mississippi. Had it not been for the civil rights struggle, Viorst wrote, the protests at Berkeley and other universities around the country would never have taken place. Prior to Berkeley, there was no student protest movement at American universities. Students were not even particularly interested in politics, but with the blacks' struggle in the South, the Vietnam War, and Berkeley's free speech movement, major changes followed.

In early 1965, the tables with political literature and brochures returned to the Bancroft Strip at Sather Gate, the main entrance to the Berkeley campus. The students had won, but their victory was short-lived.

Conservative winds, which had blown for a long time in California, and which were nourished by extremists from the John Birch Society, started to blow stronger in the summer of 1964 when the Republican Party gathered at their party convention in San Francisco - America's most liberal city - and chose the reactionary Arizona senator Barry Goldwater as its presidential candidate. Goldwater had shortly before the convention voted against the pioneering civil rights law.

"Extremism in the defense of liberty is no vice," was one of Goldwater's most famous quotations, and a petition in the Stanford Daily urged him to withdraw from the presidential election. It said:

"Few men are more unfit to be President, an ignorant war monger, gambling with our lives, repulsed by your hypocrisy on civil rights. You, Sir, are a dangerous man."

Barry Goldwater proved to have no chance against Lyndon Johnson (LBJ), who captured over 61 percent of the vote and 486 electoral votes to Goldwater's 52 -- winning in only six states, his home state of Arizona plus five states in the Deep South. Ronald Reagan had given the major nomination speech for Goldwater at the 1964 party convention in San Francisco, and in 1966, he defeated the incumbent Governor Pat Brown.

A major reason for Reagan's victory in 1966 was his campaign promise to clean house at the University of California at Berkeley, and one of his first acts as governor was to fire the University President, Clark Kerr, who, Reagan felt, had been too lenient towards the students.

LBJ's victory did not come to mean a lot for us students. Yes, Johnson had pushed through both the civil rights law of 1964 and the voting rights law of 1965, but he was also the man behind the large escalation of the Vietnam War, and his order to invade the Dominican Republic in February 1965 was more proof, as we saw it, of political cynicism and great power politics.

Fred, the son of a missionary who spent many years in Latin America and who played soccer with me on Stanford's team, was at the forefront of the demonstrations on campus against Lyndon Johnson's invasion of the small island-nation. Many years later, I met, by chance, Jim, Fred's father, in the Nicaraguan capital of Managua where he was leading weekly protests outside the U.S. embassy against the war in Nicaragua and U.S. support of the Contras.

Graduation in June 1965 came as a relief. I had now been in America for five years. I was tired and worried. We were all tired and worried. The increasingly bloody war in Vietnam had come to overshadow everything. Over half a million American soldiers now fought there. But it was not my war. I had begun to think about Sweden. What was it like there? Homesick? Maybe.

I didn't know much about Sweden, a country I had never lived in as an adult. I wondered about old friends, about my family. I decided I had to go and take a look. I could always come back to America.

So, in July 1965, I headed east, first by car on Route 66 through Flagstaff and Albuquerque and Amarillo to Oklahoma City, then down to Little Rock in Arkansas and over the Smokey Mountains to Asheville, North Carolina. Then, by bus, north. It stopped in Danville, in southern Virginia, where Jefferson Davis, the President of the Confederacy, had fled in the final days of the American Civil War after the capital Richmond had fallen to the Union troops. The doors to the toilets at the bus station toilets in Danville said "white" and "colored." I got back on the bus and continued north.

A month later, on Swedish-America Line's "Kungsholm" out on the Atlantic en route from New York to Gothenburg, I read a news telegram. Watts -- the poor, black ghetto in Los Angeles – was in flames.

Eventually, 34 people were killed, thousands arrested, and entire neighborhoods plundered, destroyed and burned down. And only half of 1960's had gone by...

Chapter 3.

I AM NOT A CROOK

"San Francisco in the middle sixties was a very special time and place to be a part of. Maybe it meant something. Maybe not, in the long run ... but no explanation, no mix of words or music or memories can touch that sense of knowing that you were there and alive in that corner of time and the world. Whatever it meant...There was madness in any direction, at any hour ...You could strike sparks anywhere. There was a fantastic universal sense that whatever we were doing was right, that we were winning ...Our energy would simply prevail. There was no point in fighting – on our side or theirs. We had all the momentum; we were riding the crest of a high and beautiful wave...So now, less than five years later, you can go up on a steep hill in Las Vegas and look West, and with the right kind of eyes you can almost see the high-water mark – that place where the wave finally broke and rolled back."
Hunter S. Thompson, "Fear and Loathing in Las Vegas," 1971.

It was Sunday morning, September 8, 1974, a dripping, sweaty summery day in New York City. I had been posted to New York by Dagens Nyheter to help with coverage from the United State for a few months, so that the newspaper's correspondents in New York and Washington would get some time off. My colleague in Washington, Kurt Mälarstedt, rang to check on what was going on. Everything was quiet, we agreed. He was going out with family and friends for Sunday brunch.

"I'll call you when I'm home again," he said and hung up.

Shortly thereafter, President Gerald Ford returned to the White House from church and announced that he had pardoned President Richard Nixon, who only a month earlier had resigned in disgrace, the first president ever to do so in U.S. history, and gone home to California.

Ford's statement meant that Nixon could never be brought to justice for his involvement in the Watergate scandal, which had begun in May 1972 and had led to the most serious constitutional crisis in the United States in modern times.

Abruptly, brutally, America awoke from the lazy rhythms of its Sunday morning. A storm of angry reactions greeted President Ford's announcement, which was totally unexpected. Reactions featured words like "conspiracy" and reflected the nation's shock.

Even some reactions within the White House reflected how controversial Ford's pardon was -- his own press spokesman, Gerald terHorst resigned with immediate effect.

"I have searched my conscience, I have sought God's help," said President Ford. "This is an American tragedy in which we all participate. It could last a long time, but only I can stop it, and if I can, I must do so."

Ford pointed out that there was no historical or legal precedent for a case like this. Serious allegations hung like a sword over Nixon's head and threatened his health. It could be months, perhaps years, before Nixon could get a fair trial, if ever. Nixon, said Ford, had already been cruelly and excessively penalized.

"We can extend this nightmare and re-open a chapter that is completed, "continued Ford in his brief statement on TV and in front of only a handful of reporters hastily summoned to the White House press room. "I am the only one who can turn this book page. Nixon and his family have suffered enough. "

A lead editorial in the New York Times the following day described Ford's decision as an affront to the U.S. Constitution and American justice, and as unwise, divisive and unfair. Ford's duty, the newspaper editorialized, was to ensure compliance with the law, that everyone was treated equally, and that those who committed crimes were punished.

There were just a few hours left until the newspaper's deadline at home in Stockholm. Frenetically, I started to write. Kurt rang again.

"Hey, is everything ok?"

"Well, not exactly," and I quickly told him.

Kurt also started to write frenetically, about the whole scandal that he had followed so closely for so many years and which had led to Nixon's historic resignation.

This is the background:

In the summer of 1970, after two years in the White House, President Nixon approved a plan to significantly expand the CIA's and the FBI's political intelligence-gathering activities.

The so-called Pentagon Papers, a secret Pentagon history of the Vietnam War, were published by the New York Times in June 1971 and then also in the Washington Post. The Supreme Court ruled unanimously against a government effort to block publication.

Some months later, a secret group nicknamed "The Plumbers" within Nixon's re-election committee broke into the offices of Daniel Ellsberg's psychiatrist in Los Angeles. It was Ellsberg who had leaked the Pentagon report to the press.

On May 28 and June 17, 1972, there were two break-ins at the Democratic Party's headquarters in the Watergate complex in Washington, DC. The purpose was to install listening devices on various office phones.

During the second break-in, five men with connections to both the CIA and the FBI were caught and arrested. One of them, James McCord, was also employed by Nixon's re-election committee and by the Republican Party.

At first it looked like ordinary burglary attempts and they were also described as such in initial White House comments. But, thanks to the hard investigative work of two young journalists at the Washington Post, Bob Woodward and Carl Bernstein, the whole story started to unravel.

In November 1972, Richard Nixon was re-elected president. Voters had not yet understood Nixon's role in the Watergate scandal, or its scope. Nixon's victory was overwhelming, capturing over 60 percent of the votes. The Democrat candidate, Senator George McGovern, won only in Massachusetts and Washington, DC. A few months after the election, McGovern, in a speech at Oxford University in England, said his loss was something of a "mystery" -- he had long believed that any reasonable Democratic candidate could defeat Nixon. But, he said, he now believed that no one could have defeated Nixon that year.

The statement showed how little McGovern really understood about the mood in America at that time and was described by Hunter S. Thompson, the eminent chronicler of those years, in his book "Fear and Loathing on the Campaign Trail '72" -- perhaps the best book ever written about an American presidential campaign -- in this way:

"The mood of the nation in 1972 was so overwhelmingly vengeful, greedy, bigoted, and blindly reactionary that no presidential candidate who even faintly reminded the typical voter of the fear & anxiety they'd felt during the constant social upheavals of the 1960s had any chance at all of beating Nixon last year – not even Ted Kennedy – because the pendulum effect that began with Nixon's slim victory in '68 was totally irreversible by 1972."

Thompson continued:

"After a decade of left bent chaos, the Silent Majority was so deep in a behavioral sink that their only feeling for politics was a powerful sense of revulsion. All they wanted in the White House was a man who would leave them alone and do anything necessary to bringing calmness back into their lives."

But the Watergate affair refused to go away after the election, mainly because Woodward and Bernstein, and the New York Times' Seymour Hersh, continued to dig. Their work was investigative journalism at the highest level.

In January 1973, the half a dozen men who were on trial for the burglaries at the Democratic Party headquarters were sentenced to various prison terms. A month later, a special Watergate committee led by the Democratic Senator Sam Ervin of North Carolina was created, and a special prosecutor, Harvard law professor Archibald Cox, was appointed.

On April 30, President Nixon dismissed his legal counselor John Dean, who had begun to reveal the embarrassing circumstances surrounding the scandal to a Senate committee's investigators. Then, Nixon's chief of staff, Bob Haldeman, and his domestic policy adviser, John Erlichman, were fired. Both were later convicted and sent to prison for their roles in the Watergate scandal.
On May 18, the Watergate committee began televised hearings. They mesmerized an entire nation and the world. John Dean testified against the president. Another White House employee, Alexander Butterfield, revealed almost casually that everything said in all the meetings at the White House had been recorded on tape.

The scandal gained a whole new, and much larger, dimension. Nixon refused to hand over the recordings and the dispute ended up in court.

In October 1973, the "Saturday Massacre" took place. Nixon's own Attorney General (Elliot Richardson) and Deputy Attorney General (William Ruckelshaus) both refused to follow Nixon's orders and fire Archibald Cox, the special prosecutor for the Watergate investigation. However, the third highest official in the Department of Justice, Robert Bork, carried out the President's order.

Many years later, after President Reagan had nominated Bork to the U.S. Supreme Court, Democrats in the Senate refused to confirm him.

Nixon continued to vigorously defend himself, including at a notable appearance in November 1973 before many hundred Associated Press journalists at which asserted that he was not a crook, and said:

"People have got to know whether or not their President is a crook. Well, I'm not a crook. I have earned everything I've got."

In the midst of these dramatic events, Vice President Spiro Agnew resigned after a corruption scandal in Maryland that had nothing to do with Watergate. The Republican minority leader in the House of Representatives, Gerald Ford of Michigan, was appointed to replace him in December 1973. On February 6 of the following year, the House of Representatives voted 410 to 4 to initiate impeachment proceedings against Richard Nixon. His fate was sealed on July 24, 1974, when the Supreme Court unanimously stated that the president could not refuse to hand over the White House tape recordings. When the tapes were made public, their damning revelations made clear that Nixon had lied about his own role in the Watergate scandal. He had, in fact, been fully informed all along, and had fully participated in trying to cover-up the whole scandal. The tapes contained what became known as "the smoking gun," and not even Nixon's most loyal supporters could doubt the president's guilt any longer.

Three days later, on July 27, the House Judiciary Committee voted 21 to 11 to impeach Nixon, declaring him guilty of attempting to obstruct justice. On July 29, the committee voted 28 to 10 to impeach Nixon for abuse of office, and on July 31, it voted 21 to 17 to impeach Nixon for defying the committee.

In the next phase, the entire House of Representatives was set to vote on the Justice Committee's recommendations and thus pave the way for an impeachment trial in the Senate. But Nixon, On August 8, in an emotional speech broadcast to the nation, declared that he intended to resign the next day, August 9. Gerald Ford was sworn in as president and spoke to the nation: "Our long, national nightmare," he said, "is over." A month later, Gerald Ford pardoned Nixon.

In a series of articles in Dagens Nyheter in the autumn of 1974, called "Voices after Watergate," I talked with Americans in various parts of the country about Nixon and Watergate and America.

Paul, 41 years old, a second-generation Greek-American teacher and author, maybe said it best during our conversation in his small apartment on Manhattan's east side:

"I'm angry, and I'm tired. I think many are tired. Not of Watergate, because it was unforgivable, inexcusable. But there is a deep, deep moral decay in this country and Watergate was just the tip of the iceberg. Watergate didn't surprise me. I sensed that Nixon was behind the burglary of the Democratic Party Headquarters though I wasn't completely sure. But maybe I was not as fooled as so many were. I did not see Nixon as a pope. But I'm surprised that no one in Congress seemed to be morally outraged.

An old American expression keeps repeating itself in my head: you know, you can do anything just so long as you don't get caught.

Those who say that the Democrats have always behaved the same miss the point. If you don't have moral leadership, you have no leadership at all. And what really scared me is that these guys, Erlichman, Haldeman, and Colson sounded like old Nazis. And when I saw them I said, shit, they are reflections of the man who hired them.

Nixon was a sort of a Frankenstein. I tried in vain to find something human in the man. Ford made a big mistake when he let Nixon go free.

I am not one of those who say that the system worked. The system, it's such a monstrous term. What can we offer the poor in this country? What are the priorities? There is such a widespread insensitivity. I don't blame the American people, but we have seen it all, we watched the bleeding and killing in Vietnam on television while we sat and ate our roast beef. What happens to a nation that is no longer allowed to yell 'stop, no more!'

Has America learned from Watergate? America is such a big word. I think the politicians have learned one thing, though I don't know how long it will last, and that thing is this: be careful. Yes, times are grim. When Kennedy was elected in 1960, there was lots of hope, lots of hope. We were naive perhaps, but since then it has gone steadily downhill. And why have they killed all those in whom we hoped? Why has it gone downhill?

I think Vietnam made this country bleed something awful. The rape and plunder of a small Asian country spread also here at home. Families were shattered. Young men were condemned because they did not want to go to war. But we did not ask why we were there; all we said was, 'let us bring our boys home.'"

Paul continued:

"I think Americans are more aware now. We have less patience. I'm not talking about the party faithful. They will always be there. But the public has become disillusioned. We've seen so much bleeding in this country, a lot of broken dreams these last ten years. I hope that during my lifetime, I am going to see a president, who not only gives us beautiful words, but who really means what they say when they say, 'come home America.'

I want to be optimistic, but I've become so tired. The defenders of the system say: this is a young country. But so many irresponsible mistakes are made and we cannot afford them. Young men and women are without hope. We need a spiritual reawakening. We need someone to tell the Pentagon that we do not need all those weapons. Our priorities are very frightening. Nixon was such a small, opportunistic man. The moral rot in this country goes so deep."

Ten years after that August day in 1974 when Nixon was forced to resign and when the American political system, indeed the whole country, was shaken to its foundations, the Watergate scandal was no longer on everyone's lips. Perhaps the silence was a sign that the fatigue that had set in after the divisive years of the 1970s that changed America? Nixon, after Ford's pardon, had tried to build a new life and had become an active writer and lecturer. Americans now spoke of his "vindication" and of "reconciliation".

But the Watergate scandal had become part of the American psyche, wrote the eminent political journalist Elizabeth Drew in the new preface to her book on Watergate. She wrote it was more than just a scandal – it came to symbolize a "fight for our constitutional form of government." She argued that Watergate had a lasting influence on the country's political system and that voters now demanded more from their politicians and that they were more wary of the abuse of power.

Others felt that the reforms after the Watergate scandal had already been eroded, that loopholes in the new laws meant there was no real reform, and that money and politics were intertwined at least as much now as before Watergate. Historian Barton Bernstein at Stanford University saw a connection between the Vietnam War that ended in 1975, and the Watergate affair. In one of our conversations ten years after Watergate, he pointed to widespread dissatisfaction with the political system in Washington before the scandal.

Watergate, he said, caused a "startling instability" in the White House. Bernstein thought that Nixon might have been able to remain in the White House if he had admitted his mistakes and intervened in time.

He felt that the Watergate affair was after all a less important event than a lot of other things that happened during the Nixon Years: the Christmas bombings against Vietnam in 1972, the coup against Salvadore Allende in Chile in 1973, the Paris peace negotiations about Vietnam the same year, the development of new types of nuclear weapons, so-called MIRV rockets.

But, added Bernstein, the Watergate scandal had led to a completely new way of resolving a deep political crisis in the United States: the President's resignation. That had never happened before.

"The Watergate affair took place because Richard Nixon did not understand our constitution and our political system," said Sam J. Ervin, Jr. when we talked ten years after the scandal in the library in his home in Morganton, North Carolina, a red brick building with white pillars at the entrance.

Senator Ervin, now 88 years old, had left Washington and retired to his home town. His library shelves were full of legal books. A bust of the old senator, which he himself declared was pretty good, stood on a side table.

He had always lived here, although his studies had taken him north, to Harvard University, and World War I had taken him to Europe's trenches where he was wounded twice and became a decorated war veteran. He had become a judge on North Carolina's Supreme Court and then elected to the Senate in Washington, DC.

That had happened in the same year that the U.S. Supreme Court had ruled that segregation in the country's public schools -- the so-called doctrine of "separate but equal," -- was inconsistent with the U.S. Constitution. As a senator from an old slave state, Ervin had fought desegregation almost his entire political career. He voted against the civil rights and voting rights reforms of 1964 and 1965. In 1974, though, he became chairman of the Watergate Committee because of his legal expertise and his thorough knowledge of the U.S. Constitution, and in the final days of his political career, he became almost a folk hero.

During our conversation, Ervin gave three reasons why he believed he had been chosen to lead the Watergate Committee: He had more legal experience than any other senator; the Republicans could accept him – well, they thought, he said, laughing, that he would take the task lightly; and, he concluded, he could not be suspected of harboring any higher political ambitions.

"Nixon and Joe McCarthy (the senator from Wisconsin who engaged in a witch hunt of Communists in the early 1950s) were the biggest abusers of power ever in the United States," said Ervin.

For him, Nixon had been guilty of something of enormous importance and magnitude. In the beginning, though, he could not believe that Nixon could have been stupid enough to get mixed up in the Watergate affair. Ervin then became convinced that the Watergate affair had been a carefully planned conspiracy and he felt enormously relieved when Nixon resigned.

Still, he added, he believed that the American people would have forgiven Nixon if he had declared that his associates had gone too far, and if he had put a stop to it in time. Nixon's fatal mistake, Sam Ervin believed, was that he refused to guarantee John Dean, his legal advisor, immunity from prosecution. This was why Dean became the Watergate Committee's main witness against the President.

"Dean's testimony was a gold mine," said Ervin.

The other big surprise of the hearings was the testimony of Alexander Butterfield, the White House staffer, who disclosed that Nixon had tape-recorded on tape all his White House conversations. Before we learned of the tapes' existence, we had no definitive evidence against the president, said Ervin.

Sam Ervin said that he had no doubt Richard Nixon was guilty. He thought Nixon would have been convicted if the impeachment process had been allowed to proceed to the end. Nixon's resignation prevented that from happening. Ten years on, he had still not been able to forgive Nixon -- "although," he said, "I do not believe in eternal punishment."

Ervin emphasized in our conversation his belief that the Watergate affair should not be forgotten. It should be remembered, he stressed, because it could be repeated if the men and women elected to higher office lack that quality called integrity, and if they do not understand this country's founding principle that it is the people who decide and have ultimate control over the direction of the country.

"At the same time," Ervin added, "the Watergate affair showed that we have a political system that can survive a major crisis and that the transfer of power from one President to his successor can take place without bloodshed."

This truly convinced me, said Ervin that the Constitution worked. It showed how wise our ancestors were when they insisted on dividing power. If all power had been with one man (the President), or a single authority, the Watergate affair would have caused the whole system to break down.

The years in America in the late 1960s and first half of the 1970s, were like one long political crisis. The civil rights movement was radicalized, there was the rise of black power – the Black Panthers in Oakland were on the other side of San Francisco Bay from Stanford University -- led by Huey Newton, Eldridge Cleaver, and Bobby Seale. Students for a Democratic Society (SDS) led a student revolt. In 1968, both Martin Luther King Jr. and Robert F. Kennedy were assassinated and Mayor Richard Daley's brutal police fought young demonstrators during the Democratic Party convention in Chicago. A year later, Chicago was also the scene of the big and scandalous political trial of the "Chicago Eight:" young radical political leaders such as Tom Hayden, Abbie Hoffman and Jerry Rubin were tried for their roles during the demonstrations at the party convention, and Bobby Seale was tied and gagged in the middle of the courtroom during the trial. It was as if the entire political left, the whole anti-war movement, was on trial.

By this time, Richard Nixon had made a political comeback with his narrow defeat of the Democratic candidate Hubert Humphrey, 43.4 percent of the votes to 42.7. Alabama governor and segregationist George Wallace - the third candidate in the election - captured 13.5 percent of the votes and won in the states of Alabama, Georgia, Mississippi, Arkansas and Louisiana.

With Nixon and Wallace capturing a total of 57 percent of the vote, the Democratic Party went down in a stinging defeat. It lost 12 million voters between 1964 and 1968.

This scenario had been made possible by President Lyndon Johnson's stunning televised announcement in the spring of 1968 that he would not run for re-election that fall. By then, the Minnesota senator Eugene McCarthy, spurred on by the Vietnam protests, had launched his candidacy and created a new sense of hope among America's youth. Johnson's decision had paved the way for Robert Kennedy's short-lived candidacy, which met its tragic end after his victory speech on primary night in Los Angeles in June 1968. His assassination, in turn, paved the way for Hubert Humphrey, Johnson's vice president, to run, and eventually losing by only half a million votes to Richard Nixon.

For Nixon, the election victory felt like sweet revenge after his losses to Kennedy in 1960 and to Pat Brown in the California governor's race in 1962. In Vietnam, the war and the bombings continued. In My Lai, it was reported, 400 Vietnamese villagers had been murdered by U.S. soldiers led by Lieutenant William L. Calley, Jr. The scandal shocked the world and further strengthened the peace movement. The invasion of Cambodia followed in April 1970, and this led to new protests throughout the country and to the tragedy at Kent State University in May 1970, when four protesting students were shot dead by soldiers from the Ohio National Guard.

Four million students went on a nationwide strike.

As Bob Dylan wrote in his book "Chronicles:"

"In a few years' time a shit storm would be unleashed. Things would begin to burn. Bras, draft cards, American flags, bridges, too - everybody would be dreaming of getting it on. The National psyche would change and in a lot of ways resemble the Night of the Living Dead."

My own view of America steadily darkened those years. I remember how, on the night of January 31, 1968, I was on duty at the Associated Press' bureau in Stockholm. I frenetically translated and edited AP's reporter Peter Arnett's minute-by-minute reporting from Saigon during the "Tet Offensive's" final hours and the attack on the U.S. Embassy in the South Vietnamese capital, and how I so wished for the war to end. It was not to come until April 30, 1975, when the last Americans fled in helicopters from the roof of the U.S. Embassy in Saigon that my wish was fulfilled.

Then, finally, the 1960s were over for me. By then, America had fundamentally changed, and so had the way the world viewed America.

Events at Stanford University, my old university, reflected those years' political radicalization, the chaos, the anxiety, even the resentment against politicians and against the Washington establishment. But what I witnessed as a Stanford student during the first half of the 1960s would prove to be like a mild summer breeze in comparison to the political storm of the next ten years with their almost continuous student anti-war protests.

The anti-war movement brought frequent occupations – and sometimes the burning-down -- of campus buildings. Bombs exploded.

The Viet Cong (NFL) flag flew from the top of the flagpole outside the campus post office, raised by members of the SDS -- Students for a Democratic Society. Constant political meetings and debates took place, some gatherings numbered as many as 8,000 students and faculty members. The special military study program, the ROTC -- Reserve Officer Training Corps -- was banned at Stanford and at many other universities in protest against the Vietnam War.

By then, the peace movement had edged out the civil rights movement and it came to completely dominate political activity at Stanford and other universities. At Stanford in the late '60s and early '70s, these two protest movements had acted in tandem. Now, members of the Black Student Union rarely attended anti-war activities.

In April and May 1970, in conjunction with the American invasion of Cambodia, there was something of a climax in the turmoil on the Stanford campus, with strikes, canceled lectures, the occupation of buildings, sit-ins, and fire attacks. Just 19 months after assuming office, Stanford's president Kenneth Pitzer resigned. In his resignation letter he referred to the continued deep divisions in America because of the Vietnam War and the lack of confidence on campus that promises of an end to the war would be met:

"The situation at Stanford represents another manifestation of the destructive nature of the current conflict. Both on campus and in society, support for reasoned discourse and nonviolent change has steadily diminished."

History professor Richard W. Lyman, who took over as Stanford's president in the autumn of 1970, wrote much later in his book "Stanford in Turmoil" about those difficult years, when the country's university leaders were tested like never before.

The civil rights struggle had by now reached the states in the north. Here, the battle was focused on school integration and school busing to achieve better racial balance in inner city schools.

In September 1974, I was in Boston, the capital of the reliably liberal State of Massachusetts. Screaming white mobs outside previously all-white schools in South Boston met in protest against the busing-in of black students from black neighborhoods, and of white students to black neighborhoods to integrate the city's schools.

The crowd threw stones and shouted "nigger, nigger" when the few black students who dared to try to go to school on that first day arrived.

Many white students stayed home that day, but Bill crossed the entire city to reach the black neighborhood of Roxbury to go to school. He was alone on the bus. Martin chose to play truant and joined the stone-throwing crowd outside South Boston High School in the center of the city's Irish working class district. Around 50 black students, and some 30 of the 1,500 white students who normally attended, showed up at South Boston High School that day.

The clash was spurred by a new law, the Racial Imbalance Act, together with a federal court decision in the summer of 1974 that ordered the city of Boston to integrate its schools through "busing." On this first day, over 18,000 students - 10,000 blacks and 8,500 whites – in 400 buses crisscrossed the city, to new schools in neighborhoods where they did not live, where they had few or no friends, and where most of them had never been before.

The screaming masses, their faces contorted with hatred, vented their anger and pain at the changes they were witnessing that hot, humid morning. But they could not do anything about them.

"I will never go to the same school as a nigger," a young white kid screamed.

"I don't care what color you are, but I won't send my son to Roxbury when he can go to school just a few blocks from his home," a distraught mother said.

Martin said he wanted to be loyal to the whole new thing. He thought about boycotting his classes for about two weeks, like everyone else, then he decided he would have to go, if he wanted to get into college the next year.

"It's mostly the older folks who are opposed to this," he said and pointed to a woman who was clearly upset.

His buddy Brian also stayed home that day. He had been assigned a school in Roxbury. He would have to go there in a couple of weeks. "I really have no choice," he said. "I want to go to school and I can only go to Roxbury High School."

For Bill, alone on his school bus, the experience turned out not to be not that remarkable. The morning in one of the city's toughest neighborhoods was quiet and peaceful. Teachers stood on the steps outside the entrance and greeted the students, every one of them black, as almost-empty buses rolled up in front of the worn-down, old school.

"My mom told me to go, because sooner or later I would have to do it and it would be just as well if I was there from the start," said Bill. This was not so special, he said. If only the parents would stay away, the students would be able to cope.

When I told Martin and Brian about Bill in Roxbury, they laughed and thought Bill was brave. Martin also admired the black students, who had come to South Boston that day. It could not have been easy, he said.

When classes began in Roxbury, 400 black students, and only seven of the 500 white students, had shown up. Kathy, a physical education teacher in Roxbury, was deeply disappointed. She had hoped for greater participation. What, I asked her, did she think of busing?

"As a means to get where we need to go and what we need to achieve, it is very important," she replied.

Overall, 67 percent of students were absent on this first school day in Boston. A week later, school attendance slowly increased, to as much as 75 percent, as compared to between 80 and 85 percent, normally. It was only at South Boston High School that the boycott continued to any significant degree.

Boston is where the American Revolution started. It is the capital of Massachusetts, the only state that voted for George McGovern for president in 1972. Boston was for a long time a city in a near state of emergency. Police on motorcycles escorted school buses and police on horses guarded the schools. In the following years, the number of students in Boston's schools decreased, and when the experiment ended in 1988, the number of students in the city had declined from 100,000 to 57,000, of which only 15 percent were white, even though the majority of the city's population was white.

The violent, even deadly days and months in Boston in 1974 and 1975 resulted in several American classics: Boston photographer Stanley Forman's photo "The Soiling of Old Glory" depicted a young white man using the American flag as a spear while trying to impale a black lawyer outside Boston City Hall, and in 1985 J. Anthony Lukas' published "Common Ground: A turbulent decade in the lives of three American families." The photo and the book both won Pulitzer Prizes. The book is one of the best books on the American society that I have ever read, a superb chronicle of a city and its inhabitants.

1976 was an election year. President Gerald Ford failed to be reelected. The Watergate scandal and a weak economy paved the way for Jimmy Carter's election victory. The choice was also a reaction against the Republicans, who by then had held the presidency for eight years. The voters wanted a change. Still, Carter won only 50.1 percent of the votes. It was a year when the entire West Coast, which today is solidly Democratic, voted for the Republican candidate, and when the South supported the Democratic candidate. No other Democratic presidential candidate, not even Bill Clinton – also a former Democratic Southern governor – has come close to Carter's success in South in 1976.

But Jimmy Carter's four years in the White House were tough years, full of conflict and crises -- oil, a weak economy with high inflation, the occupation of the U.S. embassy in Tehran and the subsequent year-long hostage crisis including a disastrous rescue attempt.

Carter also acknowledged the somber times in a speech to the nation in July 1979 that came to be known as "The Malaise Speech." Viewed today, the speech does not seem that remarkable, but the mood in an already bleak America became even gloomier. Carter spoke of a "crisis of confidence" in America which sowed doubt in every American's life and, yes, threatened to destroy the country. This doubt, this confidence crisis, the country's spiritual crisis, has evolved over a long time, said Carter:

"We were sure that ours was a nation of the ballot, not the bullet, until the murders of John Kennedy and Robert Kennedy and Martin Luther King, Jr. We were taught that our armies were always invincible and our causes were always just, only to sufferings the agony of Vietnam. We respected the Presidency as a place of honor until the shock of Watergate."

We now need to rebuild confidence, urged Carter. It was time that we took each other by the hand and together brought the American spirit back to life. Working together, he said, we could not fail.

Carter never got the chance. The anniversary of the hostage crisis in Teheran came on Election Day, November 4, 1980, and voters were reminded that 52 Americans were still being held captive in the occupied U.S. embassy in Tehran. The Democrats' loss was huge. Carter and his vice presidential candidate Walter Mondale captured only six states – their home states of Georgia and Minnesota, plus Hawaii, Maryland, Rhode Island, and West Virginia.

In New York, a month after the election, John Lennon was shot to death. And on the very same day that Ronald Reagan was sworn into office, on January 20, 1981, the hostages in Tehran were set free. The 1970s were over. A new era waited, the Ronald Reagan era.

The 1970s Watergate scandal paved the way for a new approach in the United States to politics and politicians and to the government and Congress in Washington. In addition, the role of journalism had been magnified by the assiduous investigative journalism of Woodward, Bernstein, and Hersh. There was a journalism renaissance. Journalism schools across the country were flooded with new students, who all wanted to be investigative journalists and expose scandals like Watergate.

The American public had developed a new and healthy skepticism towards all those in power.

Robert Parry, a veteran liberal journalist in Washington, wrote in his book, "Secrecy & Privilege" that the Watergate scandal also became the beginning of a conservative "backlash" against the liberal press, which the right wing thought had gone too far, and against what they called misdirected reforms in Congress. Watergate, Nixon's resignation in 1974, and the South Vietnamese regime's collapse in 1975, were low points for the conservative movement in the United States, according to Parry.

However, these historical watersheds were also the start of the new right-wing infrastructure that would reshape American politics. Wrote Parry:

"Out of the ashes of Nixon's resignation would rise a powerful network of think tanks, attack groups and media outlets, a counter-establishment financed by wealthy conservatives determined to protect a future Republican President from another Watergate."

The Watergate scandal led to a series of reforms aimed at cleaning up and repairing the political system and at restoring voters' confidence in their elected representatives in Washington. New institutions and practices became part of the American political landscape: they included tighter control over the president's personal appointments, better monitoring of CIA intelligence. There were reforms related to ethics, such as on lobbying, rules for how members of Congress should account for their income and finances, and provisions were made for the appointment of an independent counsel, like the Watergate prosecutor, whenever needed to investigate potential scandals. There was a new campaign finance law with restrictions on campaign contributions, new accounting rules for these contributions, including on campaign financing through taxes and restrictions, and limits on how much could be spent in an election campaign. In 1978, the "Ethics in Government Act" became law.

All this accelerated, according to Jeffrey Toobin, The New Yorker's legal writer, the politicization of the judicial process, or, as he put it, "the legal system's takeover of the political system."

Toobin has often written about the increasing role and power of the judiciary in American society, and he argues that this power has now grown so great that legal institutions have in fact taken over the political process. Prosecutors have become political heroes. Their power grew in the 70s and 80s after the liberals beat Nixon and after the Democrats' attempt to institutionalize this victory by creating, among other things, independent prosecutors.

During Bill Clinton's years in the White House in the 90s, this would come back to haunt Clinton and the Democrats, as the Whitewater Committee and Special Prosecutor Kenneth Starr tried to get Clinton impeached and removed from the White House.

A December 2005 comment by Dick Cheney, George W. Bush's vice president, is another indication of the deep mark that the Watergate scandal has left on American politics. Cheney, who was a proponent of expanding presidential power, is quoted by Robert Parry in his book "Neck Deep:"

"Watergate and a lot of the things around Watergate and Vietnam bothering during the 70s served, I think, to erode the authority I think the President needs to be effective, especially in the national security area. Part of the argument in Iran-contra was whether or not the President had the authority to do what was done in the Reagan years."

In March 2011, at the Richard Nixon Presidential Library in Yorba Linda -- the small town on Los Angeles' southern outskirts where Nixon was born -- a large and permanent Watergate exhibit was inaugurated despite strong resistance from Nixon's supporters. The exhibition attracted immediate attention and started a debate about the real purpose of all the presidential libraries around the country all of which are supervised by the federal National Archives.

The Nixon Library Director Timothy J. Naftali, who resigned at the end of 2011, said in an interview in the New York Times that "the library has a neutral task; it is an impartial federal institution and its obligation is to provide space for exhibits that encourage historical studies."
The exhibition describes bluntly, without excuses, how Nixon sowed the seeds that would lead to the Watergate scandal and, finally, his own departure.

And in June 2012, on the 40th anniversary of the Watergate break-in, Bob Woodward and Carl Bernstein, who had once exposed the scandal, wrote in the Washington Post that this was no "third rate burglary," as the Nixon White House had initially called it. It was something much more serious.

It was about President Nixon's "five wars" -- against the anti-Vietnam movement, the entire legal system, the news media, the Democratic Party, and history itself. They wrote:

"It all reflected a mind-set and a pattern of behavior that were uniquely and pervasively Nixon's: a willingness to disregard the law for political advantage, and a quest for dirt and secrets about his opponents as an organizing principle of his presidency ... At its most virulent, Watergate was a brazen and daring assault, led by Nixon himself, against the heart of American democracy: the Constitution, our system of free elections, the rule of law."

For R. Spencer Oliver, whose phone the Republicans tapped at the Democratic headquarters in the Watergate building, the Watergate scandal showed that people are willing to do almost anything to become and remain president, and that is also true today.

Oliver, who in June 1972 was the Executive Director of the Association of State Democratic Chairmen and who today is the Secretary General of the OSCE Parliamentary Assembly (Organization for Security and Cooperation in Europe), said in an interview with me 40 years after the Watergate break-in that the tap on his phone was designed to gather information about who would be the 1972 Democratic presidential candidate. According to Oliver, we can now see repeats of Watergate, but by other means. The Watergate lesson is to never be caught again. The problem is no longer secret money. Instead, it is the huge sums of money that millionaires – de facto oligarchs – openly pump into political campaigns to defeat candidates they do not like.

"The Republicans have advanced from Watergate to a more sophisticated and more dangerous stage in order to influence the outcome of elections, by injecting unlimited amounts of money into the campaigns and without having to report its sources," Oliver said.

"There is no need for secret money anymore, and this is very dangerous. This will destroy the democratic system if they do not do anything about it," he said.

Over the years, the campaign reforms that followed the Watergate scandal have gradually been weakened and watered down. In January 2010, the reform era could be said to have received its death blow with the Supreme Court decision, decided on a 5-to-4 vote, the smallest possible margin, in the case of Citizens United v. Federal Election Commission. The decision held that the ban on private corporations giving unlimited campaign contributions was unconstitutional and a violation of the right to free speech. The decision led to fundamental changes in how U.S. election campaigns are managed and financed but was also an enormous benefit for America's wealthy and, thus, the Republican Party, because America's business class overwhelmingly supports that party.

The decision prompted an unusual and critical comment by President Obama in his State of the Union to Congress in late January 2010:

"Last week, the Supreme Court reversed a century of law that I believe will open the flood gates to special interests to spend without limit on our elections. I do not think American elections should be bankrolled by America's most powerful interests."

"Not true," Associate Justice Samuel Alito, one of the Court's most conservative members, could clearly be seen mouthing on television in immediate response from his front row seat.

The decision is a threat to democracy, wrote Ronald Dworkin, law professor at New York University, in the New York Review of Books:

"Their decision threatens an avalanche of negative political commercials financed by huge corporate wealth ... Overall, these commercials can be expected to benefit Republican candidates and to injure candidates whose records dissatisfy powerful Industries ... It is important to study in some detail a ruling so damaging to democracy."

Judging by the 2012 Republican primary election campaign and the new so-called Super PACs (Political Action Committees), that's exactly what has happened. The PACs operate independently from the candidates and can receive and spend unlimited amounts money on political TV commercials, with no need to explain where the money came from. With millions of dollars in contributions from millionaires and billionaires - Newt Gingrich's Super PAC received, for example, over $ 10 million from a casino magnate and his wife in Las Vegas, and a Texas billionaire had, by the spring of 2012, pumped in $16 million to defeat President Obama. Most of the political ads consisted of negative attacks on opponents in a kind of shadow campaign, completely beyond any control or surveillance.

In the Republican primary election in Florida in January 2012, for example, Romney's and Gingrich's respective Super PACs spent nearly $20 million on TV attacks against each other. During the 2012 primary election campaign's first four weeks alone, the candidates' Super PACs spent a total of $44 million. It was just the kind of unlimited campaign contributions that earlier campaign laws had sought to prevent. Instead, money now more than ever dictates the American electoral process, in the name of freedom of expression.

The reforms of the Watergate era are no more. The wealthiest in America seem, finally, to have taken over America's elections.

The Supreme Court decision has led to a long series of countermeasures. New campaign laws have been proposed in Congress. In Montana, Maine, Vermont, and in other States, attempts, so far without much success, have sought to stop or alter the Citizens United decision. It has been said by many, that Watergate must not be forgotten, and that we must not return to the darkest days of our democracy. But if nothing is done, that is precisely what is happening in American politics today.

Chapter 4.

MORNING IN AMERICA

The 1980s in America was, to me, Ronald Reagan. During his eight years in the White House, he dominated the country in a way that no other president had done during my years in America. I wrestled with him, tried to understand him and the reasons why so many Americans were attracted to him. What did they see in him? Why was he so dominant? Was he good for America?

My questions and my doubts were founded in a general Swedish, and European, skepticism towards Reagan, which, in turn, stemmed from a difficulty in understanding him and what America and its voters saw in him. He was different, too American perhaps, an amateur politician, yes, an anti-politician, a movie star, who had made his name as a right-wing, anti-communist standard bearer, and who declared in his inaugural address as president in January 1981 that "government is not the solution to our problems, government is the problem." Reagan and his conservatism frightened Europeans and so did his foreign policy, or, rather, his lack of foreign policy experience. And what Reagan stood for represented viewpoints far to the right of Europe's traditional conservative parties.

That Reagan had been governor of California, America's most populous state with an economy among the world's ten largest, was noted, but it was somehow not enough. It was California, way out there on the West Coast -- "The Left Coast" -- and we all knew that it was a special place. There was a lot of prejudice, and many did not even try to take a look at Reagan with any objectivity.

Ronald Reagan came to politics late in life, at 50 years old, and after a mediocre movie career in Hollywood. He began as a liberal Democrat and was for several years the Chairman of the Screen Actors Guild of America, the movie stars' union. But during the 50's and Senator Joe McCarthy's anti-communist witch hunt, Reagan became increasingly conservative and a member of the Republican Party. His breakthrough as a politician occurred in 1964, when he chaired Barry Goldwater's campaign to become the Republican presidential candidate, and when he gave the nomination speech for Goldwater at the Republican Party's convention in San Francisco that year. Barely two years later, in 1966, Reagan was elected governor of California, and re-elected in 1970.

Goldwater's candidacy was the beginning of the Republican Party's turn to the right, which culminated with Ronald Reagan's presidential election victory 16 years later, in 1980. This conservatism still dominates the Republican Party today.

I must say that I was among those who looked very skeptically on Ronald Reagan when I arrived in Washington in September 1983 to start a new assignment as Dagens Nyheter's Washington correspondent.

It started with a bang. On my first day in my office in the National Press Building, a few blocks from the White House, the Soviet Union shot down a civilian South Korean passenger airliner in the international airspace between Japan and the Soviet Union. I landed right in the middle of a major foreign policy crisis, which was followed in quick succession by the bombing of the U.S. Marine Corps base in Beirut, which led to Reagan's decision to withdraw all U.S. troops from Lebanon, the invasion of the Caribbean island of Grenada just days after the Beirut bombing in Beirut and, of course, the up and down relations between the then two super powers, the U.S. and the USSR, and disarmament negotiations.

The Reagan years came to mean dramatic changes in U.S. foreign policy. They were years of many tragedies, but, against all the odds, ended in an almost personal triumph for Reagan. When he left the White House after eight years, the old anti-communist had dramatically improved U.S. relations with the Soviets, he had visited Moscow, and he had cemented a personal and warm relationship with Soviet President Mikhail Gorbachev. The "Evil Empire" had been transformed into a" new era" in American-Soviet relations. When Reagan and Gorbachev met for the fifth and final time in New York just days before Reagan's departure from the White House, it was almost as if two old friends and allies, full of respect for one another, were getting together for a last conversation.

Reagan's first year as president was marked by bitter attacks against the Soviet Union. When the Russians shot down the Korean passenger plane, the U.S. pulled out of disarmament talks in Geneva and, as a result of this and of the U.S. boycott of the 1980 Moscow Olympics, the Soviets decided to boycott the 1984 Olympic Games in Los Angeles, President Reagan's hometown. For a while, U.S.-Soviet relations seemed almost completely frozen.

Reagan's proposal in March 1983, for a Strategic Defense Initiative (SDI), nick-named Star Wars, meant to protect the United States against Soviet missile attacks, was received extremely negatively by Soviet leaders. They were neither capable of nor able to afford to match SDI, although there was great skepticism in the U.S. as to whether SDI would really work in practice. Still, it contributed to the turmoil in the world at the time.

Those who had warned of the consequences of having such a conservative old anti-communist like Ronald Reagan as America's president had a field day.

Ultimately, Reagan triumphed in the central American foreign policy issue -- its relations with the Soviet Union. In the process, Reagan changed from a rigid right-wing ideologue into a pragmatic foreign policy leader. After eight years of Ronald Reagan as president, the United States was at peace. The country breathed optimism. The Cold War was over. What had happened?

Many U.S. foreign policy experts that I spoke to at the time felt that Reagan had been "lucky." Those were the sentiments of John Steinbruner, then head of foreign policy research at the Brookings Institution, and Madeleine Albright, then Professor at Georgetown University and later foreign policy advisor to the 1988 Democratic presidential candidate, Michael Dukakis, and, finally, President Clinton's Secretary of State.

"Yes, he was lucky," Albright said when we talked in her home in Georgetown a few blocks from the university. It was all possible thanks to Mikhail Gorbachev coming to power."

"Gorbachev's accession to power was more important for this development than anything Reagan and the United States could achieve," said Steinbruner. "Reagan was forced to adapt to the new and constructive Soviet position.

But Condoleezza Rice, then, as once again today, a professor at Stanford University in California, saw the new superpower relationship as a result of a combination of two things: Reagan's tough policy and Gorbachev's accession to power.

"I doubt," she said on the phone from Stanford, "that it could all have happened without Gorbachev, but he (Gorbachev) could not have done it by himself either."
U.S. foreign policy during Reagan's eight years in the White House can be divided into three periods:

The first lasted between 1981 and 1983 and was characterized by hard attacks on the Soviet Union, the fiasco in Lebanon after the bombing in Beirut that cost the lives of 241 U.S. Marines, and the invasion of Grenada.

The second phase covered the years 1984 to 1986, when relations with the Soviet Union started to improve in connection with Gorbachev coming to power. During these years, international terrorism led among other things to the U.S. military retaliation against Libya in April 1986. That same year, two old dictators, the Philippines' Ferdinand Marcos and Haiti's Jean-Claude Duvalier, had to flee their countries. Reagan was commended for his actions although his critics felt that the praise was undeserved. At the end of this phase, the Iran-contra scandal occurred. Reagan's fate hung by a thin thread, but he managed to escape the degrading fate of Richard Nixon after Watergate.

During the third phase, 1987 to 1988, U.S. foreign policy achieved greater stability and a higher degree of unity. The so-called INF Treaty with the Soviet Union on nuclear arms reductions was signed. The Soviets departed Afghanistan. Reagan went to Moscow and Gorbachev came to New York. Iran and Iraq signed a ceasefire agreement. Namibia became independent and the U.S. for the first time opened talks with PLO, the Palestinian Liberation Organization.

Reagan's foreign policy outlook was based on the slogan "peace through strength." During his years, more than 2,000 billion dollars was invested in defense. The defense budget increased every year by between 150 and 300 billion dollars. This policy bore fruit, Reagan and many with him argued, for the Soviet Union could not afford similar efforts and, hence, was forced to the negotiating table. Detente was a fact, firmly rooted in the superpower relationship.

Reagan's success in other areas of American foreign policy was, however, not as great. His "constructive engagement" with the apartheid regime South Africa completely backfired, and he was forced by Congress, clearly against his wishes, to impose economic sanctions on South Africa.

In the Middle East, he failed in Lebanon, and his retaliatory action against Libya did not lead to Colonel Gaddafi's fall from power. And, above all, he did not move the peace process between Israel and the Palestinians forward. He never followed up on the Camp David Accord from 1978, when Jimmy Carter was president. According to Madeleine Albright, President Reagan threw away the chance to make progress towards peace in the Middle East.

In Central America, his Nicaragua policy was also a failure. After eight years of confrontation with the United States, Daniel Ortega remained in power, while tens of thousands of contras were without U.S. support. In El Salvador, the fighting and the death squads continued, and in Panama, the president and drug lord Manuel Noriega remained in power.

"He came in like a roaring lion, he left as a peaceful lamb," wrote the National Journal when President Reagan finally departed from the White House in January 1989.

In the autumn of 1986, President Ronald Reagan's major foreign policy scandal began to unravel. It eventually came to be known as the Iran-contra affair and it came to threaten Reagan's entire presidency as the facts became known through the investigation of a special prosecutor and Congressional committee hearings, just as during the Watergate scandal. But unlike Watergate, the Iran-contra scandal never led to impeachment proceedings against the president, although it was widely speculated at the time that such proceedings, and even Reagan's resignation, were close at hand.

The fall of 1986 was not an easy time for Reagan. He was in his sixth year as president. He had just met the Soviet President Mikhail Gorbachev at a summit in Reykjavik, Iceland, which had failed.

His veto of economic sanctions against South Africa was overturned by the Senate with an overwhelming vote of 78 to 21 -- more than enough for the two-thirds majority required to set aside a presidential veto. The mid-term elections in November 1986 were a disaster for Reagan and the Republicans. The Senate's Republican majority of 53 - 47 changed to a Democratic majority of 55 - 45, and the Democratic majority in the House of Representatives increased, to 260 - 175. President Reagan's last two years in the White house would be a time of power sharing between a Republican president and a Congress dominated by the Democrats.

It was at this time that reports began to trickle out in the American press via an article in the Lebanese newspaper Al Shafir about U.S. arms shipments to Iran, a country with which the United States had not even had diplomatic relations since the 444 day-long hostage crisis in Tehran 1980-81. The justification for arms deliveries was, it was said, to free American hostages held by various terrorist groups in Lebanon.

In November, Reagan admitted in a televised speech that he had given permission for the arms shipments to Iran, and a heated debate immediately flared up. Many wondered if this was not a violation of the export control law and of anti-terrorism laws. Reagan gave four reasons for the arms deliveries:

- resume relations with Iran;
- end the war between Iran and Iraq;
- end state-sponsored terrorism; and,
- get the hostages released.

A serious political crisis was now a reality. The attacks against Reagan came from both the right and the left.

"This is the greatest American foreign policy mistake ever," said Republican Senator Barry Goldwater.

And the Wall Street Journal wrote: "It is difficult to find anything that would be more harmful and more humiliating for the U.S. than the government secretly sending weapons to the world's premier terrorist state in exchange for a handful of hostages. But that is exactly what Reagan did."

A few days later, the whole affair took a new and sensational turn when it was revealed that nearly 30 million dollars from the arms deals with Iran had been channeled in great secrecy to the contras in Nicaragua, who, supported by the Reagan administration, had tried to overthrow the Sandinista government. John Poindexter, Reagan's national security adviser, resigned and one of his closest aides, Oliver North, was fired.

What started as a political mistake and developed into a foreign policy fiasco had now become a scandal that shook President Reagan, his administration, and, yes, the whole country. The word "Irangate" could now be heard in in Washington and many compared it with the Watergate scandal.

Many had a hard time accepting that the president did not know what was going on, especially since he had decided to manage the entire Iran operation from the White House and had kept everyone, including the State Department, the Joint Chiefs and Congress, out of the loop. And when Reagan tried to explain it all at his first press conference for three months in mid-November 1986, it increased, rather than diminished, the confusion.

Faced with a massive array of journalists in the East Room of the White House, the president gave a rare impression of uncertainty. He seemed tense and several times lost his thread of thought. One time he entirely forgot a question. In addition, some of his answers were so misleading that the White House had to issue corrections afterwards. It was an embarrassing performance, many of us who were there thought. Reagan's age, about which he had always joked earlier but which had not been used against him, now became an issue. He seemed, to put it bluntly, old.

The Reagan administration was thrown into its most serious crisis ever. Reagan's own as well as America's foreign policy credibility were deeply hurt. Just before Christmas, a special prosecutor and a special Iran committee based on the model of the famous Watergate Committee more than a decade earlier were created.

Reagan's world had come apart. After six successful years in the White House a picture of an infallible and invulnerable president had developed, based on a popularity so firmly rooted in the American people that they tolerated his mistakes. This strong wind in his back persisted…until the Iran-contra scandal.

During the winter and spring of 1986 and 1987, the political pressure increased on Reagan and his administration. The Iran-contra affair simply refused to go away. CIA Director William Casey became ill and underwent surgery for a brain tumor and would eventually die without having to testify before Congress. National Security Advisor, Robert McFarlane, swallowed a large number of valium tablets, but his suicide attempt failed.

Reagan reiterated his ignorance of the whole affair which would now be investigated by a specially- appointed commission, led by former Republican Senator John Tower. The Tower Commission's report at the end of February 1987 claimed that President Reagan had withheld information but it found no evidence that Reagan tried to cover up the whole affair.

It painted a picture of a foreign policy in utter confusion. Scathing criticism was directed towards the President and his advisors: their policy towards Iran was in direct conflict with the administration's own anti-terrorist policies; the administration's foreign policy had been handled unprofessionally and unsatisfactorily; and Congress had never been informed.

Three of Reagan's employees were deeply involved in sending secret support to the contras: Robert McFarlane, John Poindexter and Oliver North. The latter was depicted as the spider in the web.

"As I said to the Tower Commission," Reagan stated in a speech to the nation, "I did not know that all of this was going on, but, as president, I cannot escape responsibility."

The Commission's criticism was expected but its scope and weight came as a shock in the American capital. White House Chief of Staff Donald Regan resigned and was replaced by the experienced Howard Baker, former Republican Senator from Tennessee.

Meanwhile, Iran-contra special prosecutor Lawrence Walsh's work, as well as that of the two Iran committees, one in the Senate and in the House of Representatives, continued.

"We have either a president who actively engaged in an illegal foreign policy, or a president who is so incompetent that he passively can be made to agree that his staff conduct an illegal foreign policy," wrote The New Republic.

"The tragedy is that no one in the Reagan administration seems to remember the lessons of Watergate, that there are clear limits to the president's powers and that in a democracy you cannot carry on a secret policy at length," wrote the Washington Post.

In his book "Secrecy & Privilege," Robert Parry wrote:

"In crucial ways, Watergate, the signature scandal of the 1970s, and Iran-contra, the signature scandal of the 1980s, were opposites. Watergate showed how the Constitutional institution of American democracy - the Congress, the courts and the press - could check a gross abuse of power by the Executive. A short dozen years later, the Iran-contra scandal demonstrated how those same institutions had ceased to protect the nation from serious White House wrongdoing."

On Tuesday, May 5, 1987, the Iran-contra hearings before the newly formed Iran Committee started. Finally, the two key figures in the scandal, John Poindexter and Oliver North, would testify. But, after seven weeks of testimony from 23 other witnesses, the two key questions had not been answered:

How much did President Reagan know? And had he approved the secret and illegal transfer of income from the Iran arms deals to the contras?

Poindexter and North, who, until then had stubbornly refused to tell what they knew about the scandal, had by now obtained immunity from prosecution, which meant that nothing of what they told the Committee could be used against them in the event of prosecution.

Oliver North testified that he had always sought permission from his superiors and that he assumed that the president knew what was doing and had approved it. Among his superiors, according to North, were both Poindexter and the deceased CIA Director Casey.

North's performance received a huge response of the American public. Most felt North had just followed orders and that now he was being hung out to dry by his superiors. This sentimental, idealistic, somewhat politically naive and indignant patriot, the chest of his uniform bristling with medals and his wife, Betsy, mother of four - "my best friend" – sitting right behind him, grew into a kind of a folk hero. He loved America, he said, and he loved the president. He was ready to disappear quietly, ready to take the blame for everything. But his superiors didn't keep their promises even though he followed their orders. When they hung him out to dry, he did not want to play anymore and he would no longer keep silent.

Then it was John Poindexter's turn. He said he had never told anyone that the profits from the arms sales to Iran had gone to the contras. Not even the president knew it, he said.

"It was a conscious decision not to invite the President's permission and thus isolate him from the decision and provide him deniability if the whole thing leaked out," said Poindexter.

It turned out that Poindexter withheld almost everything to "help the contras," as he put it. Poindexter's testimony made it impossible to have Reagan face impeachment proceedings, although Poindexter's testimony was met with deep skepticism both among the American public and among many of the congressional committee members.

Only a slight majority of respondents in one poll thought that Poindexter had told the truth. The rest said that Poindexter's intention was to protect not only the president but also others in the administration. In another poll a few days later, a majority of respondents said they believed that both Reagan and Poindexter had lied.

Conflicts such as the Iran-contra affair between the executive power (the President) and the legislature (Congress) are built into the American political system. In the Iran-contra scandal, this conflict came to a head.

The cooperation that should have existed under the Constitution did not exist. Congress was never consulted. Instead, U.S. foreign policy was kept secret, kidnapped, by a handful of members of the White House National Security Council, who believed they possessed this right. They did not consider themselves beholden to the restrictions of the 1984 Boland Act, which prohibited the U.S. government from helping the contras in Nicaragua. Poindexter and North did not want to be limited in their actions by Congress or anyone else.

In their excellent book "Landslide - The Unmaking of the President 1984-1988," journalists Jane Mayer of The New Yorker and Doyle McManus of the Los Angeles Times, painted a frightening picture of how Ronald Reagan's entire presidency disintegrated because of the Iran-contra scandal, as Reagan completely lost control over what his White House staff were doing. The staff did as they pleased. Reagan's passivity was startling. He was unengaged, seemingly uninterested -- it was a "no-hands presidency," they wrote.

To secretly sell something that belongs to the U.S. government for a profit, and then use the profits to buy weapons for the contras, was unconstitutional. "Such action leads straight to dictatorship," a congressional committee stated much later.

Only Congress within the American system of checks and balances has the right to distribute money and approve budgets – "the power of the purse." And this was, James Madison wrote in 1788, the most effective way to limit the president's power. But Reagan, wrote Mayer and McManus, did not recognize any of those limitations.

How much Reagan actually knew about all this is still a mystery. Poindexter testified that he himself approved passing the money from the sale of weapons to the contras. He took responsibility and that saved Reagan's presidency. Poindexter was eventually convicted on five counts, but he appealed and won, by a vote of 2-1 in a federal court. Without Poindexter's testimony, though it was met with great skepticism, Reagan would probably have faced impeachment.

After having successfully led America for six years and restored the confidence in the presidency, Reagan had now ended up in a credibility- and confidence crisis. The great leader, "the great communicator," no longer led or communicated, at least not so that anyone believed him. "Project Democracy," the secret network that Poindexter and North built up with the help of CIA Director William Casey had not only been created to keep Congress out but also without the knowledge of Reagan's own cabinet members. Casey and his allies - "the junta" - had launched what became an almost secret coup d'état, wrote Mayer and McManus.

It has never really been established how much Reagan knew about "Project Democracy," but he remained largely passive during the events of November 1986. It was clear that his sympathies lay with Casey and the others – after all, they had helped to get hostages released and made sure that the contras survived. Ollie, Reagan said once on the phone to Oliver North, as described by Mayer and McManus, you are a national hero, there will be a great movie about you one day. The president still saw nothing wrong with selling weapons to Ayatollah Khomeini in exchange for freeing American hostages, according to Mayer's and McManus's book. And he never apologized for what had happened.

Actually, they added, he never ever apologized, whether for public or private mistakes. For Reagan, it was always someone else's fault.

The budget deficit was Congress's fault; the failure to conclude a nuclear agreement was the Soviet Union's fault; the issue of his business associates' "sleaze" was either the media's or nobody's fault -- until the arms sales to Iran.

The American public, which had long accepted these sunshine success stories and admired the president's self-confidence, no longer did so. In just one month, everything changed. Now, instead, people began to wonder if Reagan was able to do his job as president. And, for the first time, the public questioned the president's integrity.

"He lives in a dream world," a close associate said, according to Mayer and McManus, who said that other employees were shocked by the president's ignorance. He did not remember his own decisions. A chaotic White House no longer had a leader. Reagan's poll numbers plummeted, from 67 percent to 46 percent. And 90 percent of those polled did not think he had told whole truth about the Iran-contra affair. The majority of respondents concluded that the president lied.

The Reagan era was now largely over and his remaining two years in the White House became a period of inactivity and powerlessness. His ability to get his proposals approved by Congress declined to the lowest level since the beginning of the 1950s, according to Congressional Quarterly's statistics. In February 1988, Congress put a stop to all further military aid to the contras in Nicaragua. Relations with Iran never improved, and in Beirut, where there had been seven American hostages when Reagan began selling arms to Iran, there were now nine hostages.

The Congressional hearings reached a conclusion not to start impeachment proceedings against Reagan, because it could never be stated with certainty whether Reagan had authorized the clandestine diversion of income from the sale of weapons to Iran to the Nicaraguan contras.

But a bipartisan majority on the Iran-contra committee stated that Reagan had violated the presidential oath to uphold the country's laws. North and Poindexter had not sold weapons secretly to Iran and funneled money to the contras on their own. Their actions had been the result of the president's policies. Laws had been violated and this was Reagan's fault.

When Reagan became president in January 1981, he promised a new era of optimism, lower taxes and a strong defense. He lived up to the promises. His optimism never failed, not even after the assassination attempt against him only three months after he entered the White House. His popularity increased even more. He talked about Americans as the "chosen people" and he said, repeatedly, that it was "morning in America."

It had an effect. When Reagan left the White House, Americans were satisfied with their lives. Over half of them were positive about developments during the past few years, and 87 per cent said they were satisfied with their personal lives. They were pleased that America had turned to the right and with their election, and re-election, of the first ever ideologically conservative president, who then enacted the biggest political changes in the United States since Franklin Delano Roosevelt in the 1930s.

Domestic political developments during the Reagan years were full of paradoxes and contradictions. One of the first actions by the president in the spring of 1981 put a clear stamp on his presidency – he fired thousands of striking air traffic controllers and crushed their union. Congress had approved a law prohibiting public employees from striking because public safety could be threatened.

The strike was illegal, said Reagan, and announced that if the 13,000 air traffic controllers did not return to their jobs within two days, he would fire them. The public and private sectors are different, he explained. Government just cannot close, it must continue to perform its duties. Reagan did what he said and dismissed over 11,000 air traffic controllers, who refused to return to work.

During the Reagan years, the presidency was strengthened after being weakened during the years after the Watergate scandal and Richard Nixon's resignation. The recession in the early 1980's had turned into record-long economic expansion with low inflation and near full employment, albeit with a gigantic budget deficit because of tax cuts and the billions in new money for defense.
But environmental problems worsened, race relations deteriorated, and poverty and inequality in the American society increased. The homeless flooded the cities. More murders were committed in New York and Washington, DC than ever before. There was talk of America's decline, but there was also the feeling that Reagan had restored the presidency and a sense of pride in America after Vietnam and Watergate.

In fact, he changed the whole debate about the federal government and its role in America. "Reaganomics"- - the ideological belief in free markets and in an increasingly smaller role for the federal government -- guided the direction of the country. This created an image "of a heartless administration that ignored the problems in society," according to Isabel Sawhill of the Urban Institute.

Bill Clinton eventually came to call the Reagan years "the politics of nostalgia," and Clinton's former staffer in the White House, Lanny Davis, added many years later:

"Reagan created an irresponsible economic model. Initially, George H. W. Bush called it 'voodoo economics,' and he was right. It plagues both parties today. We can borrow and spend, pay for two wars and massive bailouts, stimulus programs, pork, and national health care –cut taxes all the while adding three trillion more dollars to the national debt. Let our grandchildren pay the tab. This is immoral - both parties today are complicit - and it all began with 'Morning in America' and Ronald Reagan."

A revised picture of the Reagan years has begun to emerge, albeit slowly. For many in contemporary America, its deep problems are a result of the Reagan era, when selfishness and greed dominated and the idealism of the 60s seemed so distant. The Reagan years were the "triumph of the upper-class," wrote the leading conservative political analyst Kevin Phillips in his book, "The Politics of Rich and Poor." It was a time, he wrote, of ostentatious worship of money and of glorification of capitalism and free market forces. They were years when the rich became richer. In fact, not since the late 1800's, when Rockefeller, Vanderbilt and Morgan founded their enormous wealth, have similar kinds of new fortunes been created.

Thomas Edsall, a Washington Post political writer at the time, wrote that the economic stagnation at the bottom of the wage scale was a threat to the social order, even to Americans' own identity. At stake, he argued, was the entire American experiment, threatened by growing political cynicism and alienation and by a fundamental uncertainty about the future. Americans' interest in politics had decreased. Voter turnout had fallen steadily since 1960, and not even half of the country's voters voted any longer. Fatigue had for many turned into frustration and cynicism. Did voting make any difference?

Whoever had the most money seemed to win anyway, and all politicians were the same -- their only interest was to stay in power as long as possible and profit as much as possible during that time.

America's policy crisis could also be seen in a record-low trust in politicians and government in Washington. Only 36 percent of Americans during the Reagan years, as opposed to 75 percent in the 50s, had confidence in Washington and its politicians.

In his book from 1991, "Why Americans Hate Politics," E.J. Dionne, Jr., a columnist at the Washington Post, warned that the survival of American democracy was at stake. We hate politics, he wrote, because politics is no longer about solutions but to gain short-term political advantage. While Japan and Germany capture market shares globally, Americans are waging a series of ideological battles over abortion, flag burning, allegiance, school prayer, racial quotas, and the right to bear arms. In the battle between conservatism and liberalism, the political debate has polarized and limited the American voters' choice.

"Morning in America" became Reagan's slogan - full of myth and romance. He was the constant optimist about America -- "the shining city on the hill". Criticism, until the Iran-contra scandal, did not seem to affect him. He became the "Teflon president," a term coined by Patricia Schroeder, a congresswoman from Colorado. Not even when the 257 Marines died in the terrorist attack on their barracks in Beirut did Reagan's popularity decline. The invasion of Grenada cemented his popularity -- "America is standing tall," said Reagan.

Reagan depicted himself as anti-government, both as governor of California and as president in Washington. He said that everything was possible -- lower taxes, more money for the military, counter-terrorism, the rolling back of communism, ending the threat of nuclear war. He seemed to offer America everything good, without costs or sacrifices.

The final judgment on the Reagan years is not easy and there is wide disagreement. Lou Cannon, a veteran journalist from California and expert on Reagan after covering him for many years, said when I spoke to him shortly before Reagan left the White House that he regarded Reagan as a serious person, who read a lot, had a great sense of humor and self-irony and always treated everyone with respect and consideration.

His greatest success, according to Cannon, was that he managed to restore the feeling that the U.S. was a nation, after the agonizing years of the Vietnam War and the Watergate scandal.

It is important for the United States, Cannon argued, to have symbolic leaders who created a personal relationship with the American public. And Reagan did that. As Cannon saw it, Reagan succeeded in his foreign policy but failed in his domestic policy, especially with the economy, because he never dealt with the huge budget deficit. Cannon was also critical of Reagan in terms of race relations in the country -- they deteriorated during the Reagan years.

Clayborne Carson, an African-American history professor at Stanford University, did not mince words, when I talked to him, saying that the Reagan years were a "low point" for race relations after the 1960s. Progress not only stopped, it turned around, he said. And Carson's black colleague, Roger Wilkins at George Mason University just outside Washington, was brutally critical of the Reagan years, calling them a "disaster," a time when "all the worst values in our society were glorified."

For many critics, the Reagan years became a legacy of "despair," in which wealth was increasingly concentrated among a small group of people at the top, in which the middle class disappeared and in which the numbers of the poor swelled, wrote Robert Parry on his website in connection with the centenary of Reagan's birth.

The eight Reagan years began with the worst economic downturn since the 1930s. Unemployment of 7.5 percent rose to 10.8 percent by December 1982 -- the highest since the 30s. Inflation was over 12 percent. The recession during Reagan's first years in the White House lasted 16 months, until the middle of 1983.

In 1981, he had succeeded in getting the "Economic Recovery and Tax Act" (ERTA) through Congress, a tax reform political scientists Andrew S. Hacker and Paul Pierson in their 2010 book from "Winner-Take-All-Politics" called Reagan's "greatest legislative triumph." The reform represented a fundamental change in the country's tax laws to the benefit of America's high earners.

In 1983 and 1984, the economy turned, growing at a stunning 7 percent. 73 months of uninterrupted expansion followed. At the time, it was the longest peacetime expansion period in the United States. Not even the stock market crash in October 1987 could dampen growth. Unemployment fell to its lowest level in 14 years, inflation was halved to 4.5 percent, 17 million new jobs were created, and interest rates were drastically reduced. Defense spending rose by 7 percent a year, federal spending rose relative to GDP between 1981 and 1985.

Meanwhile, taxes were drastically cut and the national debt tripled during Reagan's time in the White House - the United States became the world's largest debtor country - and the budget deficit grew to alarming proportions.

But Reagan never suffered politically for the deficit or the national debt. In 1984, he was re-elected, beating Democratic candidate Walter Mondale by an overwhelming margin. Mondale, along with Geraldine Ferraro - the first female vice presidential candidate - won only in his home state Minnesota and in Washington, DC. Reagan received over 58 percent of the votes.

It was difficult to understand, I remember, how a man like Walter Mondale -- almost "one of us" -- of Norwegian descent from historically Scandinavian Minnesota, an experienced and pragmatic politician, a solid liberal, with a female vice presidential candidate -- did not have a chance against a 74-year-old conservative former movie actor. And I remember how difficult it was to explain that to readers back home.

What was it that we did not understand about him and about America? American voters apparently thought highly of him, they believed and trusted in him, they were charmed by him and his optimism and love and faith in America, and they wanted to keep him in the White House.
Ronald Reagan's goals during his years in the White House were to reduce the size of the government, its role and influence, and to restore economic prosperity and improve national security. Tax cuts and a larger defense budget were more important than balancing the budget, and curbing inflation was more important than moderating the recession.

During his time as governor of California 1966-1974, Reagan had failed to drastically lower state taxes. Then, in 1978, a big tax initiative in California called Proposition 13 was introduced in response to skyrocketing state property taxes. California's voters supported the proposal with a 65 percent majority and paved the way for the largest property tax reduction (60 percent) in California's, and yes, the country's history.

The new law froze property tax at 1975 levels and tightly regulated future tax increases on both private and commercial properties. Proposition 13 came to cost California more than 7 billion dollars in lost tax revenues, losses which have mainly affected the state's schools. The school system has still not recovered from the effects of Proposition 13.

The lessons of Proposition 13 formed the basis for Reagan's approach in the White House when "tax cut fever" came to play a major role, according to California journalist Peter Schrag in his book "Paradise Lost." Reagan lowered marginal tax rates for the wealthy from 70 to 28 percent. He introduced the "trickle down economy," where prosperity would trickle down through the ranks as the rich paid less in taxes. But that was not to be.

However, Proposition 13 still rules in California and over the years it has negatively affected the state's public sector across the board. Despite this, it has its successors in virtually every American state. And "Reaganomics," or "trickle-down economics," is still the goal for Republicans, still their solution to America's economic problems.
In the Urban Institute's "The Reagan Record" about those years, the election of Ronald Reagan in 1981 ended the long period of social activism that began during Franklin Roosevelt's New Deal in the 30s. What mattered now were budget cuts, not social policy.

As a result, the poor became poorer during Reagan's years in the White House as income between 1980 and 1984 grew by only 1 percent for a typical middle-class family. Incomes fell by almost 8 percent for the poorest fifth of Americans while they increased by 9 percent for the most prosperous. Thus, the inequalities increased during the Reagan years.

Professor Hugh Heclo of Harvard University wrote in "Perspectives on the Reagan Years" that Reagan said what Americans wanted to hear, that the future was bright. Reagan urged Americans to dream, but it was dreams of individual progress, not of success for the common man.

"The Reagan years will be remembered as the turning point, from liberal to conservative ideas and conservative politics," wrote Isabel Sawhill of the Urban Institute in the same book.

During Reagan's years religion made its entry into American politics in a more organized way than ever before. The religious right was born with strong ties to the Republican Party. Anti-abortion and school prayer, pro-Israel and a strong defense, were some of their political obsessions. Those were the years when powerful television preachers formed a political movement called the "Moral Majority" with leaders such as Jerry Falwell and Pat Robertson.

Jimmy Swaggart and Jim and Tammy Bakker were others. The founding figure for all of them was Billy Graham, the legendary preacher. Millions of new evangelical voters registered.

Pat Robertson, a Southern Baptist and founder of the Christian cable channel Christian Broadcasting Network, was a Republican presidential candidate in the primary election of 1988. He did pretty well, with seven million revivalist Christian voters supporting him during the primary campaign, which George H. W. Bush eventually won. Robertson is still active on their TV channel, and the program he once started, "The 700 Club," still has millions of viewers.

Many of these TV preachers became very rich, but for some, it did not go well. That included Jimmy Swaggart in his vast church in Baton Rouge, Louisiana, where he also started a Bible College, and Jim and Tammy Bakker's Christian theme park "Heritage USA" in South Carolina.

Swaggart and Jim Bakker were both involved in sex scandals. Bakker was forced to resign and was eventually convicted of fraud and spent a half dozen years in prison. Both Bakker and Swaggart still preach, but you don't hear much about them anymore.

Jerry Falwell, the TV preacher who died in 2007, was for many years a political and religious power in America, like no other TV evangelist. He worked from a base in Lynchburg, Virginia, which has a church, a Christian elementary school, a University -- Liberty University -- and "The Moral Majority." Today, the university has 12,000 students and the church thrives.

"We are waging a holy war and we will win," said Jerry Falwell, a round and friendly man, who readily acknowledged his great interest in politics when I met him in the spring of 1987 in Lynchburg. He supported George H.W. Bush in the 1988 election, not Pat Robertson. The country is not ready for a preacher as president, he said. Behind the statement, there was likely a whole lot of personal rivalry between him and Robertson. For Falwell, television was a way to recruit followers and raise money. The Christian fundamentalist movement's rapid growth was completely thanks to television, Falwell told me after a church service in his Thomas Road Baptist Church.

At the end of the Reagan era, the Christian Right was in decline. "The Moral Majority" had financial problems and it was dissolved in the late 80's. Falwell said that it had accomplished what it set out to do, it had reached its goal, and the religious right was now firmly rooted in American politics.

At his retirement in 1989, Ronald Reagan was more popular than all his predecessors when they left office, and in all elections thereafter Republican presidential candidates have attempted to be as close and faithful to Reagan as possible.

It is still the ticket for success in the Republican Party.

"Of our modern presidents, Reagan left the largest footprints," said David Kennedy, professor of history at Stanford University, when I interviewed him in the autumn of 2011.

Reagan shifted the emphasis of U.S. policy and made conservatism the dominant political movement in the country. No other politician is as associated with what happened in the 1980s as Ronald Reagan is. It was a time when American politics changed in a fundamental way and a new, unequal economy was created, wrote political scientists Hacker and Pierson in their acclaimed book "Winner-Take-All-Politics:"

"Reagan was simultaneously the conservatives' most eloquent advocate and their most successful candidate. He was, in a word, a game-changer. There was American politics before Reagan, and American politics after Reagan. Full stop."

Even Obama acknowledged Reagan's importance during the 2008 presidential election campaign:

"Ronald Reagan changed the trajectory of America in a way that Richard Nixon did not, and in a way that Bill Clinton did not. Reagan put us on a fundamentally different path, because the country was ready for it ... he tapped into what people were already feeling, which Is, we want clarity, we want optimism, we want a return to that sense of dynamism and entrepreneurship that had been missing."

Ronald Reagan died in 2004, at 93 years old. He had suffered from Alzheimer's disease for many years. His presidential library is located high on a hill in Simi Valley, north of Los Angeles, with sweeping views of the treeless, sun-parched hills. The Pacific Ocean can be inferred on the horizon in the west. The library is one big tribute to America's 40th president, with a large bronze statue of Reagan as a cowboy at the entrance, a piece of the Berlin Wall on the lawn, and, for some reason, a large collection of antique cars, and his old plane, Air Force One.

"One man had the courage" ... "he fought for freedom"..."He set out to change the nation," "he refused to surrender ..."

Not one negative word to be read…anywhere. The Iran-contra scandal was long not mentioned at all, and has now a modest place in the exhibits. The Reagan library has become a place of pilgrimage for America's conservative movement – it is holy ground. It's about preserving Reagan's memory and keeping the myth of Ronald Reagan alive.

Chapter 5.

OH, BILL...

The post-Reagan years were not years of reassessment for America, at least not at first. The new president, George Herbert Walker Bush, showed no signs of seriously addressing the many problems that had piled up when he entered the White House in January 1989. Reagan's optimistic message of "morning in America" certainly still had resonance, but Reagan had gone home to California and Bush proved unable to assume his mantle.

In the spring of 1992, calls for reforms came one after the other. The same calls had had been heard before. In Congress, the mood was somber, also not for the first time. However, the crisis this time was caused by something more than scandals and the privileges of those in power. The crisis was caused by Washington's increased isolation from the rest of America.

Fewer and fewer citizens around the country, in California, Montana, Iowa, Texas, Florida, cared anymore about what was happening or being accomplished, if anything, in Washington. America's government was in the grips of paralysis. It was as if nothing of importance was getting done. What was accomplished was only of marginal importance. The White House and the Senate were controlled by Republicans, but the Democrats ruled in the House of Representatives. They all fought one other. The result was stalemate.

The U.S. Constitution calls for "checks and balances," and it is usually celebrated. But when times are difficult, the American political system's effectiveness can be called into question.

A parliamentary system with a prime minister backed by a solid parliamentary majority seems infinitely more effective, at least for many foreign observers.

In the spring of 1992, nearly 80 percent of respondents in an ABC-Washington Post poll said that America was heading in the wrong direction. They asked themselves: "America: what went wrong?" True, opinions can changes fast in America. When things go well, they are seen as going very well, and when things go badly, they are seen as going very badly. Subtlety and nuances are often lost. Yesterday tends to be quickly forgotten. History is last week's issue of People Magazine, as one of the main characters in the TV series "Thirty Something" once put it. Even so, there was now little doubt that America was facing a leadership crisis, both in the White House and in Congress.

During his nearly four years in power, George Bush seemed unable to tell the American people what direction he wanted to take the country. He had no vision, either domestic or foreign. He was a president without initiatives of his own. He did not lead, he only reacted.

It's was as if Bush was idling, wrote the Washington Post, and as if all of America's huge problems were being pushed aside. A weak Republican president with Democrats in the majority in the House of Representatives was not exactly the ideal recipe for political cooperation and for joint decisions on long-term solutions.

In March 1991, in Los Angeles, the world saw via television how four policemen, on television, severely abused Rodney King, a black man. It had been filmed by a bystander. But, after a high profile trial, three of them were acquitted and the jury could not decide if a fourth was guilty.

The verdicts led to riots in Los Angeles in the spring of 1992. They resulted in 53 dead, over 2,000 injured, and nearly a billion dollars in property damages.

The unrest shook Los Angeles much in the same way as the riots in Watts had done 27 years earlier.

The feeling was of "a country unraveling," as John F. Harris aptly wrote in his book, "The Survivor." Not even on foreign policy, which had always been president Bush's love and strength, and where he had wanted to appear an expert, was he able to formulate a new post-Cold War U.S. policy. The golden opportunity that followed the breakup of the Soviet Union was lost. Instead, wrote the New Republic confusion in our foreign policy seemed infinite.

Finally, in the spring of 1992, under pressure not only from critics, but from within his own Republican Party, Bush presented a proposal for how the U.S. might help its old enemy, the Soviet Union, in its difficult transition to a modern, democratic state. This was another example of Bush's failure to act until he was accused of passivity, and even as his proposal met with praise it also reinforced his image as a weak leader.

Americans had by now not noticed any economic benefits in the new post-Cold War era of détente. Talk of a "peace dividend", i.e. that defense spending could now be reduced and the money spent on needed civilian projects, proved to be mostly rhetoric. While there was broad consensus that the defense budget was too big, there was also the new insight that cuts in defense spending would be painful, because they would cost jobs, perhaps several hundreds of thousands, in the first year alone.

For the first time since World War II, new jobs now had to be created outside the defense industry. For the first time, the economy would now have to grow without the help of an ever-expanding defense system. The transition would be severe and painful. And if money was actually spent on problems in the big cities, and on schools and health care, what was Bush's plan then? No one knew, and Bush, himself, gave no guidance.

In his 1993 book, "Who Will Tell the People: The Betrayal of American Democracy," a deeply concerned William Greider wrote that U.S. domestic policy was no longer addressing the country's problems. Instead, he wrote, everything was being done to hide them, risking social chaos. It could determine if the American experiment really was unique or only a new chapter in the rise and fall of nations. America was being tested as perhaps never before.

The story of Victor reflected the times. Victor got married in the mid 60's and bought a small house on Long Island for 16,000 dollars. That was what one was supposed to do, he said at the time, get married, buy a house and a car, and have children and dogs and cats. He earned up to 35,000 dollars a year and he and his family lived well, until he was fired. His wife Ginny began supporting the whole family. His son, Scott, a draftsman who earned 30,000 dollars a year, was about to get married. He could not afford a house in the neighborhood, which now went for about 140,000 dollars. His other son, Greg, could not get a job without a college degree, so he had to go back to school. And a new car cost more than the house Victor bought in 1965, so they had to settle for an old car, at least until he got a new job. Victor just knew one thing for sure: life would never be as good again.

The income gap in America widened dramatically between 1980 and 1989, and the shrinking middle class, to which Victor and his family belonged, saw living standards drop. Although total middle class wages of between 20,000 and 50,000 dollars a year rose by more than 40 percent, total income in that same period for those earning over one million dollars per year increased by 2,184 percent (two thousand one hundred eighty-four percent). And while the average wage for those earning less than 20,000 dollars a year rose 1.4 percent, the average wage for those earning over a million dollars a year increased by nearly 50 percent.

The spring of 1992, which was the twelfth year with Republican presidents in the White House -- eight years of Ronald Reagan and now almost four years of George Bush -- was characterized by a deep uncertainty. Americans were confused. They did not know where their country was heading. They knew that something had gone wrong, and must be corrected. But they did not know exactly what and exactly how. And they lacked leaders.

This was a time when confidence in the paralyzed government steadily diminished and cynicism towards politics and politicians steadily increased. It was a time when the cities' inhabitants were held hostage by crime and drug abuse and decay, when the budget deficit continued to skyrocket, when the debt burden continued to grow and the country's competitiveness eroded. It was a time when fewer and fewer people wanted to buy the foremost symbol of America – a car – and when Japan got richer and Europe stronger and more independent. It was a time, when today's children no longer took for granted that they would be better off than their parents.

A series of articles at this time in the Philadelphia Inquirer entitled, "America: What Went Wrong?" became, by far, the most widely read series in the history of the paper. Readers asked the same question: what had happened to their country?

For millions of people, life had become more difficult and more uncertain. And, suddenly, the self-confidence, such a defining American characteristic, began to fail them, and ever fewer believed anymore in the American dream. It was no longer in "morning America", as Reagan had insisted. The bill for the Reagan years had arrived, and it was expensive.

Like Victor, John, his wife and three children were victims of these times. They lived in a borrowed trailer on the outskirts of Seattle. After John lost his job as a computer programmer and had been forced to sell his house, and with only 1,000 dollars in his pocket, the whole family went west, looking for work. It did not go well. For a while, the whole family lived in a tent until they managed to borrow the trailer. For the first time in their lives, the family had to accept food stamps of just over 300 dollars a month in order to survive. In addition, they received social benefits of 700 dollars a month. To get by without depending on social assistance, John needed to find a job that paid at least 11 dollars an hour, but although he was looking full time, he found nothing.

It shouldn't be this way, people said. Only yesterday, America had been full of optimism and self-confidence, the economy had been growing, unemployment had been low and inflation had barely existed. In addition, the Cold War had ended and -- a devastating nuclear war between the two superpowers was off the table. Peace prevailed, both inside and outside of America's borders. There was no longer a Vietnam War that had almost torn the country apart, no longer the race war that had seemed so threateningly close during the 60's civil rights struggle, and no longer the kind of gloomy uncertainty that the political system's would fall apart, as had been the case after Watergate.

But peace had not yielded any dividend. Instead, problems spread over the country like a big dark cloud. Infrastructure was neglected. An educational crisis deepened. Violence and crime – 24,000 murders in 1991 alone -- increased steadily. In the big cities, a black underclass grew, ever more separated from the rest of the United States -- the median pay of a black family was only 56 percent of that of a white family, and one third of the blacks lived below the poverty line.

Only three percent of the country's university students were black. In the spring of 1992, unemployment was, officially, 7.3 percent, or some 8.9 million Americans were without work.

Jonathan, who was white, well-educated, and 22 years old, was unemployed. He lived in Philadelphia and had been out of work for almost a year after graduating with a degree in economics from Harvard University. His parents -- his father was a music teacher and his mother a shop assistant -- had had to make major financial sacrifices so that Jonathan could go to Harvard. His four years there cost about 100,000 dollars, even after he received scholarships and other help. Jonathan's father had for years supplemented his teacher's salary by playing the piano twice a week in a bar in town. Although his mother enjoyed her work, she would have preferred to stay home with her children.

Neither Jonathan nor his parents understood what had gone wrong in America. A Harvard degree, once, automatically, led to a job. What had happened? And what was going to happen? Many young people in the early 90s faced similar predicaments, and many had come to the same painful conclusion, that a basic college degree was no longer worth much. A higher degree, even more education and training, were now required to compete in the labor market.

In January 1991, the United States went to war again, this time in "Desert Storm." But in contrast to the Vietnam War, the war against Saddam Hussein was short, it didn't even last two months. Kuwait, which had been invaded by Saddam Hussein's Iraq, was liberated, but President Bush let Saddam Hussein remain in power in Baghdad.

In America, the euphoria after the victory in "Desert Storm" quickly evaporated. With the steadily deteriorating economy Americans looked increasingly inward and lost their confidence in Washington.

In Eisenhower's time in the 1950s, 75 percent of Americans believed that the government did what was best for them, but in 1991 that figure was down to 36 percent. Seven out of ten Americans said that the country was on the wrong track.

When Bush broke his election promise, -- "read my lips, no new taxes" -- he lost the support of the Republican right wing. With Bush's U-turn on taxes, the Republicans' election strategy, based on firm opposition to any tax increases, fell apart. The rug had been pulled from under all Republican candidates and the success in the 1990 mid-term election that the party had hoped for did not materialize. Instead, Democrats expanded their previous majorities in both the Senate and the House of Representatives. For George Herbert Walker Bush, whose victory in 1988 had been seen as a third term for Ronald Reagan and everything he stood for, things turned out differently.

Maybe Bush just never believed in "Reaganomics," which Bush in the 1980 election campaign had called "voodoo economics"?

The slogan "don't get mad – get revenge – elect no one," symbolized the voters' mood in the early 90's. After the Reagan and Bush years, leading Democrats had also failed to demonstrate any ability to tell the country and its people how they saw the future and where they wanted to take America for the rest of the decade. The only truth about President Bush, Newsweek wrote, is that he is willing to do anything to win the election in November.

After "Desert Storm" and Kuwait's liberation, 88 percent of Americans approved of how Bush handled the presidency. But then his poll numbers started to fall. The Democrats saw their chances of recapturing the White House increase. There was even talk of a "historic" opportunity for the Democrats.

Conservative author Kevin Phillips wrote that Bush does not deserve to win, but the Democrats do not yet deserve to defeat him. This was the irony of those years. Americans sought a new direction for their country, they wanted to hear the truth about its problems and about how they could be solved, and they thirsted for leaders who could carry them through these difficult times. But they found only weak and misguided politicians with simplistic answers to difficult questions. In the final weeks of the 1992 primary election campaign, two-thirds of the American electorate said they were dissatisfied with all the current presidential candidates.

Instead, the eccentric Texas billionaire H. Ross Perot was mentioned every more frequently as a serious, possible third candidate. This only served to further emphasize the weakness of the leaders of the two main political parties.

For Bush -- "the foreign policy president" and the archetype of the Republican political establishment – the political signs were not encouraging. Suddenly, he seemed very vulnerable. Among Democrats, the relatively unknown governor from Arkansas, Bill Clinton, eventually became not only the Democratic candidate, but he definitively defeated Bush, by 43 percent to 37. In addition, almost 20 million deeply discontented voters, or 19 percent of the total, voted for Ross Perot, the third candidate. That was the most votes for an independent presidential candidate since 1912, when former Republican President Theodore Roosevelt tried to get elected president as an independent candidate.

The discontentment of the time cost Bush the victory, and the Republicans lost the White House for the first time in twelve years.

Bill Clinton entered the White House in January 1993. He was to become the first president since Andrew Johnson shortly after the Civil War to face an impeachment trial in the U.S. Senate. Like Johnson, he won in the end.

Clinton's problems began a year after his accession, when the first news reports were published about something that would come to be called the "Whitewater Affair." It was over a large chunk of land in his home state of Arkansas that Bill and Hillary Clinton had bought in 1978 as an investment for more than 200,000 dollars through a good friend, Jim McDougal. It was McDougal who had handled the deal and the plans to develop the land and make it into some kind of vacation spot. Clinton was not involved in any of the details, and when the land was sold in 1985, it sold at a loss.

For the Clintons, Whitewater was a most unsuccessful investment. Still, news reports implied that irregularities had occurred, and that Clinton had tried to help his friend McDougal for whom the transaction resulted in tax benefits. In the middle of all this speculation, Clinton's close friend and White House staffer, Vincent Foster, committed suicide. Was this connected to Whitewater?

Republicans started to request that the whole matter should be investigated and that a special congressional committee be formed with a special prosecutor as during the Watergate affair. In the end, the Democrats gave in and in January 1994, Clinton asked Attorney General Janet Reno to appoint a special Whitewater prosecutor. A Whitewater Committee was formed with Alfonse D'Amato, the tough, conservative Republican Senator from New York as Chairman, and with the prominent, moderate Republican Robert B. Fiske as special prosecutor.

Fiske did not last long. He was replaced after six months, during what could only be described as murky and highly politicized circumstances, by Kenneth Starr, a conservative judge. The decision was driven by impatient Republicans who were frustrated that Fiske had not yet obtained decisive evidence against Clinton. And they did not like Fiske's conclusion that Vince Foster had committed suicide for personal reasons.

For the Clintons' friends, "Whitewater" became synonymous with false accusations, partisan revenge and prosecutorial abuse. The appointment of Starr, a pronounced conservative, who opposed Clinton and his policies at almost every turn, came to dominate Clinton's six remaining years as president, which, in turn, led to a relentless partisan battle in Washington.

The Republican Speaker of the House, Newt Gingrich, became Clinton's main opponent. Gingrich was once heard saying during a visit to the White House, "Mr. President, we are going to run you out of town." Gingrich, who had been a Congressman from Georgia since 1979, had been elected Speaker of the House after the Republican election victory in 1994. He had built his career in Congress by using ethics and morality as a weapon as he launched a "civil war" against Democrats and liberals, so the New York Times reported in a long profile of Gingrich during the Republican primary election campaign in 2012.

The ultimate victim of this "ethical campaign" was the Democratic Speaker Jim Wright, who was forced to resign after being given an unusually large advance for his book "Reflections of a Public Man."

Many years later Gingrich came under fire for his own large book advance from HarperCollins, which is owned by Rupert Murdoch.

Gingrich's "Republican Revolution" and his proposal for a "Contract with America" paved the way for the sweeping Republican election victory in 1994, when the Republicans captured the majority in the House of Representatives for the first time since 1954.

In 1996, the Republicans retained a majority and Gingrich was re-elected Speaker. He worked successfully with Clinton: they achieved welfare reform, tax cuts and a balanced budget.

But Gingrich's aggressive style offended many and in 1997 he was convicted of ethical irregularities, especially on his taxes, by his colleagues in the House of Representatives. Gingrich was forced pay fines of 300,000 dollars. Nothing like it had ever happened before and it spelled the end of his career as Speaker.

When the 1998 election went badly for the Republicans, and Clinton easily won reelection, Gingrich resigned, not only as Speaker but also as a member of the House of Representatives.

It was not widely known then, but it has later emerged, that Gingrich, while pursuing Clinton for his sexual transgressions and while supervising the impeachment process against Clinton, was himself involved in a romantic affair with Callista Bisek, a much younger congressional staff member, even though he still was married to his second wife. In 2000, Callista Bisek became Gingrich's third wife.

Over time, fewer and fewer people took the Whitewater affair, which had occurred before Clinton became president, seriously. The Whitewater Committee in Congress never came up with anything that could prove that Bill Clinton had abused his office. Yet, its investigations continued until Clinton's final year in the White House.

Evidence was totally lacking, wrote Richard Ben-Veniste, the Democratic General Counsel on the Whitewater Committee, in his book "The Emperor's Clothes - Exposing the Truth from Watergate to 9/11."

However, the Whitewater prosecutor Kenneth Starr never gave up. His investigation took a new direction. It no longer came to be about whether Clinton was guilty of irregularities and illegalities in the Whitewater affair, but rather about President Bill Clinton's personal sex life, both before and after he became president.

The parade of women, all the way back to Gennifer Flowers and others from Clinton's time as governor of Arkansas, seemed never to end.

In May 1991, in Little Rock, the then Governor Bill Clinton met a woman named Paula Corbin. What took place between the two has never been completely established, but three years later, in May 1994, Paula Corbin Jones, by then married, sued Clinton for sexual harassment and demanded 700,000 dollars in damages. In July the following year, Monica Lewinsky began to work as an intern the White House and in November of that year the intern and the U.S. President started a sexual relationship. It lasted 16 months. According to Ben-Veniste, it was the Lewinsky affair, not the Whitewater affair that almost led to Clinton's resignation.

The saga revealed to the American public and the whole world was jaw-dropping. Paula Corbin Jones and her lawyers did not give up and investigators continued their stubborn prying into Clinton's sex life. In May 1997, the Supreme Court unanimously rejected the president's request for immunity in the Jones case which he had argued for on the grounds that, as president, he had no time for these things. Parallels were inevitably drawn between the Supreme Court's decision against President Nixon during the Watergate scandal when the Supreme Court unanimously denied a sitting president's request on the grounds that Nixon was not "above the law" and that he had to hand over the White House tape recordings.

In December 1997, Clinton learned that Monica Lewinsky was to be one of the witnesses in the Paula Corbin Jones case. Who was she, his staff wondered? Clinton flatly denied to his lawyers that he had had sex with her. "Do you think I'm fucking crazy," he said, according to similar accounts in John F. Harris' book, "The Survivor" and in Jeffrey Toobin's book "A Vast Conspiracy."

Clinton made that claim even though he had met with Monica Lewinsky just moments before he met with his lawyers. He lied. How could Clinton be so "brazen," Harris asked in his book, "so brazen, so bold?"

Oh, Bill...

The president continued to lie even though his lawyers warned him that if it was discovered that he had lied, he would be impeached. In a series of media interviews, and in interrogations during preliminary investigations in the Paula Corbin Jones case, and in a speech in White House in January 1998, Clinton denied having had an affair with Monica Lewinsky.

"I'm going to say this again. I did not have sexual relations with that woman, Miss Lewinsky. I never told anyone to lie, not a single time - never. These allegations are false. And I need to go back to work for the American people."

The following evening, on January 27, 1998, President Clinton gave an extra-ordinary State of the Union speech in Congress. In subsequent days, his approval ratings skyrocketed, to 67 percent -- the highest ever during his years in the White House.

In April of that year, the president was called to testify before a grand jury, and it was then, finally, that he acknowledged his affair with Monica Lewinsky. In a subsequent televised speech he confessed what he had done and said that he was "deeply sorry" and apologized. But he also said: "It's time to stop the pursuit of human destruction and the prying into private lives and get on with our national life."

By this time, the nation was tired of Clinton, Paula Corbin Jones, Monica Lewinsky, Kenneth Starr, Whitewater and all the other things that, month after month, year after year, had dominated the political discourse in Washington and captured the headlines all over America.

Clinton himself had paid a heavy toll and his entire presidency was threatened. Richard Ben-Veniste described in his book how extremely disappointed he was with Clinton and he urged him to publicly apologize to the American people: "The American people are the most forgiving people in the world - we have built a nation in which one can have a second chance - - and if he apologizes quickly people will forgive him."

Despite his disappointment, Ben-Veniste did not feel that the president's refusal to admit his extra-marital affair under oath was enough to impeach a man who had twice been elected president. That was hypocrisy. Clinton's mistake did not come even close to the "high crimes and misdemeanors" that the Constitution stated was required to impeach a president.

Kenneth Starr's 445-page report about Clinton and Whitewater and Monica Lewinsky was published in September 1998 and a month later Republicans in the House of Representatives decided to start impeachment proceeding against the president. The vote was 258 to 176. The Republicans clearly aimed not only to harm the president but to destroy him, to get him out of the White House. But their strategy did not have broad support politically or from the American public. In the days after the Starr report was published, polls showed support for Clinton at a steady 60 percent.

There had been 15 impeachment proceedings in American history before Bill Clinton's. They had included a judge, a Cabinet member, a former president. Congress now sought to use its constitutional authority to impeach a president and remove him from office after he has been declared guilty of "treason, bribery or other high crimes and misdemeanors."

The impeachment of a president had only happened once before, in 1868, a few years after the Civil War, when President Andrew Johnson was impeached but acquitted by one vote following a trial in the Senate.

The reason for that trial was that he had fired the Secretary of War, Edwin M. Santon, despite a law that radical Republicans had pushed through forbidding the president to dismiss members of his Cabinet. Johnson considered the law unconstitutional and ignored it.

The impeachment proceedings against President Richard Nixon in 1974 as a result of the Watergate scandal was never completed, because Nixon chose to resign after his convictions in the House Judiciary Committee but before the House of Representatives as a whole could vote on the question of proceeding to an impeachment trial in the Senate. In Clinton's case, the case proceeded to the full House, where a majority concluded the following:

Article 1: perjury before the grand jury - Yes! 228 voted for and 206 against. Only five Democrats voted for impeachment, while five Republicans voted against.

Article 2: perjury during the preliminary investigation - No! 229 voted against and 205 for. 28 Republicans voted with the Democrats.

Article 3: impeding the course of justice - Yes! 221 voted for and 212 against.

Article 4: Clinton's answers to questions from the Committee - No! 285 voted against and 148 for.

Clinton's defenders were not particularly worried after the votes. They argued that there was no "smoking gun," and that it had absolutely nothing to do with "high crimes and misdemeanors." It was about sex and not about whether Clinton had damaged the United States and the American society.

The six-week impeachment trial in the Senate began in January 1999. Supreme Court Chief Justice William Rehnquist presided. It was of a little interest, actually it was quite unexciting.

Everyone knew how it would end and that the 67 votes needed to impeach Clinton were not there because the Democrats continued to support their president -- the 55 Republican votes were not enough. Democratic Senator Dale Bumpers, Clinton's old friend from Arkansas, expressed what many thought when he tried to provide a perspective on the whole matter:

"We're here today because the President suffered a terrible moral lapse, a marital infidelity; not a breach of the public trust, not a crime against society, the two things Hamilton talked about in Federalist Paper number 65 -- I recommend it to you before you vote - but it was a breach of his marriage vows. It was a breach of his family trust. It is a sex scandal."

Yes, this was not enough of a reason to convict Clinton, the 100 Senators appeared to think when they voted, and acquitted, the president:

Article 1: perjury before the grand jury -- 45 votes for and 55 against.

Article 2: Prevention of justice - 50 votes for and 50 against. Five Republicans, all from the northeastern United States - Susan Collins, Olympia Snowe, Jeff Jeffords, Arlen Specter and John Chafee - voted with the Democrats.

In the middle of the ongoing trial, Clinton gave his State of the Union address to Congress. It served to underscore how strange this whole story was and how it lacked all proportions. This was different from the Watergate scandal or for that matter from the Iran-contra affair, both infinitely more damning than Clinton's personal lies. It was a matter of "public vs. private morality."

Jeffrey Toobin asked many questions in his book "A Vast Conspiracy."

How was the investigation of the Whitewater affair allowed to go on so long? Why was Kenneth Starr allowed to continue when it was clear that after three years he had found no evidence of irregularities in the Whitewater affair? And why was Starr given permission by Attorney General Janet Reno to begin examining what happened between Paula Corbin Jones and Governor Clinton? How was it that the investigation came to be about whether Clinton had "prevented the course of justice" in ways that had absolutely nothing to do with the Whitewater affair? Starr took the view that this occurred when Clinton instructed Lewinsky on how she should answer questions about their relationship.

For Toobin, this was yet another proof of the judiciary's "takeover" of the political process.

Bill Clinton's political success seems even more remarkable because it took place during these years of investigation, of special prosecutor, special committee and impeachment. There is no doubt that the Clinton years were successful, albeit turbulent, years, full of with both advances and adversity, of crisis after crisis.

The proposal to introduce a comprehensive health care reform was a major failure. It immediately met with intense opposition and accusations that Clinton wanted to introduce "socialized medicine" and that "big government" would now take over the health sector. The proposal never even came up for a vote in Congress.

The failure was to be a warning to all who advocated health reforms, right up until to President Obama's successful health care reform was approved by Congress in March 2010.

The basis for Clinton's economically successful years as a president was laid in August 1993, just seven months after he entered the White House, when Congress approved his economic plan albeit with an extremely slim majority. The victory was eventually seen as the catalyst for the subsequent years of extraordinary economic prosperity. Not a single Republican voted for the plan, which was approved in the House of Representatives by a vote of 218 to 216, and by a 50-50 in the Senate, only after Vice President Albert Gore, as President of the Senate, cast his 51st and deciding vote. After years of huge and irresponsible budget deficits, the country now took a major step towards restoring the health of the economy.

However, the victory did not seem to have helped Clinton and the Democrats, who failed to pass the big health reform proposal. The mid-term elections of 1994 became a triumph for the Republicans, who, for the first time in 40 years, won control of the House of Representatives and who were now led by a tough new speaker named Newt Gingrich. Gingrich saw as his task to build on the conservative gains that the "Reagan Revolution" had initiated. Gingrich's "Contract with America," which Clinton mockingly came to call "Contract on America," dominated the debate in the years that followed.

1995 was a most eventful year. In April, terrorism shook Oklahoma City and the whole country; in August, NATO launched its largest military operation ever against Bosnia; in November a peace was concluded with the Dayton Agreement. It was a major foreign policy triumph for Clinton, who had suffered setbacks both in Somalia where he had unwisely sent American troops, and in Rwanda's great human tragedy, with 800,000 deaths, and where Clinton had failed to intervene. Clinton's inaction in Rwanda can be attributed to his failure in Somalia, but passivity during the Rwandan genocide has remained his darkest hour as president.

That fall, the U.S. government was forced to close -- twice. Millions of federal employees were prevented from to going to work. The furloughs were a result of Speaker Gingrich's and the Republican congressional majority's ultimatum to President Clinton about the new budget, an ultimatum to which he, simply, said "no." Public opinion agreed with him and the Republicans committed a costly political mistake that still haunt them 17 years later in the fierce battles between Congress and President Obama. Republicans, all those years on, want at all costs to avoid another government closure and getting blamed for it.

Clinton was politically strong in late 1995 and after his successful State of the Union in January 1996. The mid-term elections in November 1998 were a success for the Democrats, although the Republicans retained their control of the Senate and the House. But the steady strengthening of the U.S. economy was a main reason for his political success. In 1997, the year of a major budget agreement that had Republican support, the economy grew, for example, by 8.2 percent. Just after New Year of 1998, the budget deficit turned into a surplus, something which the New York Times termed "the fiscal equivalent of the fall of the Berlin Wall."

Many have questioned if Clinton personally had anything to do with the great economic successes that occurred during his eight years in the White House. Regardless, the figures are inescapable: 22 million new jobs, hundreds of billions of dollars in budget surpluses, more Americans than ever owning their homes, median incomes among blacks and Latinos steadily increasing. These were good years for America, the country was strong, even though the scandals, or alleged scandals, followed President Clinton during almost all of his years in the White House.

In the Paula Corbin Jones case, Clinton refused for the longest time to make a deal but made one in the end, in his Presidency's eleventh hour, and paid 850,000 dollars in damages without having to issue an apology to her. And on his last day in the White House, on January 19, 2001, he approved a settlement with the Whitewater special prosecutor, now named Robert Ray. Clinton would not be prosecuted after for his presidency, but in return he had to pay 25,000 dollars in fines and he was deprived of his license to practice law in Arkansas for five years.

Despite all this, despite the fact that his eight years in the White House were marked by crisis after crisis, Bill Clinton, both so loved and so hated, succeeded in remaining in office. But his years in the White House also led to sadness among many of his supporters, over so much promise never quite met, and over so much wasted time and effort. Yes, he had "made it to the end," as John Harris wrote in his book, but...

For Harris, there were three main reasons why Clinton not only managed to remain in office but that his eight years also became extremely successful for America: he was serious in his duties as president and he brought sound policies; he had a genuine populist ability to create a close relationship with the electorate; and he was a "survivor."

Today, Bill Clinton, 67 years old, is a statesman, an extremely popular and successful ex-president. He looks great and many miss him in a somewhat nostalgic way and wish that he could run again for president. With a wife, Hillary, who was elected senator for New York State and then Secretary of State under President Obama, it is difficult to imagine a more successful political couple in modern America, fully comparable with Franklin D. and Eleanor Roosevelt.

For Newt Gingrich, Clinton's demagogic opponent during his years as president, things have not gone as well. His career as a lobbyist in Washington has brought him millions of dollars, but his message is as negative as ever and he is as unpopular as ever, even within his own party. He still thinks highly of himself as a statesman, rivaling both Ronald Reagan and Margaret Thatcher, and he still believes that he would be the best president in America. His problem is that few agree with him. After his short, victorious moment in the Republican primary election in South Carolina in January 2012, his political fortunes have slowly but surely diminished.

His time in American politics, as opposed to Bill Clinton's, is today over.

Chapter 6.

THE DARK YEARS

I will never forget the morning of September 11, 2001. As fate would have it, I was at 80 John Street in lower Manhattan in New York City, just three blocks from what would come to be called "Ground Zero."

It had begun as one of those clear, beautiful, blue-sky mornings, even though we had to imagine much of it in our apartment in the shadows of skyscrapers and giant office blocks. My wife, daughter and I were getting ready, eating breakfast and reading the newspaper before departing for work, classes, meetings, expecting another ordinary day in New York City.

Suddenly, about a quarter to nine, we heard a loud bang, much louder than the usual noise from exhaust pipes, firecrackers, garbage trucks so common in lower Manhattan. What was it? I rushed down and out into the street where people had begun to gather, they were looking up at the sky, where, high up, one of the gigantic twin towers of the World Trade Center was on fire. It seemed that a plane had flown straight into the north tower. My first thought was that it had been an accident. But how could it have happened?

I rushed back inside and turned on the television. There was chaos and confusion. Then, another large explosion sounded. A second plane had flown straight into the South Tower. It was now clear that something out of the ordinary, something big, was happening.

I hurried out into the street again and started walking up John Street towards Broadway and the Twin Towers.

Both were now on fire up there in the blue sky, and then, something even more unimaginable happened: the gigantic North Tower simply started to crumble, top to bottom, almost effortlessly and with an enormous roar, and then, seconds later, a huge, dark mass of debris and smoke and dust, like a giant dark wave between the skyscrapers on both sides of our narrow street, rushed towards me.

I had fortunately not gone very far, so I managed to run back and reach our entrance before everything disappeared in a pitch-black cloud. Coughing, shocked people filled our foyer. We could not see anything, we could barely breathe. Eventually, the sun shone through again and the air was easier to breathe, but then the second tower collapsed - again from top to bottom with a roar and we were swept back into dust and smoke and total darkness. There was a sense of panic, new people crowded into our building to take shelter, coughing and covered in dust and debris.

A young woman, who had been on the 53rd floor of the North Tower into which American Airlines 11 had crashed just above her office, sat quietly in our foyer and cried with her cell phone in her hand. She had finally managed to call her father on Long Island to tell him that she was alive.

Out in our street, more and more people appeared. They came out of the smoke and the dust and the darkness from "Ground Zero" as if from another world. Many were immediately helped. Staff from shops along the street and residents from the apartments along John Street turned up with protective masks and water bottles. Many had no idea where they were and how they could escape this madness and head home. Go north, go north, we said and pointed to the Brooklyn Bridge, which could be seen when the dust settled and daylight returned.

Our deep sense of concern, of worry, turned into real fear when we heard via radio and television that a third plane had crashed into the Pentagon in Washington, DC. This was bigger, much bigger, than just where we were, in lower Manhattan. What was happening?

By now, we were without electricity and telephone service and an order came to evacuate the entire apartment building. We hurriedly packed up necessities and went out into the street, which was now covered in foot deep dust and debris, almost like dirty snow. We turned right, away from "Ground Zero," and headed north. Soon, we were out in the sun and under a clear blue sky, but behind us, where the Twin Towers had been part of our neighborhood and our world, there was now nothing, only emptiness. I had often walked in their shadow and looked straight up, trying to see the top of them. They were enormous. I never went up there, to the top. A wonderful view, I had been told. Now it was too late.

Thousands walked north with us, while many turned east, across the bridge to Brooklyn. Block after block of people walking in almost total silence. Mobile phones did not work and telephone booths, now so seldom used, had suddenly become essential. Long lines to use them stretched around the corners. We had to wait a long time before we got our chance to hear the reassuring news that our three sons were alive and well.

One of them, a reporter for Bloomberg News, was already reporting on what had happened and he was concerned for people he knew, among them sources who were bond traders at Cantor Fitzgerald on the 101st floor of the North Tower. The firm, as we came to learn later, lost almost 700 employees that day. Another son was still at home in Brooklyn, and followed everything from the roof of his house. And a third, a student, was still home further up on Manhattan.

We continued walking north, to a bar in Greenwich Village and a couple of stiff drinks.

Late that afternoon, we went south again to see how things were around our home on John Street. There were no buses, no metro, hardly any taxis. The streets were practically deserted. We were tired, very tired. John Street was like a war zone. Not a soul was around, except for a few police officers and rescue personnel. Dust, ash and debris lay ankle deep in the streets and everything was dark – there was no water, no electricity. Our building was empty except for the manager. You can't stay here, he said.

We picked up a few more necessities and walked north again, in search of a bed for the night and found one way up on Manhattan. Not until over a week later could we return home for good, although it all still looked like what could only be described as a war zone. Our building was in such poor condition that the tenants protested and proposed a rent strike if the landlords did not clean it up properly and lowered rents. When they refused, and refused even to allow those who wanted to move to terminate their leases, a rent strike broke out. It lasted for months. There was a trial and then, finally, a settlement, in March 2002. The landlords cleaned up the building, washed the facades, dismantled and cleaned all the air conditioning units in the windows, which were found to contain everything from asbestos to human remains.

Life on John Street in lower Manhattan had now changed. I remember how even a few months after 9/11 there was a sense of anxiety, uncertainty, of anticipating a new horror. We tried to return to everyday life, but it was difficult. Every time a plane flew a bit low over the city we were reminded of that fateful day. Any loud noise, or bang, made us flinch. A distinct odor from "Ground Zero," an odor of burnt steel and other metals and perhaps of human remains, hung in air for months and met us as soon as we came out from the subway into the daylight.

We could not forget. Actually, we did not think of anything else. For us, 9/11 was still so present, and it was still so hard to understand and comprehend what had happened. We all had our own memories of that day and we had all our own way of moving on and trying to find a way back to how we were before 9/11, which may not always have felt so exciting but which, now, was, oh, so eagerly hoped for.

Every morning when I stepped out on John Street and turned west towards the subway I was reminded of "Ground Zero" a few blocks away, where the Twin Towers had dominated the skyline. Now, there was only sadness and emptiness. All of New York was different, more subdued, but also friendlier and with a new sense of cohesion after all we had been through together.

In June, as soon as our lease allowed, we moved up uptown, to the Upper West Side of Manhattan, near the greenery of Central Park, and a new life. But it did not happen without a serious discussion. We had started to get attached to lower Manhattan - the Financial District. Not too many people lived down there, and what we had been through, together, had forged a new sense of solidarity among us. There were good restaurants; we enjoyed our walks along South Street or on the promenade along the Hudson River in Battery Park City. We liked the proximity to the water. But the large hole where the World Trade Center once stood reminded us of every day of that fateful day, and we realized that our home and our neighborhood would become a giant construction site for years to come.

Sadness overtook us as we, like thousands of others, moved. And in the autumn of that year, we left New York City and moved west, to a new job and a new life in San Francisco.

It was said at the time that New York and the United States would never be the same after 9/11. It turned out to be true, perhaps more so than we ever imagined. We asked ourselves if this would be the catalyst for a new American foreign policy, if now we all would look at the world differently, with new eyes. Maybe we would witness a new American involvement in foreign affairs and there would be a new focus in the media on the world beyond the United States, a focus that for so long had been absent.

We cannot afford to "close our borders and take care of ourselves," said a friend, almost wistfully. No, the time when America could "go-it-alone" was past.

I remember that we were hoping for a vigorous, imaginative new American engagement in international affairs, one in which the United States would realize that military solutions were not the answer to every international problem, and that there would now be an emphasis on cooperation, patience and perseverance. But we also realized that this would depend on the United States embracing the new goodwill that the world was showing America after 9/11 and understanding that the fight for democracy and freedom must be a joint fight waged within existing international political and economic institutions.

Meanwhile, in lower Manhattan, the relatives of the thousands of missing waited and hoped, but there came a point when hope ran out. All of America waited to see what would now happen, whether there would be war, new terrorist attacks, whether we would know who the enemy really was, what would happen in the stock market, what would be the future for our friends and our jobs.

There was an uncertainty about the future such as I had never before experienced in America. There were only questions, no answers.

This waiting tore at the American public. Americans have never been known for their great patience. They want things to happen fast and they want quick results, even in war, and, ideally, without costing any American lives.

As always, when something big happens in America - as in 1963 when John F. Kennedy was shot, or in 1968 when both Bobby Kennedy and Martin Luther King Jr. were assassinated, or during the Gulf War, or after the Columbine massacre, the Oklahoma City bombing, the death of Osama bin Laden -- a big debate, from coast to coast, started. Television led. Many commercials were dropped. Programs focused on the same thing. The nation turned itself inside out. I remember Ted Koppel saying on television one evening after 9/11 that "we are very good the first five days" after a tragedy. That is so right. That's when America is at its best -- open, questioning, willing to debate, ready for reassessments and changes. But what Ted Koppel also meant was that with time, this all goes away, and, in the end, spurs very little positive change.

President George W. Bush's remaining seven years in the White House were unexpected and shocking in ways few could have imagined. These became the years of the "War on Terror" -- in Afghanistan and Iraq, years when a strong and healthy U.S. economy with a large budget surplus crumbled into large deficits, years when the property market crashed and a financial crisis shook Wall Street.

They were years when America at Abu Ghraib, at Guantanamo, and in secret prisons around the world, violated the fundamental principles of human rights set down in the U.S. Constitution and in all international conventions of war on how prisoners of wars are to be treated.

For America, the first decade of the 21st Century's became the dark years, a time when "America was losing its moral authority as a nation of laws," when America "lost its way," as Eric Lichtblau wrote in his book, "Bush's Law - The Remaking of American Justice."

Just a few weeks after 9/11, a secret order by President Bush paved the way for the widespread wiretapping of phones, across the whole world. It came without the participation of the FISA Court (Foreign Intelligence Surveillance Act), which had been created in 1978 - after the Watergate scandal – and which was intended to prevent the wiretapping of American citizens without special court orders. Bush's decision was made without the knowledge of the FBI, the federal police. Bush, simply and secretly, expanded the NSA's (National Security Administration) mandate and allowed spying on American citizens. This happened without debate and without Congressional approval.

It's still not known how many phones were tapped in those days. When the New York Times revealed the NSA's wiretapping in October 2005, reactions were sharp and there was even some talk of initiating impeachment proceedings against President Bush. According to Lichtblau, the NSA wiretapping was Vice President Cheney's idea. The United States was at war and Cheney demanded that the Commander-in-Chief (Bush) should have unlimited powers. This became the basic philosophy of the Bush presidency.

The New Yorker journalist Jane Mayer wrote in her book, "The Dark Side - the Inside Story of How the War on Terror Turned into a War on American Ideals," that Bush's and Cheney's basic positions were that the terrorists struck because they regarded the United States as "soft."

Within the Bush administration, many thought that there were too many international laws, too many civil liberties, too many restrictions on the President's powers, and too much openness and interference from Congress and the media.

On January 8, 2002, this led President Bush to violate the Geneva Convention and its rules on treating prisoners, which had been observed since 1949, including during the Vietnam and Gulf Wars. The United States became the first signatory of the Convention to make such a decision. Ten days later, Secretary of Defense Don Rumsfeld issued a new order to the military: they no longer had to adhere to the rules of the Geneva Convention.

"The brightest interpretation of the Bush years is that this was an unfortunate episode, and the bleakest interpretation is that this Administration changed America in a fundamental way," said Karen Greenberg, director of the Center on National Security at Fordham University Law School in New York, in an interview with me in January 2012. For Greenberg, an expert on human rights and the Guantanamo prison, the important issue was whether the pendulum that Bush moved would ever swing back. She deeply doubted this would happen. The sad truth was, she said, that Bush got solid support. Remember, she added, Abu Ghraib took place just months before the November 2004 election. We had the chance, then, to defeat Bush, but we didn't do it. Instead, we re-elected him.

"In fact," continued Greenberg, "we still debate the torture issue -- just look at what the Republican presidential candidates said during the 2012 primary election. Guantanamo is still open, despite President Obama's efforts to make the pendulum swing back and close the prison. He might have succeeded in this if he had acted quickly, after the election victory in 2008, but the whole thing dragged on and he failed."

This means, Greenberg said that we still have a system of indefinite detentions without trial, and that is "unacceptable" to me.

America changed quickly after 9/11. Just five weeks later, Congress approved a new law called the "USA Patriot Act." It passed with overwhelming majorities – in the House of Representatives by 357 votes to 66, and in the Senate by 98 to 1. The new law restricted Americans' rights and freedoms in a number of areas, as a consequence of President Bush's declaration that the United States was at war, although no war had officially been declared. Still, he called himself a "War President" and he started two wars, the first was against Afghanistan on October 7, 2001, less than a month after 9/11, and the second against Iraq a year and a half later, on March 20, 2003. The war in Iraq lasted over eight years, until the last U.S. troops left Iraq on December 15, 2011.

Here are the final statistics about that war:
- Between 110,000 and 120,000 military deaths, including 4,500 Americans, 4,800 coalition forces, and 10,000 Iraqis.
- 32,000 American soldiers wounded.
- Over 100,000 Iraqi civilian casualties.
- More than 1.6 million refugees and 1.2 million internally displaced Iraqis.

In Afghanistan, the war is still raging and we don't yet have any final numbers. By August 2013, 2,161 American soldiers had died there.

The two wars have cost enormous sums, over two trillion (two thousand billion) dollars. And in the coming years the care for the 32,000 wounded soldiers is expected to cost between 400 and 700 million dollars.

Those who led America into those two wars, President Bush, Vice President Dick Cheney, Defense Secretary Don Rumsfeld, National Security Advisor and later Secretary of State Condoleezza Rice, have written memoirs about their years in the Bush administration.

None of them "regretted" anything. Bush wrote in "Decision Points" that although no weapons of mass destruction were found in Iraq, we did not lie, we were just wrong. He wrote that he sent U.S. troops into a war that was based on intelligence information that turned out to be incorrect. He added that no one was more upset than he was when it turned out that there were no such weapons.

In James Mann's excellent book from 2004, "Rise of the Vulcans," one is struck by how long these protagonists had known each other and how closely they had worked together over many years, starting when first Ronald Reagan and then George HW Bush were in the White House. Far from being newcomers or beginners, they were experienced foreign policy experts who had long thought about America and about America's role in the world, and the George W. Bush presidency gave them the opportunity to implement their ideas and plans.

Bush's foreign policy advisers called themselves "The Vulcans" after the Roman god of fire and metalwork. Led by Cheney and Rumsfeld, they were mainly focused on military power and on rebuilding the military and restoring it to its post-Vietnam role. For them, the collapse of the Soviet Union was not an end, just one step on the way. America was not a country in decline. The country's power and leading role in the world would be preserved and its values and ideals would spread for the good of the world.

Multilateral diplomacy, as in the United Nations, was of no interest. Instead, they relied on American military power, on the U.S. as a superpower, ready to act unilaterally. The Iraq war was the last step in a foreign policy that they had been developing since Vietnam, according to James Mann.

Robert Parry wrote in his book, "Neck Deep-- The Disastrous Presidency of George W. Bush," that the "Neocons" – the neo-conservative foreign policy experts in the Republican Party -- praised the first President Bush for having pushed Saddam Hussein out of Kuwait.

But at the same time they mocked him for not having pushed on, not having invaded Iraq, marched on Baghdad and overthrown Hussein. Even in the mid-1990s, when Bill Clinton was president, they still felt that Bush had not completed his mission, and in 1998 they demanded in a letter to Clinton, through their "Project for a New American Century," that Saddam Hussein be deposed. All of the letter's 18 signatories, among them Rumsfeld, Richard Arbitrage, Paul Wolfowitz, Elliott Abrams, John Bolton, Paula Dubinsky, and Robert Zoellick, were veterans of previous Republican administrations. And when George W. Bush returned the Republicans to power in the 2000 election, the "Neocons," led by Cheney and Rumsfeld, marched into the White House to execute a foreign policy they had so long advocated.

As the United States marked the tenth anniversary of 9/11, articles and comments reflected how much America was still grappling with what happened during the eight Bush years.

In an article in The New Yorker entitled "Coming Apart," George Packer summed up the situation at the time of 9/11: about an America characterized by two ideologically irreconcilable camps in Congress after the impeachment of Bill Clinton and after the 2000 presidential election, decided by the Supreme Court. The Republican Party came to be controlled by its extreme right wing. Instead of reconciling the contradictions and building national unity and kinship, America became even more divided; the country was in recession, income inequality grew -- the richer became richer while the middle class and the poor lost ground; the dotcom crash was a fact, and Wall Street speculated ever more wildly.

9/11 and subsequent years came to constitute a failure of all America's institutions, concluded Packer.

Intelligence did not foresee 9/11; the media was wrong about weapons of mass destruction in Iraq; the military could not prevent chaos in Iraq after the invasion; Congress neglected its oversight role; and businesses concentrated on short-term and ever bigger profits.

With Hurricane Katrina and the disaster in New Orleans in 2005, the Bush administration collapsed. The picture of Washington and a government that committed mistake after mistake was reinforced, and then came the crash on Wall Street, caused by completely rampant and irresponsible speculation in the property markets and with criminal loan issuance policies, where people without income who should never have been given a mortgage, could borrow big money. Everything was built on sand. The only success of the Bush administration those years, according to Packer, was that no new terrorist attack on America occurred.

The conservative New York Times columnist, Ross Douthat, named Bush "the most unpopular president in 50 years." In contemporary opinion polls Bush won the approval of only 22 percent of the respondents. In comparison, Bill Clinton and Ronald Reagan won 68 percent approval after their eight years in the White House. For George W. Bush, who had 90 percent support immediately after 9/11, and who was at that moment one of the most popular presidents in U.S. history, one can speak of a presidency in total collapse.

Were the Bush years the worst decade ever? National Journal's political commentator Ronald Brownstein posed the question and replied, "Yes"…at least since World War II. And in an article called "Our State of Exception" in the New York Review of Books, journalist Mark Danner focused his criticism of the Bush years on how the war on terrorism changed America.

Prior to 9/11, he wrote, torture was officially illegal and banned. Under Bush the limits of what was legal were expanded under the definition "enhanced interrogation techniques.

There were:
- 5,000 arrests by immigration authorities.
- 10,000 imprisoned at Abu Ghraib and in other prisons in Iraq and Afghanistan.
- Hundreds held at the Guantanamo Bay prison on Cuba.
- Dozens of prisoners in the so-called "black holes" -- secret CIA prisons in at least eight countries, including Poland and Romania. At least 150 were sent under the so-called "rendition" program to be tortured in other countries, including in Egypt, Syria, Morocco, Uzbekistan, Jordan and Afghanistan. No one knows for sure the total number of people or where they were sent.
- In total, there were upwards of 100,000 prisoners in all the prisons around the world.
- The National Security Administration (NSA) intercepted and listened to the phone calls of thousands of American citizens, without permission from any court.

Some individual examples:

Abu Zubaydah, an alleged al Qaeda leader, was subjected to torture, known as waterboarding, 83 times. He was secretly transported to Guantanamo in 2006 and has been imprisoned there without trial ever since. Khalid Sheikh Mohammed, the "brain" behind the 9/11 attack, was waterboarded 183 times.

Joe Padilla, an American citizen was arrested in Chicago in 2002, was declared an "enemy combatant" and is still in a U.S. prison and has never been tried in a court.

The Canadian citizen Maher Arar was arrested during a stopover at John F. Kennedy Airport in New York and then detained and held incommunicado without being formally charged for twelve days and then and then sent to Syria, where he was tortured for a whole year before released. Arar sued the United States without success, but the Canadian government paid him over 10 million dollars in damages and the country's parliament issued a formal apology.

What was behind all this? What was the reason for this behavior?

Mark Danner quoted the author Ron Suskind and the so-called "one percent doctrine." It dates from Vice President Dick Cheney's statement that even if there was only a one percent's chance that terrorists could lay their hands on a weapon of mass destruction, the United States needed to act as if this were a fact.

President Bush's public message was different. In June 2003, on the UN Day dedicated to supporting torture victims, he said the United States was determined to eliminate torture in the world and at a press conference in March 2005, he said that America does not believe in torture. The reality was different. According to Mark Danner, the U.S. is today a symbol of a society where breaking the law is condoned by the country's highest leaders and where those same leaders are not punished.

Those who were behind this knew that the day would come when everything would be made public, and they prepared for it brilliantly, through various legal memoranda. Cheney has argued in his memoirs that what was done was legal despite statements by the International Red Cross to the contrary. Bush wrote proudly in his memoirs that when he was asked if Khalid Sheikh Mohammed should be the subject to enhanced interrogation techniques, he replied, "damn right!"

We are still waiting for the debate about this in America, wrote Danner, but instead it is as if all this has become part of our normal life.

In his book, "Secrecy & Privilege," Robert Parry described what happened during the Bush years as the result of a longer progression towards a more authoritarian form of government in America. It was a system that, with help from a sophisticated right wing press, emerged after the Watergate scandal.

But, he asked in his other book, "Neck Deep," how did it come about that that the American public granted Bush virtually "unlimited" powers during several years -- a kind of a "blank check" that, as Bush said in his West Point speech in 2002, gave him the right to overthrow any regime that constituted a threat to the United States.
It was not until 2006, when the Democrats took back the majority in Congress that the president's powers began to be questioned.

Previously, in June 2004, the Bush administration had encountered a stinging setback in the Supreme Court when a majority struck down plans to establish military tribunals for the Guantanamo detainees. In its "no," the Supreme Court referred to the Geneva Convention and said that Congress had not issued a blank check to the president. The Bush administration could not keep someone imprisoned in Guantanamo indefinitely. Prisoners were entitled to due process. Guantanamo was part of the United States and a state of war was not a blank check, said Sandra Day O'Connor, one of the nine justices.

Even conservative Antonin Scalia voted against Bush. Hamdi, a Guantánamo prisoner who had both American and Saudi citizenship and was said by the Bush administration to be too dangerous to have contact with other prisoners, was never charged. Instead, in October 2004, Hamdi was allowed to quietly return to his homeland of Saudi Arabia.

But the Supreme Court did not deter the Bush administration. It continued on the same path. Cheney wrote in his memoirs "In My Time" that he had "no regrets." Torture, he wrote, is safe, legal and effective.

For Dahlia Lithwick, Slate magazine's legal commentator, only "fools" discuss if illegal actions "work" -- the same fools that stand behind the illegalities. Commenting on Cheney's memoirs, Lithwick wrote that the former vice president had escaped justice -- "he got away with it" -- by referring to meaningless legal memoranda from the Bush administration's own lawyers, who claimed that torture was legal. And, she continued, Cheney can continue to pretend that torture is legal for as long as this does not lead to any legal consequences.

Today:
- 600 of the 775 detainees at the Guantanamo Bay prison have been released.
- Torture is no longer official U.S. policy.
- NSA wiretapping is now under judicial control, as before 9/11.
- Preventive arrests of Arabs and Muslims in the U.S. no longer take place.
- No extradition - rendition - to allies for special treatment and torture is taking place.
- The CIA black holes have been closed.

"The Torture Memos - Rationalizing the Unthinkable" is a book by law professor David Cole at Georgetown University in Washington, DC. The legal memoranda issued by the Bush administration's lawyers constitute "the smoking gun" in the torture debate, Cole wrote. The Obama administration published four of the six memos in April 2009, a few months after he became president. The remaining two had previously been leaked and become public.

All were issued in secret by the Bush administration between August 2002 and May 2005, and they originated, according to Cole, in a meeting at the CIA on July 13, 2002, when plans to use waterboarding and other "enhanced interrogation techniques" were approved.

Cole wrote that the torture memos do exactly what George Orwell predicted in his book 1984 -- "they distort the language and the law to rationalize the unthinkable." Bush's lawyers allowed the CIA to do whatever the intelligence agency suggested. They justified predetermined and illegal results. They did not demand that the CIA follow the law, but, rather, that the law be adapted to the CIA's requests. This was official policy, approved by the Bush administration, and was not something done by a few "bad apples," or agents, who took matters into their own hands. It is difficult to understand how experienced lawyers, schooled at Harvard University and other prominent law schools, could have approved torture, wrote Philippe Sands, law professor at University College London, in the foreword to Cole's book. The consequences, Sands continued, were that serious crimes were committed which America should investigate and bring those involved to justice.

But, unlike at the Nuremberg Trials, at the International Criminal Court in The Hague, or in Phnom Penh or Kigali, where those who issued the orders that brought death and destruction were brought to trial, there was no criminal prosecution of any member of the Bush administration.

To date, only ten low-ranking men and women in the U.S. military have been prosecuted and convicted for what happened at Abu Ghraib. A staff sergeant and a corporal were given eight and ten-year prison sentences, respectively. But their superiors have not been punished, and the CIA agents, who interrogated and tortured, and who, according to Jane Mayer in her book "The Dark Side" were behind at least four deaths, have immunity from prosecution.

How could this happen and how could the torture continue, despite leaks in the press, despite assurances to the contrary, despite bills like the one sponsored by John McCain, who himself had been tortured during the Vietnam War?

International and U.S. laws state that torture is never justified, under any circumstances, for any reason, in war as well as in peace. The Convention Against Torture has been signed by the United States and over 150 other nations, but if such laws are to work it requires that lawyers say no to torture.

During the Bush years, some of the country's most powerful lawyers simply did not live up to their ethical and legal responsibilities, wrote Cole. The lawyers in the Justice Department during the Bush years said "yes" over and over again: Jay Bybee, John Yoo, Daniel Levin, and Stephen Bradbury. All of them failed to live up to their obligations to prevent illegal acts from taking place. They gave the green light to all that the CIA proposed, all ten interrogation methods the CIA wanted, including waterboarding. On this basis, and with approval from the highest levels in the Bush administration, at least 27 prisoners were subjected to torture in various CIA prisons. Eventually, this behavior reached the Abu Ghraib prison in Iraq. Shocking photographs from the prison were published in April 2004.

Still, as recently as May 2005, two new legal memos again approved all of the CIA's interrogation methods. They were, according to Cole, "get out of jail" cards for the CIA. In other words, they served to ensure that the CIA could never be criminally liable for this. It was a matter of protecting members of the Bush administration and the CIA agents from prosecution, at all costs.

"Their memos resembled the advice a Mafia lawyer provides his clients so that they can avoid jail," wrote Anthony Lewis, the New York Times' legendary legal columnist.

None of Bush's lawyers have officially recognized that what took place was illegal, no one has apologized, no damages have been paid, not one has been disbarred or even suspended, none have been denied teaching positions in the country's leading law schools, and not one has been denied employment in the nation's premier law firms. Of Bush's lawyers, Jay Bybee is now a federal judge and John Yoo is a tenured professor at the University of California at Berkeley, while Daniel Levin and Stephen Bradbury both are lawyers in Washington.

What happened during Bush's war on terror, wrote constitutional expert and law professor Bruce Ackerman at Yale Law School in an article in Foreign Policy in the spring of 2011, "was a more sweeping violation of what the Constitution permits than what Richard Nixon ever tried during Watergate."

That those involved have still not changed their minds, or renounced torture and everything else that took place during these years, became apparent after President Obama ordered the killing of Osama bin Laden in 2011. A new debate about the use of torture broke out. In The New Yorker, Jane Mayer criticized Republican commentators who claimed that Obama finding and killing bin Laden was really a result of the previous intelligence work done during the Bush administration, including the "enhanced interrogation" methods -- torture -- used on Al Qaeda members. She wrote:

"Well, that did not take long. It may have taken nearly a decade to find and kill Osama bin Laden, but it took less than twenty four hours for torture apologists to claim credit for his downfall."

Mayer referred to the organization "Keep America Safe," where Cheney's daughter Liz and conservative journalist Bill Kristol published a "victory statement," praising the Bush administration's interrogation techniques without even mentioning President Obama.

Slate's Dahlia Lithwick also wrote of "torture apologists" in her commentary, "Closing Pandora's Box," and that no one can ever prove or disprove whether the Bush administration's interrogation techniques led to bin Laden's death. All we can say with certainty, she wrote, is that we tortured, and that we must now determine if we want to continue to live in such a way:

"With bin Laden's death, let's simply agree that the objectives of the Bush administration's massive anti-terror campaign have finally been achieved, and that the time for extra-legal, extrajudicial government programs -- from torture, to illegal surveillance, to indefinite detention, to secret trials, to non-trials, to the prison camp at Guantanamo Bay -- has now passed. There will be no better marker for the end of this era. There will be no better time to inform the world that our flirtation with a system of shadow- laws was merely situational, and that the situation now is over."

In other words: a better America!

Today, it is almost as if those dark years never happened. But I was reminded of it all when I visited New York City on September 11, 2011, ten years after the attacks on the World Trade Center. It was a day of memories and sadness, but also a reminder, a kind of encouraging reassurance that New York City was still there, in all its glory. The day was not as stunningly beautiful as ten years ago. Just as we had suspected, Ground Zero in lower Manhattan had been turned into a gigantic construction site and the re-building was still unfinished. World Trade Center 1 stretched to the sky and you could imagine how it would look when it was completed.

It will stand next to a new museum and two deep basins with its rippling water right where the Twin Towers once stood with the names of all the 2,977 victims carved into the black marble surrounding the basins' edges.

And all around in the open space, many hundreds of newly planted oaks stood, which, with time, will provide shade and coolness to the visitors.

On this day so full of memories, all the cranes stood silent. So far, 24 billion dollars had been invested in lower Manhattan. When we lived there ten years ago, there were only a few thousand residents in the apartment buildings around Wall Street.

Today, more people live there than ever before. And much is the same as ten years ago. The view across the water from Manhattan's southern tip is still magnificent, with the Statue of Liberty in the southwest, in the middle of the entrance to the harbor. Battery Park City is full of sailboats, and as the sun sinks in the west, children play and ride their bikes and their parents and grandparents sit there and enjoy the stillness of the evening, along the Hudson River.

For a moment, one could almost forget Ground Zero and the sadness and the fear we felt then, ten years ago, if it were it not for the three thousand special flags from countries around the world carrying the victims' names planted in the park by the water, lit up by evening headlights. A Swedish flag, my country of birth, stands there among them, in memory of David Tengelin, 25 years old, who was high up in the North Tower at the time of the attack, and who perished there.

In other parts of Manhattan that day, the Museum of Modern Art (MOMA) was full of visitors. The restaurants were packed and the boardwalk on the High Line, the new wonderful promenade along the old train tracks high above the streets on Manhattan's West Side, attracted thousands to a slow walk among greenery, with cars and traffic thundering underneath their feet.

So, in a way, this day was not only one of melancholy and sad memories, it was also a day of joy, that New York City continues to be a city of constant renewal, always exciting, and, in a way, still our home.

Chapter 7.

OBAMA – FAREWELL TO THE OLD AMERICA

We had all left home early that beautiful but chilly January morning in 2009 in Washington, DC. We wanted to be sure to be there. The last stretch down to the National Mall in the middle in the U.S. capital, where all motor traffic had been prohibited and the streets were full of eager and smiling people on their way on foot towards the heart of the capital.

"The walk of my life," said a young black man from Atlanta, Georgia, to me.

We were among the around two million people who that day wandered down to the monuments of the American nation's more than two hundred years of history to be part of something historic, something that we still found difficult to comprehend that it had really happened, and something we certainly do not want to miss now. A black American, an African-American, had for the first time in history been elected President of the United States. We thought it might happen sometime, in the distant future, not this year, probably not for many years yet, not in our life time.

Still, I had begun to understand that something unusual, something historic, was going on a few months earlier, a November evening in 2008, in Manassas, Virginia, a few miles west of the capital in the old Southern stronghold, from which so many of the country's first president, and large slave owners, had come--George Washington, Thomas Jefferson, James Madison ...

It was Obama's last election rally, late in the evening before Election Day, and perhaps 100,000 people had turned out, waiting patiently until 11 pm in the chilly evening to hear him speak, perhaps for the first time, perhaps again.

The atmosphere was festive, but the candidate looked dead tired, and sad. His beloved grandmother, who had raised him and taken care of him during his childhood and adolescence in Hawaii after his father returned to Kenya and his mother stayed with her new husband in Indonesia, had died that morning. He had so much wanted her to witness these last days and to experience the verdict of the American voters about her grandson the very next day.

All of the new America seemed to be there that night in Manassas, Many of them had only a short ago probably ever even have imagined that they'd be at a rally to express their support for a young black candidate with the strange name of Barack Hussein Obama. But they arrived early and parked far, far away, and the stayed well past after midnight, patient and expectant and good-natured. No brawls, no conflicts, only joy that they could attend that rally that night, and experience something historic.

"Virginia," Obama said, "I have only one word to you, just one word – tomorrow! After decades of broken politics in Washington, eight years of George Bush's failed leadership, twenty-one months of campaigning, we are less than a day away from changing America. We are all here – together: Black, white, Latinos, Native Americans, Asians, Democrats and Republicans, young and old, rich and poor, gay and straight, handicapped and non-handicapped -- all have contributed."

And then he told the story of the old lady at an election rally in the early stages of the campaign in Greenwood, South Carolina, which got a whole room going with her words, "fired up" -- "ready to go." She stood there, said Obama, small and delicate, a bit over 60, and smiled at me in her best church hat, and repeated, "fired up" -- "ready to go." And all the others in room began repeating the same words and the whole atmosphere in the room was transformed in a flash. I was "fired up" and "ready to go".

"That's how a voice can change an entire room. And if one voice can change a room it can change a city, and if it can change a city it can change a state, and if it can change a state, it can change a nation, and if it can change a nation, it can change world. Virginia, your voice can change the world tomorrow."

Manassas is historic ground, perhaps a somewhat strange choice for Obama's last election rally. Here the South reigned not so long ago, and this was where the South fought to preserve its traditions, its way of life…slavery. This is bloody land. In the village, which is now steadily changing into a liberal suburb of Washington, DC with a completely different population than the conservative small farmers who lived here 150 years ago, two big battles took place during the Civil War 1861-65. The first, "Battle of Bull Run" in July 1861, became the then largest and bloodiest battle during the four-year war, with almost a thousand dead and thousands wounded. In August 1862, it was time for the second "Battle of Bull Run," the culmination of the Confederate offensive. 10,000 of the North's men were killed or wounded, while the South lost 1,300 dead and 7,000 were wounded.

All those that night in Manassas who heard Obama were part of the historic change that took place on Election Day, the next day, for Virginia's voters, for the first time since 1964, gave their support not only to a Democratic presidential candidate, but to a black Democratic presidential candidate. And when the vote count was finished, it turned out that Obama had won in two other Southern states, North Carolina and Florida. He had also won in Republican Indiana, among the farmers in Iowa, in all-white Vermont and Maine - yes, throughout New England, along the entire Pacific Coast, in New York and in the old "Rust Belt" -- in Pennsylvania, Ohio, Michigan, and Illinois.

And he won in the north, in Minnesota and Wisconsin. He won in the desert, in Nevada, and in Colorado and New Mexico in the Rocky Mountains.

The Republicans stayed entrenched in the deep South - Alabama, Mississippi, Georgia, Louisiana, South Carolina and Arkansas - where Obama's support turned out to be the weakest, with only between 38.7 and 47 percent of the vote. The Republicans remained victorious also in the States of Wyoming, Utah, Oklahoma and Idaho, where Obama's support was even weaker -- between 32 and 36 percent of vote, because there were not African-American voters like in the South, where they so overwhelmingly voted for Obama.

"Yes, it was a historical event, something quite unthinkable 50 years ago," said David Kennedy, professor of history at Stanford University when I interviewed him in autumn 2011. "The victory showed how far we have come in this country in our race relations and in our relations with minorities. As with John F. Kennedy, who became the first Catholic president, Catholicism is no longer an issue in U.S. presidential elections, and I think that with Obama becoming the first African-American president, race will no longer a be factor in future presidential elections."

For Clayborne Carson, the African-American history professor at Stanford University, Obama's election victory was not entirely unexpected. There were signs, he said in an interview in autumn 2011 that something was about to happen in American society, politically, culturally and socially. People like Jesse Jackson and Colin Powell had opened doors for Obama even if Jackson could never get more than 30 percent of the vote and Powell chose never to run. There had also been Tom Bradley, for 20 years the mayor of Los Angeles, and Andrew Young, mayor of Atlanta and UN Ambassador during Jimmy Carter.

"But Barack Obama became the first African-American politician who American voters could seriously imagine as the country's president," said Carson. "The sad thing was that the conditions for Obama's breakthrough were such that he could not be seen as an advocate for the black America. His campaign therefore became a difficult balancing act."

Carson spoke about the great concern and skepticism regarding Obama's candidacy among America's black population. They wished him well, of course, and they wished him success. But they did not know him very well and they were concerned that if he lost, it would lessen the chances of another black candidate to be president, maybe for a hundred years. They also worried for his life. I do not think, admitted Carson, that there was a day during campaign that I was worried about the possibility that he could be murdered.

On election night in Grant Park in Chicago, Illinois, Obama's hometown, joy knew no bounds. Half a million people from all America's races cheered the country's new first family, a handsome African-American family, and they could hardly believe it was true.

"The hour of change has struck," Obama called out before the hundreds of thousands of cheering in the park in downtown Chicago next to Lake Michigan. "And if anyone is still in doubt that in America all things are possible, who still wonder if our ancestors' dream is alive today, who still questions the power of our democracy, they have the answer tonight. We have proven that a nation's true strength is not from our weapons or our wealth, but from the power of our ideals: democracy, freedom, opportunity, and hope."

In a powerful, almost thundering voice, the newly elected president ended by inviting everyone in Grant Park and in front of the television sets to reclaim the American dream and reaffirm the truth of this dream.

Amid the cheering, singing, laughing, the TV-cameras time and time again zeroed in on a man, now with graying hair, who cried and cried, for joy. It was a man who had fought long for a long time, long before Barack Obama was even born, a man who in two exciting election campaigns himself had tried, but failed, to be elected America's first black president, but who had paved the way for what happened in the election of 2008.

That man was Jesse Jackson.

Maybe Jesse Jackson also found it difficult to understand what happened, that Obama had succeeded where he had fought for so many years, ever since the 60s and the major civil rights and voting rights reforms of 1964 and 1965. Obama never participated in that long struggle. How could he? He was born in 1961, before Martin Luther King Jr.'s famous "I have a dream" speech in August 1963 in front of the Lincoln Memorial on the National Mall in Washington, DC. Obama was only two years old then.

In the autumn of 1983 King was honored with his own official holiday, even if a few senators from the South, led by North Carolina's reactionary Republican Senator Jesse Helms, fought against this to the end. It was in a way the old South's last battle and it took place almost exactly 20 years after King's great speech and 25 years before Obama's election victory in 2008.

Perhaps Jesse Jackson was thinking about all of this and all that had happened during struggle in the previous decades, in cities such as Montgomery and Selma, Alabama; Philadelphia, Mississippi; Greensboro, South Carolina; Nashville, Tennessee; Atlanta, Georgia, but also in the north, in cities like Chicago and Boston.

Perhaps he was thinking of that tragic day on April 4, 1968, in Memphis, Tennessee, where he witnessed Martin Luther King Jr. being shot to death by a white man named James Earl Ray. And maybe Jesse Jackson thought about suck local black leaders like Harold Washington, here in Jackson's and Obama's hometown, who became Chicago's first, and to date, only black mayor?

In his autobiographical "Dreams from My Father," Obama wrote that Washington's portrait appeared everywhere in Smitty's barbershop in Hyde Park on Chicago's South Side, where Barack Obama went and cut his hair for many years. When Harold Washington won the mayoral election in 1983, it was, Smitty told the young Obama, like when Joe Louis knocked out Max Schmeling. Before Harold, we were always second-class citizens. Now that we have Harold, we are proud of ourselves. The morning after his election victory was the most beautiful day of my life.

Harold Washington was supported by 97 percent of Chicago's black voters, but his years as mayor were not easy. That was evident when I met him in Chicago in summer of 1985, after two years as the city's leader. With humor and eloquence he told of tremendous opposition from the Democratic Party apparatus - Mayor Richard Daley's old organization - and how the city's population had been traumatized by this political fight because it was not used to this. For year, the mayor explained, the opposition had been defeated, beaten to the ground, and into silence.

"What is no going on is a power struggle between an old, well-entrenched organization and a reform movement," he said, but he would not characterize the struggle as a racial struggle, even though a local newspaper described Chicago as "the symbol of racist obscenity and political division. "I see changes every day. Today, we have changed the entire political dialogue in Chicago."

Harold Washington himself got good marks as the city's leader. And he was honest. He was re-elected mayor in 1987, after another tough election campaign. But his heart gave up, and six months after his election victory, he suddenly died in his office at City Hall, only 55 years old.

In 1986, on January 21, Martin Luther King Jr.'s new holiday was celebrated for the first time. America turned its gaze to little Ebenezer Baptist Church in Atlanta, Georgia. America reminisced and celebrated that the country had changed and become a better country, much thanks to King. The day was filled with powerful and jubilant celebration of the "freedom prophet," who had now taken his place in history alongside presidents like George Washington and Abraham Lincoln.

King was born in Atlanta and became pastor of its Ebenezer Baptist Church. It's where his memorial center, museum, and grave are located. The mayor in 1986 was black. His name was Andrew Young and he had marched and demonstrated for years with King. So many had come this sunny January day to Atlanta and its old worn down neighborhood, "Sweet Auburn:" Vice President George Bush, Ted Kennedy, Jesse Jackson, John Lewis, Andrew Young, and all the way from apartheid South Africa, Bishop Desmond Tutu. They laid a wreath on King's tomb and filled the old church with peeling paint in the ceiling and on the walls, but where the choir sang so beautifully to clapping hands and stomping feet.

Rosa Parks sat in the front row, the black woman who on that day in 1955, in Montgomery, Alabama, refused to give up her seat in the front of the bus to a white man and go back to the back of the bus. Her defiant act was the signal of a year-long bus boycott by Montgomery's black residents, a fight they eventually won. That fight was led by Martin Luther King, Jr. and it made him well-known all over America and in many parts of the world.

In 1984, the year after the U.S. Congress decided to institute a holiday in to King's memory, which President Reagan reluctantly signed the new law, Jesse Jackson decided to run for president. Initially, it brought no major headlines. Nobody expected any greater success for pastor from Chicago, and, by the way, he was not even the first black presidential candidate. Before Jackson, the comedian Dick Gregory had run. So had Black Panther Party leader Eldridge Cleaver and Congresswoman Shirley Chisholm – all without any greater success. And after Jackson, Republican Alan Keys, Democrat Al Sharpton of New York, and Carol Mosley Braun of Chicago had all tried, but they were marginal characters in the great battle for White House that takes place every four years in America.

Only Jesse Jackson achieved some success. In 1984, he was one of eight Democratic candidates and at the party's convention that summer in San Francisco he was one of only three remaining candidates. He had done much better than anyone had predicted.

In Harlem in New York City, stronghold for black American, the crowds that met up with Jesse Jackson on the corner of Lenox Avenue and 125th Street were large and enthusiastic - "win, Jesse, win." The tens of thousands at one of the last campaign events before New York's primary elections in April that year would not let him stop speaking, would not let him go. He got them to cheer and laugh and cry. It was a day that mirrored the "Rainbow Coalition" Jackson was trying to build, from the homosexual community in Greenwich Village through Chinatown and up here - - "home" -- to Harlem, in an amazing, chaotic, celebratory march along streets lined with poverty and hopelessness, but still a center for black America, rich in culture, music and history. They received him as their own, although he was born in South Carolina and resides in Chicago. That year, 1984, he was black America's undisputable leader.

The "Rainbow Coalition" never quite became the success that Jesse Jackson had hoped for. The support from white voters was never quite big enough. Instead, his campaign developed into an enormous African-American manifestation. Jesse Jackson was able to enthuse and engage the black voters in a way that had never been done before. About 200,000 new black voters had registered before the primary election in New York. That was the political significance of Jesse Jackson's first presidential campaign and such figures resulted in votes, in New York and across America.

Although Walter Mondale won the primary election in New York, Jesse Jackson received 26 percent of the vote, primarily because he captured 86 percent of the black vote. A new center of power had been born in the Democratic Party.

This was further evidenced in the starring role that Jackson came to play at the Democratic convention in San Francisco in July 1984. His magnificent voice confirmed not only that he was a magnificent speaker but also that he contributed greatly to giving the Democratic Party a new voice by registering so many new voters.

"I'm not perfect," he told the convention delegates, "but I am trying to do my best. Be patient, God is not finished with me yet. This campaign has taught me a lot, and if I have accomplished something good, created understanding, healed some wounds and created new hope, then this campaign has not been in vain."

The Democratic Party and its presidential candidate Walter Mondale had no chance against Ronald Reagan in November that year and lost big. Nothing helped, not even Jesse Jackson.

A few years later, just before Christmas 1987, Jesse Jackson re-appeared on the national political scene, in the State of Iowa, in America's "Heartland."

In the small village of Tipton, Jackson filled the little church to the breaking point. The audience was as white as the snow that covered the prairie in all directions. And in a school auditorium in Clinton, another small Iowa village, several hundred people gathered to hear him in the middle on a sunny Sunday, filling up the banquet room at Muscatine. Everywhere, he was greeted enthusiastically, by the old farmers, housewives, priests, teachers, workers, school children -- all white. They had come to hear his message of economic justice and peace on earth in the midst of the Reagan era and about his campaign as a "moral and political challenge" to build a "coalition of those who cannot win."

Something had happened, not just in America after almost eight years of Ronald Reagan's presidency, but also with Jesse Jackson himself. Then, in 1984, he was the newcomer, the fresh outsider. The blacks flocked around him and gave him their overwhelming support. But his crusade scared many white and Jewish voters. At the party convention, in the end he won only 465 of the nearly 4,000 delegates. But in the 1988 presidential campaign, he was no longer the outsider, no longer only the black candidate. He had become something more.

"We have broadened the campaign, and people now cross the traditional borders," said Jesse Jackson to me during an interview in a hotel room in Iowa's capital Des Moines. "More and more people seek us out, workers whose wages are driven down or whose factories closed, and farmers who lost their farms. People turn to me for help because my leadership and my ideas are based on action. We have constantly tried to extend our support, including voter registration. We have tried to build a coalition of people whose interests coincide. We have tried to change the nation's priorities."

In 1984, everyone said that Jesse Jackson could not win. Many said so, also in 1988. But that year he was much stronger than before. Already in the first battle in Iowa in February 1988 he won 11 percent of the vote.

The goal had been reached, the base had been broadened. He had proven that a black candidate could win white votes out here on the prairie, in the middle of white America.

When the 1988 primary election campaign came to a close, Jesse Jackson was the only remaining competitor to the winner Michael Dukakis. He had gathered 1,135 delegates after winning a total of 14 primary elections in his two presidential campaigns. A total of seven million Americans had voted for him. He had been a major player in the Democratic Party and he insisted now that his voice would be heard as the Democrats geared up for the final battle against George HW Bush, who was supposed to take over the mantle after Ronald Reagan. Jackson would have liked to be Dukakis' vice presidential candidate, but it was not to be. Instead, Dukakis chose the conservative Texas Senator Lloyd Bentsen, and Jesse Jackson could not hide his disappointment.

At the Democratic Convention in Atlanta in the summer of 1988, Dukakis and Jackson patched up their differences, and Jackson spellbound the convention delegates in his speech. The dream about a victory in November against Republicans was still alive.

"My friends, said Dukakis, "if anyone says to you that the American dream belongs to the privileged few, say to them that the Reagan era is over and that a new era has started."

But, as in 1984, the Democrats proved to be without chance against the Republicans, and George HW Bush with Indiana Senator Dan Quayle as vice presidential candidate won a big victory – 54 percent against 46 for Dukakis and Bentsen.

The Republicans won in 40 States against only ten for the Democrats. The White House was secured for the Republicans for another four years.

Jesse Jackson would never run for president again.

But, as journalist Gwen Ifill wrote in her book, "The Breakthrough," his campaigns were the start of a breakthrough for black candidates in American politics. Until then, there had only been one black senator in the U.S. Congress, Republican Edward Brooks from Massachusetts. Carol Mosley Braun and Barack Obama, both from Illinois, came in much later, not until the 1990s. Brooks had by then retired.

At the beginning of Barack Obama's presidential election campaign, shortly after he had announced his candidacy in January 2007 outside the Old State Capitol in Springfield, Illinois, where President Abraham Lincoln began his Senate campaign in 1858, Obama went to Selma, Alabama, to give a speech on the anniversary of the great, and bloody, civil rights march there in 1965.

It was the first time Obama participated in the memorial activities in Selma, as David Remnick, the editor of The New Yorker, wrote in his book, "The Bridge - The Life and Rise of Barack Obama." His participation was Obama's attempt to find his place, his role, in the long black struggle for equal rights in America. In his speech, Obama praised those who fought before him. He admitted he was a little nervous and said that he understood those who thought he was too new, with insufficient experience in Washington, to run for president.

I admit, he said, there is some arrogance in my decision to get into the presidential fray and he tried to make a connection to the battle that so many in the audience not only participated in, but had led.

"We are here today in the presence of giants whose shoulders we stand on today," Obama said. "These people fought not only for all African-Americans, but on behalf of all Americans, for America's soul. I stand here today because you marched. I am here today because you sacrificed yourselves for my sake. I stand on the shoulders of giants."

And then he told them about his background, about his grandfather in Kenya, cooking and cleaning in the British colonial families, called "house boy," and about his son, Obama's father, who received a scholarship to study in America and how he met Obama's white mother from Kansas, whose great, great, great grandfather had owned slaves. When they married in 1960 in Honolulu, Hawaii, mixed marriages were still illegal in half of America's 50 states.

"So you see," he said in Selma," I have the same experience as you and that's the connection to Selma, Alabama."

Obama mentioned some names in his Selma speech: King, John Lewis, Joseph Lowery -- but not Jesse Jackson's. The two were never close, even though they both lived in Chicago. After some snide remarks by Jackson during the campaign, the distance between them seemed to grow even more.

I'd like to cut off his balls, Jackson is quoted as saying about Obama when he felt that Obama spoke condescendingly to the black voters. Jackson's comments, which were not intended to become public, forced him to apologize, and they came to harm him more than Obama, because Obama had soon realized that he could not conduct election campaigns like Jesse Jackson's. Obama spoke, like Jackson, about hope and change, but Jackson had engaged in election campaigns with the black voters as a base from which he tried to build a progressive "rainbow coalition," consisting of all races. Obama was never a "black" candidate.

"Obama is an American who happens to be black, not a black American," said the former Secretary of State Colin Powell, himself black, who broke with his Republican Party colleagues when explaining his support for Obama.

But Obama was more than black. When he won the election, he became the first president whose father was born abroad (Kenya), the first from Hawaii, and the first to grow up in a developing country (Indonesia). Obama's extended family is black, white, Asian, Christian, Muslim, Jew. They speak English, French, Cantonese, German, Hebrew, Swahili, Luo and Ibo. His half-sister has an Indonesian father and is married to a Canadian of Chinese origin. His wife Michelle's ancestors were slaves in South Carolina and Alabama and her family belonged to the millions of blacks, who left the South in the great migration north in the early 1900s to find work and more tolerant surroundings, away from poverty, racial discrimination and tragic memories. America had never had such a president before.

As Remnick wrote, Obama turned his own black and white background to a metaphor about how he wanted to build a broad coalition and get Americans to back his talk about moral and political progress.

Obama was not the hero of the civil rights movement, but he became its greatest success. He was not the result of the traditional struggle that King and Jackson had led. His background was different -- African father, white mother, raised in Hawaii, schooled in a series of private schools, from Punahou High School in Honolulu, to Occidental College in Los Angeles, Columbia University in New York and Harvard University Law School in Cambridge, Massachusetts.

He was different, new, and in the beginning he had great difficulty in gaining support among blacks, especially the older blacks, who had been involved in the civil rights struggle and who thought that Obama's time had not yet come, and that he should wait a while, bide his time a little longer.

But Obama himself saw it differently. He never saw himself as only a "black" candidate, but as a representative for the "exceptional" America. Only in America is his story possible, as he so elegantly described it in a major speech at the Democratic Party convention in Boston in 2004, when he still was only a member of the Illinois State Senate, and Obama warned those who tried to divide the country and its inhabitants and he concluded to thunderous applauses:

"There is no liberal America, no conservative America, there is only the United States of America. There is no black America, white America, Latino America, Asian America, there is only the United States of America... The political commentators talk about red states and blue states, red for Republicans and blue for Democrats, but I want to say to them ... we are one people and we promise everyone to be faithful to The Stars and Stripes and to defend the United States of America."

For Stanford professor Clayborne Carson, that speech was the foundation Obama's election victory four years later:

"The speech represented many Americans' yearning to get away from the Bush years, the intense partisan confrontations and the increased tensions between the red and blue states. The speech set him apart from all previous black candidates."

Obama's goal during the campaign was also to constantly seek support from white voters. He succeeded in Iowa, in the first battle of the primary election campaign, and after that the black voters around the country flocked to their new leader.

In the primary election campaign's first major battle in the South, in South Carolina, a fourth of the white voters and nearly all of the blacks voted for Obama.

The only time race became a central issues in Obama's campaign was when his old pastor from his church in Chicago spewed hateful rhetoric. Until then, Obama and his campaign staff had carefully avoided discussing race or making race a major issue in the campaign. But now, race had ended up in the center of the election campaign and Obama took the bull by the horns and gave a speech, live on TV, on race and relations between blacks and whites. It was hailed for its intelligence and eloquence.

The speech in Philadelphia in March 2008, called "A More Perfect Union," was based on the fact that in no other country in the world would his own personal story and history be possible. It is an "American story," he said. I don't that we can solve today's problems if we don't do it together and understand that we all have different stories and backgrounds and that we don't look alike, but that we want the same thing: a better future for our children and grandchildren. And we know one thing: America can change. We have no alternative to working together to heal the wounds of past times.

And now, we stood on the National Mall in the middle of Washington, DC in January 2009 and we saw something almost unfathomable. Even old civil rights activist Joseph Lowery, who had helped Martin Luther King, Jr. form the Southern Christian Leadership Conference, and who had now been asked to speak at Obama's inauguration, was deeply taken by the moment, as he later told David Remnick and as he had looked out over the huge crowds, all the way to the Lincoln Memorial in the distance.

He thought he could hear Martin Luther King Jr.'s voice from there, far away, from 46 years earlier, in 1963, in his famous "I have a dream" speech urge the country to leave the whole race issue behind. Now, finally, America had heeded that call by installing a black man as America's 44th president.

When I stood there in the cold in the shadow of the Washington Monument along with a couple of million people and looked up at the huge displays that showed what was going there in front of the Congress and saw and heard Obama swear the presidential oath and speak to the nation, it was like a dream had come true. I can't say that I had been dreaming that a black American could become the country's president. I had never thought much about, maybe because I never thought it would happen in my life time. I had been looking for other signs, looking for other evidence that America was headed in the right direction, away from is violent and unjust past, away from slavery, racial discrimination and segregation. And, of course, the country has changed, and improved, during my years in America when it came to race relations. However, this I had not imagined, and certainly, not now.

It felt, as Obama himself said later to David Remnick, as if we celebrated America and how far we have come in this country.

"We African Americans are Americans. Our story is an American story and by strengthening our rights, we strengthen our Union," said Obama in the interview.

President Obama's inaugural address was not the grandiose speech that we had become used to from the election campaign. Not quite. It did not contain any quotes that became famous, like John F. Kennedy's "ask not what this country can do for you, ask what you can do for this country." It was a speech in the middle of a deep economic crisis and when America was fighting two wars, in Iraq and Afghanistan.

However, Obama said in a firm voice, we will meet our challenges. We remain a young nation, but as the Bible says, it is time to put childish things aside. The time has come to choose our better history. Our history is our strength, civil war, segregation ... but we have left that period behind us more united, and we believe that the old hatred will one day disappear.

"So let us, today, remember who we are and how far we have traveled, and that we will continue to bring the great gift of freedom and deliver it safely to future generations." Barack Obama's victory was big. There was no doubt who won. The symbol of the new America beat John McCain of the old America, by 10 million votes, with 52.9 percent of the vote to 45.7 percent. He captured 365 electoral votes to 173, far more than the 270 needed to win.

Farewell to the old America.

Chapter 8.

ON THE ROAD

> *"So, in America when the sun goes down and I sit on the old broken-down river pier watching the long, long skies over New Jersey and sense all that raw land that rolls in one incredible huge bulge over the West Coast, and all that road going, all the people dreaming in the immensity of it, and in Iowa know by now the children must be crying in the land where they let the children cry, and tonight the stars'll be out, and don't you know that God is Pooh Bear? the evening star must be drooping and shedding her sparkler dims on the prairie, which is just before the coming of a complete night that blesses the earth, darkens all rivers, cups the peaks and folds the final shore in, and nobody, nobody knows what's going to happen to anybody besides the forlorn rags of growing old, I think of Dean Moriarty, I even think of Old Dean Moriarty the father we never found, I think of Dean Moriarty."*

Jack Kerouac, "On the Road," 1959.

America is a big country. That's easy to forget. Over 3.7 million square miles. In comparison, Sweden, one of the largest countries in Europe, is only slightly larger than the State of California. It takes between five and six hours to fly from the Pacific to the Atlantic, and at least three days by car, and then you have to drive hard, almost around the clock. When it's twelve noon in Washington, DC, it is only nine in the morning in Los Angeles, and Hawaii, out there in the Pacific, is another three hours away.

Gertrude Stein once wrote:

"In the United States there is more space where nobody is than where anybody is. That is what makes America what it is."

It is precisely the size and geographical differences that make America so fascinating and that make traveling in America such a grand adventure. I started my discovery of America from the west, from the shores of the Pacific Ocean, and over the years I have traveled countless times back and forth between the two oceans. America and Americans are characterized by the desire to move, change jobs, try something new, and start over somewhere where no one knows you.

To travel, to be "on the road," is natural, nothing unusual, and nothing exceptional. It's reflected in such books as Jack Kerouac's "On the Road," John Steinbeck's "Travels with Charley" and "The Grapes of Wrath," William Least Heat Moon's "Blue Highways," Mark Twain's "Roughing It," Larry McMurtry's "Lonesome Dove," and in films like "Thelma & Louise" and "Easy Rider."

*

I have a special fondness for "The West" – America west of the 100th meridian that runs straight north to south, down the center of America, from the State of North Dakota up at the Canadian border down through Texas to the Mexican border. West of the 100th meridian, "The Great Plains" -- the American prairie – starts, and runs westward until it bumps up against the Rocky Mountains. Then, the deserts in Utah, Arizona and Nevada take over, eventually reaching the long coastline that runs from San Diego up to Seattle all along the Pacific Ocean.

Archibald MacLeish wrote that "America is west, and the wind is blowing." The West is wind, distance, loneliness and lack of water.

It rains less than 20 inches a year west of the 100th meridian, which is not enough to farm without irrigation. In many places, in cities like Phoenix, El Paso, and Reno, it rains only seven inches in a year. The only exception in this vast, dry part of America is the country's northwest corner, west of the Cascade mountain range, where it rains copiously and the forests are reminiscent of the Amazon rainforest.

California and Arizona have only become populated and prosperous thanks to irrigation. The many dams in the West have become legendary: Grand Coulee, Shasta, Hoover, Glen Canyon, and Bonneville. But, still, it's only a tiny part of the West that has benefited from the water drawn from such rivers as the Colorado, Green River, Snake, Sacramento, and the Columbia. When there is not enough water in the rivers, water gets drawn from ground water which is steadily disappearing. The West is still desert, or semi-desert.

If we are to judge from history, the odds that this desert civilization in western United States will survive are poor, wrote Marc Reisner in his classic book "Cadillac Desert - the American West and Its Disappearing Water."

The land in the states of the West, with the exception of Texas, was owned by the federal government when they became part of the United States, and it still owns nearly half of all the land in the West's eleven states. So, ironically, in this bastion of American individualism, where man is alone and has only himself to rely on and where no one is going to tell him what he must do or not do or how he should live his life, the power of the federal government is greater than in any other part of America.

The West is populated by drifters, wrote Wallace Stegner, the Stanford University English professor and writer and one of the great storytellers of the West, in his "The American West as Living Space." These immigrants created a "civilization in motion, driven by dreams."

They marched westward, starting in Europe, and these Americans became wanderers: leaving the old behind, the laws and regulations and religious oppression, with renewal as the goal. It became part not only of the American Dream, it became part of reality. And the road always headed west, Stegner wrote.

"Land gave Americans their freedom. It also gave them their egalitarianism, their democracy, their optimism, their free-enterprise capitalism, their greed, and their carelessness. It is an ambiguous and troubling legacy."

The Homestead Act of 1862 handed out land for free, 160 acres to every person who was willing to move west and settle in the emptiness of the prairie and begin to cultivate the land. People out there fought a daily struggle to survive, since it turned out to be impossible to survive on such a small piece of land. John Wesley Powell, the famous one-armed discoverer of the West, found that farmers on the vast prairie needed 2,560 acres, with irrigation and other efforts, to survive.

In "Giants in the Earth: A Saga of the Prairie" by the Norwegian-American writer Ole E. Rölvaag, many of the Norwegian farmers in North Dakota lost their battle for survival out on the prairie. Some went mad in their solitude and in the constant wind. Those who were able, sold their farm and moved on, and those who could not sell left anyway, never to return. Today, deserted farms litter the Great Plains.

Few of those who live in the West were born there. Most people there have lived their lives as a series of departures. The literature of the West is about place as much as about movement. This has created a certain rootlessness that has prevented sustained communities and traditions from taking hold. The rootlessness, in turn, has led to "the illusion of independence," according to Stegner:

"American individualism, much celebrated and cherished, has developed without its essential corrective, which is belonging. Freedom, when found, can turn out to be airless and un-sustaining. Especially in the West, what we have instead of place is space. Place is more than half memory, shared memory. Rarely do Westerners stay long enough at one stop to share much of anything."

In 1893, the historian Fredrick Jackson Turner declared the Frontier officially closed. There was no more free land. There were four million people in the West's eleven states at that time. Today, nearly 70 million people live there, most of them along the Pacific coast and in cities such as Phoenix, Denver, El Paso, Las Vegas, and Albuquerque. The rest is almost empty.

*

The West has been full of violence, death, and exploitation, not least of America's Indians – the original Americans, now also called Native Americans… bitter memories, as Ian Frazier, a journalist at The New Yorker, wrote so passionately in his book "Great Plains:"

"This, finally, is our punch line of our two hundred years on the Great Plains: we trap out the beaver, subtract the Mandan, infect the Blackfeet and the Hidatsa and the Assiniboin, overdose the Arikara; call the land a desert and hurry across it to California and Oregon; suck up the buffalo, bones and all; kill off nations of elk and wolves and cranes and prairie chickens and prairie dogs; dig up the gold and rebury it in vaults someplace else; ruin the Sioux and Cheyenne and Arapaho and Crow and Kiowa and Comanche; kill Crazy Horse, kill Sitting Bull…"

"...harvest wave after wave of immigrants' dreams and send the wised-up dreamers on their way; blow the topsoil until it blows to the ocean; ship out the wheat, ship out the cattle; dig up the earth itself and burn it in power plants and send the power down the line; dismiss the small farmers, empty the little towns, drill the oil and natural gas and pipe it away; dry up the rivers and springs, deep-drill for irrigation water as the aquifer retreats."

The landscape at Little Bighorn is magnificent. Soft, rolling hills stretch as far as the eye can see. Montana's sky – The Big Sky – is constantly shifting, its clouds changing color and chasing each other as its weather turns quickly from sunshine to rain, hail, thunder, and lightning, and back to sunshine. Down at the Little Bighorn River, cottonwoods shine all green. Were it not for the white gravestones scattered everywhere in the tall, yellow prairie grass, it would be hard to avoid a sense of idyllic perfection.

For it is here, in the rolling hills of what is now the Crow Indian Reservation in southeastern Montana, that the U.S. Army suffered its most humiliating defeat, and is today still its most painful military memory. For the American Indians, by contrast, Little Bighorn is the site of their grandest victory and proudest moment.

It was here, on June 25, 1876, that General George Armstrong Custer and his 263 men rode straight to their deaths, down to the very last man – known as "Custer's Last Stand." What happened here on that hot summer day will never be fully known. No white soldier survived the attack on the vast Indian camp at Little Bighorn with many thousands of Lakota Sioux and Cheyenne warriors. There are so many different versions of what happened that no completely clear picture has been established. The myth lives on and grows each year with the many tens of thousands of new visitors.

Custer and his men had left Fort Abraham Lincoln at the Mandan Indian village on the western bank of the Missouri River next to Bismarck, North Dakota's current capital. The fort is now a memorial complete with traditional Indian dwellings and with a splendid view in all directions out over the prairie. The air here is thin, hot and dry.

Outside the State Capitol building in Bismarck, there is a statue of Sacagawea, the Indian woman and mother, who guided Lewis & Clark on their improbable three-year voyage of discovery in the early 1800s from St. Louis on the Mississippi River to what is today the small seaside village of Astoria in Oregon by the Pacific Ocean and back again. Then, for the first time, America came to realize how big it really was.

At Little Bighorn, Custer found the Indians. "Hooray, now we have them, boys," Custer is said to have shouted as he spotted the Indian camp through his binoculars. Then, he and his soldiers from the Seventh Cavalry rode straight into the largest band of Indians ever assembled, led by the famous chiefs, Sitting Bull, Crazy Horse, Gall, and Two Moons. Custer and his men never had a chance.

The American Indians' big victory was the beginning of the end for free Indians in America, and the beginning of one of the "most shameful chapters" in American history, as the Crow Indian guide at the Little Bighorn Battlefield National Monument. The culmination of that chapter came in 1890 with the massacre of hundreds of Indians, including women and children, at Wounded Knee, on the Lakota Pine Ridge Indian Reservation in South Dakota. By then, both Sitting Bull and Crazy Horse had been captured and murdered by U.S. soldiers.

There is a long line of books about General Custer and Little Big Horn. In one of them, "The Son of the Morning Star," Custer is described as arrogant and cruel. He was already a General at 23, after winning big Union victories during the Civil War.

As the Civil War ended, Custer moved out west and started fighting Indians. The Indians never forgot his attack one morning in 1868 on a peaceful Indian camp at the Washita River, where Black Kettle was chief, at which over a hundred Indians were killed. For them, the great victory at Little Bighorn eight years later was their revenge.

For Sitting Bull, Custer was a "fool who rode straight to his death."

*

America's national parks are jewels, scattered across an entire continent. I'm not a big nature lover. I don't go camping, and I know little about plants and animal life. Still, the American national parks hold a big attraction for me. Their beauty and nature serve as a calming refuge from America's commercialization, from traffic and noise, from McDonalds and Burger Kings, from gas stations and billboards, from movie theaters and shopping centers.

The 58 national parks almost equal the size of Sweden. I have my favorites, Bryce Canyon in Utah, Canyon de Chelly in Arizona, Mesa Verde in Colorado and Glacier National Park up in northern Montana adjacent to the Blackfeet Indian Reservation on the border with Canada. There, if you ever row out to the middle of Lake McDonald on a hot summer day in water so clear you can see the bottom tens of feet down and gaze up at snow-capped mountain peaks majestically lining up in all directions, and experience the silence, the silence, and then take a quick dip in the chilly water, well, then you know what I'm talking about...

The National Parks had over 281 million visits in 2010, so you have to choose your visits carefully to avoid the crowds. Their popularity is really the parks' big problem. But the weather can also be a problem, as it was in the summer of 1988 when big fires broke out at Yellowstone National Park, America's first national park. Smoke spread to Washington, DC on the east coast and to San Francisco on the west coast. The fires burned all summer, until the first autumn rains extinguished them. By then, almost half of Yellowstone had burned down.

Fires in Yellowstone are not uncommon, but the summer of 1988 was like no other in Yellowstone's 116-year history due to the extreme drought. Firefighting was politicized as the ranchers around Yellowstone started to question the "let it burn" policy, and the dispute reached Congress in Washington, DC. But the fires that summer in Yellowstone did not turn out to be the catastrophe that many had feared. The park management got its "let it burn" policy endorsed -- forest fires are a natural part of the wild ecosystem.

The Grand Circle is a trip of several hundreds of miles through four states, Utah, Arizona, New Mexico, and Colorado, a journey through geological history. There are 14 national parks here and include one discovered by a Swedish archaeologist in 1881, as well as the vast Navajo Indian reservation, and prehistoric Indian ruins.

The journey on the Colorado Plateau takes you through mountains, forests and deserts, through a naked and dramatic landscape shaped by wind and water over millions of years. Three mighty rivers, the Colorado River, the Green River and the San Juan River, cross the plateau and here is also one of the world's largest artificial lakes, Lake Powell, created by a dam in the Colorado River.

The morning is still dark and it's totally quiet in the vast amphitheater in Bryce Canyon National Park as the sky slowly brightens behind the Canaan Mountains in the east. With the first rays, strange, almost human stone columns become visible. They light up in pink and then in red, then white and gray as they fill up the whole valley. In the foreground is Thor's Hammer.

These columns, "Hoodoos," give a mysterious, almost human impression, as if the valley is full of old men. The Paiute Indians called the valley "Unka-timpe-wa-wince-pock-ich" or "Red rocks standing like men in a bowl-shaped valley." The sky remains deep blue, crossed occasionally by white lines from silent jet planes high up. Ravens call. A woodpecker is heard in the distance. Chipmunks wake up and jump out of their holes.

From Bryce Canyon, it's off to the south, to the northern edge of the Grand Canyon, which is only open half the year due to the severe winters. Between the northern and southern edges it's about ten miles as the crow flies, but by car it's 250 miles around this enormous opening in the earth. The whole scene is so immense and so beautiful that you immediately feel small and insignificant.

Then, it's eastwards through forests filled with ponderosa pines and out into the semi-desert on the vast Navajo Indian reservation – home to America's largest Indian tribe. The Navajo Nationwide Network on the car radio plays Native American and cowboy music, out here in the middle of the stunning Monument Valley, so familiar from John Ford's classic Western movies. The sky is cloudless, and the sun lights up the ever present red rocks. Here and there a Navajo family lives, perhaps 500 families in all. It's poor and lonely, and their homes are little more than shacks surrounded by majestic stone monuments -- Three Sisters, Elephant Butte, Rain God Mesa, Totem Pole.

It's not easy to get to Canyon de Chelly on the Navajo Indians' vast reservation. But it is worth the effort, for it's a quiet and beautiful place. The Navajos returned here after Kit Carson's attack in the 1860s and after their long forced march to a concentration camp in eastern New Mexico. It was the era of ethnic cleansing.

Now, Navajos live in Canyon de Chelly, farming and ranching while a few tourists respectfully wander deep into the valley, though only in the company of Indian guides. They come to see the Anasazi's' 900-year-old monuments from a bygone era, monuments that over the years have been made famous by the photographs of Timothy H. Sullivan, Ansel Adams, and Edward S. Curtis.

Four Corners is the only place in the United States where four states meet, Arizona, Colorado, New Mexico, and Utah. Nearby lies Gustaf Nordenskiöld's big discovery, the Mesa Verde National Park, high up and covered in forests, as the name indicates -- Mesa Verde, the green table.

Nordenskiöld was the son of the great Swedish polar explorer Adolf Nordenskiöld, known from his voyage on the "Vega," the first ship through Northeast Passage.
The son studied chemistry and mineralogy before coming to the southwest corner of the state of Colorado. He was consumptive and came for the climate. He began the excavation of the 500 cliff dwelling the Anasazi built but eventually abandoned in the 1200s. His archaeological effort was groundbreaking.

Nordenskiöld was not actually the first to see the cliff dwellings – that had been done a few years earlier, between 1874 and 1886, – but he performed the first scientific excavations. The dwellings had by then been abandoned for 600 years. The Anasazi came to Mesa Verde around the year 550. Their lives were hard with harsh winters and a constant search for food.

It was during the classic pueblo period -- during the golden years of the Mesa Verde culture between 1100 and 1300 – that the cliff dwellings were constructed --a total of 38. Many of them were named by Nordenskiöld, the Balcony House with 40 rooms, the Long House, Spring House, Mug House, and Spruce Tree House. The jewel of the collection is the Cliff Palace with 220 rooms.

At sunset, the Cliff Palace is golden yellow and pink. In the silence after the last visitor leaves for the day, there is a sense of mystery in the air. There was life here 700 years ago, but then they all left the plateau and moved down to the dwellings carved out in the steep cliffs. They probably felt some sort of threat and needed to defend themselves. In 1274, a 24-year-long drought began, and in 1300, Mesa Verde was abandoned. No signs of strife or struggle have been found, but the departure seems to have been hasty. In the end, the lack of water made life impossible.

Gustaf Nordenskiöld's visit became the defining moment in his short life -- he died in 1895, 27 years old, never having seen Mesa Verde a second time.

*

Texas arouses strong emotions. No American state is less liked by outsiders – they tend to find Texans insufferable in their hats and boots and full of swagger, see them as caricatures. At the same time, few people love themselves as Texans do, few are prouder of themselves.

Texas is "barbarically large," wrote Texas writer Billy Lee Bremmer once, a thousand miles from north to south and even more from east to west. Even dawn takes an hour to cross Texas, wrote William Least Heat Moon in his "Blue Highways."

Texas, unlike all other American states, was an independent nation before it became part of the United States. And when Texans don't get what they want, they threaten to become independent again.

The capitalist and the entrepreneur are hailed in Texas. Everything is outsized. There is still a lot of "boom and bust" – as with James Dean in the film "Giant."

Once, I had lunch with Molly Ivins in a small Mexican restaurant in Austin. Ivins, now unfortunately dead, was a legendary Texas journalist and a wonderful storyteller, humorist, and, in Texas, something as unusual as a liberal Democrat.

Here is what she said about her home state:

"The motto in Texas is to start again, from scratch. Here, no one jumps out of a window and commits suicide just because he/she has failed and gone bankrupt. We lack shyness and self-consciousness and we are never afraid to make a fool of ourselves. We brag, but there are always those who are ready to put reality behind the bragging. We are friendly, yet not so civilized -- we fight and we kill each other. But there are three things almost everyone in Texas likes, and that's football, country music and beer. And everything we dislike, we see as a communist conspiracy."

*

In his book "Sidor av Amerika," Swedish writer Thorsten Jonsson, who at the end of World War II was the daily Dagens Nyheter's correspondent in New York, wrote during a trip through the South in 1946 how difficult it was to like it there, because "so much of the old and beautiful contains so much that is unhealthy and unproductive" -- there is a "smell of oppression that seeps out from the daily relationships between whites and coloreds" ..." a piece of gangrene in the body politic that must be removed.

Today, the South has changed, of course, and the gangrene has healed. But I remember that even in the 1960's, the South was a strange and frightening part of America, and not just for blacks. If you were a young, white student and drove a car with license plates from a northern state -- be careful! Anything could happen.

My picture of the South, the eleven states that fought for slavery in the great Civil War from 1861 to 1865, has long been influenced by the 60's, when so much injustice and violence and death was part of everyday life in that part of America. Still, today, I cannot completely get away from this picture when I travel through the South, because I am constantly reminded of the past. The South lost the Civil War and as a result, the slaves were freed. But what followed was one hundred years of institutionalized discrimination and oppression. Everywhere, monuments remind the visitor of the past, and the scenes of the major battles are holy ground. But they are all monuments to a lost cause.

In Washington, DC, on the border between the North and the South, the Confederate General Robert E. Lee's old home is visible on the hill above the Arlington National Cemetery across the Potomac River in the state of Virginia. Here, one is constantly reminded of how far south Washington actually is situated and how close one is to the bloody history of the Civil War. The trip from Frederick, Maryland through Leesburg and Culpepper in Virginia down to Monticello is called the "Journey through Hallowed Ground." It is a journey through this country's most historic part, where nine Presidents had their homes. History is often more alive in America than in Europe - perhaps because the history of the United States is so much briefer than Europe's...

The American Civil War between 1861 and 1865 was a war with many names, depending on whether one was for the Union or sympathized with the eleven States in the South, known as the Confederacy. Names like the "War Between the States," the "War against Northern Aggression," the "Second American Revolution," the "Lost Cause," the "War of the Rebellion," the "Brothers' War." Whatever the name, it was a war for the preservation of slavery in the South, and it was bloody.

During nearly four years of fighting, from Fort Sumter in South Carolina to Appomattox, Virginia, over three million soldiers fought and 620,000 of them were killed. Not far from my home in Maryland, at Antietam, one of the bloodiest battles of them all took place --- 23,000 soldiers on both sides died.

The free black population in the North consisted of only one percent of the total population, but in the final stages of the war 180,000 black soldiers fought for the Union, or ten percent of its forces. Their victory was the slaves' victory, and America's victory, even if the war cost President Abraham Lincoln his life and even if the blacks in the South had to wait another 100 years for their true emancipation.

When the North's commander Ulysses S. Grant met his counterpart from the South, General Robert E. Lee, at his surrender at Appomattox, Virginia, Grant wrote the following memorable words about the South's cause:

"I felt like anything rather than rejoicing at the downfall of a foe who had fought so long and valiantly, and had suffered so much for a cause, though that cause was, I believe, one of the worst for which a people ever fought, and one for which there was the least excuse."

Yes, so it is...one of the worst reasons, ever, to go to war.

On August 29, 2005 Katrina blew in over New Orleans, flooded 80 percent of the town and killed nearly 1,500 people. Over 240,000 people, half of the city's population, lived in houses that were flooded with more than three feet of water. Thousands of homes were completely destroyed and more than 100,000 people left New Orleans. Many have still not returned, and New Orleans is today a smaller city in size, 29 percent smaller than twelve years ago, and it has fewer people – 350,000 – compared to 485,000 seven years ago.

The scars from the huge disaster remain, especially in the Lower Ninth Ward, the poorest, almost entirely black neighborhood that was hardest hit by Katrina's enormous powers. The scars are made up of emptiness and decay. Here and there, for example, a part of a chimney or fireplace is all that remains of a house. One third of the inhabitants live below the poverty line.

It is a sad sight. Block after block of deserted, overgrown plots. But, suddenly, just off a reinforced dam wall where North Claiborne Avenue Bridge crosses the canal that flows into the Mississippi River, a series of new homes stand, modern and colorful. Downtown New Orleans skyscrapers are visible in the west, not far away.

The new houses stand on stilts to avoid being flooded during the next Katrina. They are part of "The Pink Project," started by Brad Pitt, the architectural firm GRAFT and environmental activists in the "Make It Right Foundation." A score of other architects, including David Adjaye, Thom Mayne, Shigeru Ban, and Frank Gehry, have pitched in for free.

"Why pink? Because it screams the loudest," said Pitt, who became involved in the project during a film shoot in New Orleans in 2007.

It started with 450 pink tents in different sizes and shapes that, day and night, lit up the area where 150 new green and environmentally friendly homes would eventually be surrounded by canals, rivers and water on almost all sides. Many millions of dollars have rolled in and the pace of construction is frantic. The project is, of course, just a drop in the ocean in the Lower Ninth Ward, where 5,000 homes were destroyed by Katrina, where a new super market was greeted with jubilation, but where everything progresses oh, so slowly, and where there still are no hospital or police and fire stations.

Other parts of New Orleans are pretty much the same, as before Katrina. The French Quarter is full of tourists as usual, and at Preservation Hall and the Palm Court Jazz Café, New Orleans jazz is played, as always. It's nice to see that Lars Edegran, who came here from Stockholm as a young man in the 60's to play jazz and who never left, not even after Katrina, still plays his piano.

In Tremé, the oldest black neighborhood with its Cultural Backstreet Museum full of Mardi Gras Costumes and its African American Museum, it's sunny and warm this January day and full of people. More and more young white yuppies have moved here for the houses are inexpensive and Tremé is comfortable, almost right in the middle of New Orleans but still far enough away from the madness of the French Quarter, especially during Mardi Gras.

The Garden District with all its fine old buildings was spared almost entirely by Katrina and traveling on the old streetcar along the St. Charles Avenue is the same great experience as always. Along the beach in Lakeview and Gentilly, between City Park and the vast ocean-like Lake Ponchartrain, there is the quiet of suburbia and the sun shines warmly. The Lower Ninth Ward and Katrina feel far away.

*

In Montgomery, Alabama, where Jefferson Davis was declared President of the Confederacy on February 18, 1861, the Confederate flag no longer flies on top of the State Legislature, visible all over the city. When it was finally taken down, in 1993, after many years of bitter struggle, it seemed as if Alabama had, finally, joined the rest of America.

A young black policeman smiles but says nothing when I revisited Montgomery in early 2012 and commented on the fact that the Confederate flag no longer flies up there, but only the Star Spangled Banner and Alabama's state flag.

I had seen the flag as late as in the late 1980's. It had been put there over 20 years earlier by Governor George Wallace, the old segregationist, not only in protest against the Kennedy administration but also as a humiliating message to all blacks, not only in Alabama but across the South. Montgomery is the cradle of the South. It was here that the Confederacy was declared and Montgomery became its first capital before it moved north, to Richmond, Virginia. Across the street where I met the young black policeman there is an elegant old house that dates back to 1835. It once served as the Confederacy's White House.

But Montgomery also has its symbols for modern Montgomery and modern Alabama. The city is the home of the Rosa Park's Museum and of Dexter Avenue Baptist Church, where Martin Luther King Jr. was a pastor from 1954 to 1959, and from which he led the successful year-long bus boycott after Rosa Parks had refused to give up her seat for a white man and move to the back of the bus.

Montgomery now also has a new museum about the recent struggles, the Civil Rights Memorial Center. Its slogan is "The March Continues." Maya Lin is the Center's architect, the same Maya Lin who designed the powerful Vietnam Memorial in Washington, DC.

The new center did not exist when I was in Montgomery last, and, back then, I would probably never have imagined its existence twenty years later.

Those who worked at the Southern Poverty Law Center back then would also have had a hard time imagining that such a museum could ever exist in Montgomery. The Law Center, once a small civil rights group founded by two young idealistic Alabama lawyers. One of them, Morris Dees, became in time a legend for his fight against white hate groups like the Ku Klux Klan, and in support of the poor blacks of the South. The new civil rights museum, now sponsored by the Law Center, is a fine memorial to the struggle of the past and to those who died in that struggle.

The Southern Poverty Law Center is no longer housed in a little house but in a new, large office building. Its fight against the Ku Klux Klan has been very successful.
But there are still over 1,000 hate groups in America, and the new building is reminder that the battle is not yet won, even though the Confederate flag is no longer flying from the top of Alabama's State Capitol.

*

America's big roads make traveling easy. They came about through a decision by President Dwight D. Eisenhower in the 1950s to build a nation-wide Interstate freeway system that would span the whole country. The system has revolutionized car travel for all Americans.

The advent in 1970 of commercial-free, public radio, National Public Radio (NPR), revolutionized radio listening. I remember the days when the programs on American radio stations consisted of advertising, music, more advertising, with occasional news reports.

Many stations are still like that, but, today, 920 NPR stations all over America have almost 27 million listeners every week. NPR has become America's second-largest radio network and an invaluable contributor to and shaper of America's cultural and social debate. I find it difficult today to imagine America without NPR, cut off from serious information and debate, and less connected to the big world out there.

Around the country, where it is often difficult to get hold of a good newspaper or even a good cup of coffee, you can almost always find a local NPR station, often near a college or university, and its many stimulating and informative programs, such as "Morning Edition;" "All Things Considered;" "Fresh Air with Terry Gross" from Philadelphia; and "A Prairie Home Companion" with Garrison Keillor from St. Paul, Minnesota. Or news from the BBC, "Market Place" from Los Angeles with economic news, "Car Talk" with everything about cars from Boston, and, of course, lots of classical music.

Many on the political right wing hate NPR, calling it leftist and elitist, and the Republicans constantly try to stop government funding for NPR. So far, they have thankfully failed, which makes me very pleased in my car as I travel through by America.

In some parts of the country, NPR has had serious competition in recent decades from Christian radio stations, which feature religious music and reactionary political talk show hosts like Rush Limbaugh, Laura Ingraham, and Glenn Beck. Limbaugh is the most dominant. He is on 600 stations around in the country, especially in the South where he can be heard on 22 stations in Georgia alone. I tried to listen to him driving through Georgia, in part to attempt to understand his immense popularity. But his demagogic nonsense soon became too much, and I switched stations.

*

As I crossed the border into the State of Georgia, the sign "Georgia on my mind" welcomed me. I immediately came to think of Ray Charles's version of the song, which has now become Georgia's state song. Ray Charles came from Georgia, like Martin Luther King Jr., and both are now among Georgia's most famous native sons, two black legends of the Old South.

In the middle of the small town of Albany, at the Flint River, on Ray Charles Plaza, there is a statue of Ray Charles, sitting at his piano as his singing and his music are heard in the heat out over the river and the city, and as the statue slowly spins, round and round ... "Tell Me What'd I Say" ... Albany has 75,000 inhabitants -- almost 70 per cent of them are black. The economy was once dominated by the large cotton plantations, which relied on the black labor force. The city museum, once built with Andrew Carnegie's money, was closed to blacks until the new civil rights law of 1964. In the early 60s, the Albany Movement was an important part of the civil rights struggle. Martin Luther King, Jr. came down here from Atlanta, but he was met with fierce resistance from the white establishment, which still controls Albany even though the mayor is black. He is the only black member of the City's Golf Club.

There is something forlorn about downtown Albany, even though some new buildings and a new museum and aquarium have attempted to revive the city center after the new shopping centers in the suburbs lured away most customers. Poor blacks have remained, living in miserably poor districts not far from Ray Charles Plaza, on block after block with dilapidated homes. Both old and young sit in their chairs on their porches of their "shotgun shacks "and wait ...this is America's dark side.

In Atlanta, a few hours' drive north, Martin Luther King, Jr. was born, in 1934. It was here, in Ebenezer Baptist Church, where King was pastor until his death in 1968, and his grandfather and father had been pastors before him. The church, built in 1922, on Auburn Avenue with the skyscrapers of Atlanta's downtown within sight, has just reopened after extensive renovation. It is now a museum and part of the Martin Luther King, Jr. National Historic Site, which includes a new large church, the Center for Nonviolent Social Change, and King's and his wife Coretta Scott's graves.

I had visited Ebenezer Baptist Church before, on January 21, 1986, when Martin Luther King, Jr.'s national holiday was celebrated for the first time. Everyone seemed to have come to Atlanta and to its old, worn down "Sweet Auburn" neighborhood on that sunny January day. They filled the old church. Many memories...where tourists today sit in the pews and listen attentively to recordings of King's speeches from a different time in America.

*

Over the years, America has become more homogenized. The different parts of this vast country look more like each other, with the same fast food chains among the same gas stations and the same cheap motel chains.

Finding good food can be problematic outside of the America's big cities. Food tends to be not only monotonous but often spectacularly bad. Coffee has its own and sad history of watered-down tastelessness, all over America, be it along the freeways or in motel after motel. The more recent advent of Starbucks and its coffee has revolutionized coffee drinking in America and become the great salvation for coffee lovers. A Starbucks sign along the freeway often means it's time to stop. Finally, a good cup of coffee, and a New York Times on top of that to read. That's happiness.

The British-American historian Tony Judt once wrote that the best thing about America was the country's universities. I agree, and when I travel in America, I always try to visit them.

Judt did not mean Harvard or Yale or Stanford, or other prestigious, private schools - those with all the money. No, he was referring to the large public universities, encountered in almost all states, intellectual anchors and oases surrounded by the often vacuous American countryside. The large public university with its beautiful campus, its students and professors, guest lectures, conferences, adult education, libraries, concerts, theater performances, and football and basketball games make the small town out on the prairie or among the corn fields so infinitely attractive. What would such towns as Boulder, Colorado be without its great university, or Madison, Wisconsin; Ann Arbor, Michigan; Iowa City, Iowa; Missoula, Montana; Austin, Texas; Chapel Hill, North Carolina; Lincoln, Nebraska; Laramie, Wyoming; or Burlington, Vermont?

America's seniors have discovered the benefits of America's college and university towns, and they have moved and settled there in the thousands to get access to all that these college towns have to offer.

Maybe I will, too, one day...

*

Not far from where I live, in northwest Washington, DC, is the home one of America's premier bookstores, "Politics & Prose."

Recently, I was reminded how important it is to maintain great bookstores in what, for all booksellers and booklovers, are bleak times. I had gone there to hear one of my favorite American writers, Richard Ford, talk about and read from his new book "Canada."

He was on a book tour, visiting some of the best bookstores that this country has to offer: first "Barnes & Noble" at Union Square in New York and then here to Washington, DC, and then on to "Books Inc." in Palo Alto, California; "Powell's" in Portland, Oregon; "Elliott Bay Book Company" in Seattle, Washington; "Square Books" in Oxford, Mississippi; "Parnassus Books" in Nashville, Tennessee; "Tattered Cover Book Store" in Denver, Colorado, etc.

Ford's tour reminded me of what Tony Judt had said about American universities as intellectual oases out there in America, for the same is true of American bookstores if you are traveling, and if you love books, which I do. To enter "Powell's" in Portland or "Elliott Bay" in Seattle, or to walk around and discover the many floors of the "Barnes & Noble" in New York, or grab a coffee at "Politics & Prose," and then listen to Richard Ford, is a true treat, and an important part of travel and life in America.

We are fortunate still to have a "Politics & Prose," and every time I visit San Francisco, I am happy to see that "City Lights Books," founded in the 1950's by the old beat poet Lawrence Ferlinghetti, is still there on Columbus Avenue in the city's North Beach, and that Ferlinghetti, himself, still seems to be running at full speed. And I am pleased that a new bookstore such as Garrison Keillor's "Common Good Books" in St. Paul, Minnesota, founded in 2006 even expanded this year, and that small bookshops, especially with used books like my old friend Ed's "Bookends" in tiny Florence, Massachusetts, have survived for so many years, even though Ed, himself, sold the business a few years ago.

At the same time, we mourn those who perished along the way, such as our "Borders" in downtown Silver Spring, Maryland, where I live, and "Hungry Mind" in St. Paul, Minnesota, and "Cody's," the legendary bookstore in Berkeley, California, and many more, too numerous to mention. Amazon can never replace them.

*

Over the years, I have traveled north more and more. On one trip, Detroit is behind us and the countryside and fields spread out along the road as we head north in the sunshine, through Michigan and up over the big bridge leading to the state's Upper Peninsula, or the "U.P." as it's called.

Then by boat to nearby Mackinac Island, a delightful excursion out on Lake Huron, one of the five large great lakes along the border with Canada. The whole little town on the island smells of white paint. The old Hotel Iroquois, down by the harbor, graced by a long, wide porch, is reminiscent of the elegance of a bygone era, when one still had to wear a coat and tie to the whitefish dinner.

So westward, like a journey through a summerlike Sweden. No traffic on the narrow, two-lane roads. Lake Michigan's water glitters in the sun on the left as we head through meadows with buttercups and bluebells, and birches mixing with spruce and pine.

And then north, far from everything, to North Dakota, along the border with Canada, where the capital is Bismarck and where the city of Fargo gave its name to the Cohen brothers' unforgettable film. There, on a summer day on Interstate 94 where everything is sky and where the road is as straight as a needle, from Fargo through Bismarck and Mandan and on west towards the Montana border, the car goes a little fast and a friendly police officer stops us. We are driving a Swedish Saab with license plates that read "Diplomat" instead of the usual name of the State, because my traveling companion is a diplomat at the Swedish Embassy in Washington, DC, where all diplomatic cars carry those license plates.

When he reaches our car, the police officer, pen and notebook ready, asks, politely, "where is Diplomat?"

Vermont is also way up north, near Canada, and Montreal, not Boston, not New York, is the nearest big city. It's a bit of America like no other, a small state, the smallest in the whole country with only half a million inhabitants. The "Green Mountain State" is pastoral, with fields and meadows, birch and maple forests, and with mountains high enough to provide a serious challenge even for the best downhill skiers. The villages, with their white wooden houses and churches with slender steeples complete the idyllic picture.

When I was in Vermont the first time the State had a female governor, born in Switzerland, a Jewish woman who once, as a child, fled the Nazis and came to America. Vermont was the first state that prohibited slavery and the first to introduce universal suffrage. Half of all able men in the State joined the Union forces in the Civil War, and one in seven was killed. In Vermont, annual town meetings still play an important role in local politics, and the environment is a main issue. Big advertising billboards, so common along all America's roads, are prohibited. And it is in Vermont that America's healthiest people and least religious people live, according to statistics.

Vermont has the U.S. Senate's most liberal member, the Brooklyn-born, democratic socialist, Bernie Sanders. He is officially an independent, but he votes with the Democrats and is a breath of fresh air in the staid Senate. The other Vermont senator is also a Democrat, just like the governor.

A truly progressive stronghold, in other words, although Vermont's liberal tradition is fairly new. For many years, the state was a Republican bastion. In fact, it was one of the few states that voted against Franklin D. Roosevelt as president in 1936. But in the 1950s and 60's, the State's politics changed drastically and today, Vermont is second to Hawaii as the most Democratic state in all of America, the only state that George W. Bush never visited during his eight years as president.

In Blue Hill, Maine, the Atlantic coast with its pine trees, bare rocks and icy ocean water feels just like Sweden on a hot summer day.

We always stop at the "Lobster Shack" on our way home from the daily swim and buy a lobster or two for the evening meal. And in Belgrade Lakes, not far from Blue Hill, where the lake water is warm and clear and soft, my swim reminds of those in my childhood's Lake Siljan in Dalarna.

*

When the temperature reaches 100 degrees and Washington is so hot and humid and disgusting that it's impossible to be outdoors and you rush between the air-conditioned buildings longing for an evening shower, it's time to get out of town, preferably out west, to the other side of the Mississippi River where the heat is dry, but also eastward, over the long bridge across the Chesapeake Bay and across the flat Eastern Shore of Maryland to Delaware and the Atlantic Ocean. There, the waves roll in, day after day, and the salty wind blows cool while the sandy beaches extend north and south as far as the eye can see.

It takes a little over two hours to drive to Delaware, where the first Swedish immigrants arrived in 1638 on the ship "Kalmar Nyckel" and founded the New Sweden colony. A replica of the "Kalmar Nyckel" was completed in 1997 in conjunction with the 350th anniversary of New Sweden, and she now transports tourists in the waters along the Delaware coast.

Sometimes the ship anchors up in the ferry terminal in Lewes, from where ferries run between Lewes and Cape May, New Jersey, on the other side of the Delaware Bay.

The old fishing village of Lewes, which dates back to the early 1600s, is particularly charming with its small historic center of Victorian houses, quaint shops and good restaurants and near Cape Henlopen State Park's pristine nature and wide open beaches.

It is no wonder that the Delaware beaches of the Seashore State Park have become such an attraction, not only for Washington's inhabitants, but also for those in Baltimore, Wilmington and Philadelphia. That's the negative side of the Delaware beaches -- their popularity. But if you avoid rush hour traffic on Friday afternoons and Sunday evenings, or simply come in late spring or in the fall, then you cannot avoid being charmed and returning, again and again.

*

I like America's old industrial cities where steel and automobiles once ruled. There's something special about them, they have tradition and character, cities like Pittsburgh, Cleveland, Detroit, right there in the Rust Belt, in Pennsylvania, Ohio and Michigan. They have long struggled, through the steel and automotive crises, through the mortgage crisis, as people have moved away as a result of unemployment, poverty and crime.

Detroit's numbers tell the sad story of a once-lively, even glamorous city -- once America's fourth largest city and its industrial center -- and its disastrous economic decline. Between 2000 and 2010, Detroit's population sank by 25 percent, from 951,000 to 713,000, and from 1950 by 60 percent, when American cars ruled in the world, and when Detroit had 1,850,000 inhabitants.

The flight from Detroit between 2000 and 2010 was bigger than the 140,000 people who fled New Orleans after Hurricane Katrina in 2005. 38 percent of the people in Detroit are poor, the highest rate of all American cities, with Cleveland in second place and Pittsburgh at 26th.

In the book, "Ruins of Detroit" by the two young French photographers Yves Marchand and Romain Meffre, their photos tell the tragic story of Detroit's decline and the creation of a city of neglect and decay better than any words. The photos are heartbreaking -- how could America let this happen?

Pittsburgh, in western Pennsylvania, tells another and more hopeful story, although it is difficult to believe that when you travel along the river in the Mon Valley, where the abandoned steel mills are monuments to a bygone time. They stand side by side, wall to wall, mile after mile, with ovens long ago cold and with chimney stacks without smoke.

In the 1980's, in McKeesport, Braddock and Homestead and all the small towns along the Monongahela River, President Reagan's slogans about a "prouder, stronger, better America " felt like an insult. Here, the American dream turned into a nightmare for many, a professor at the University of Pittsburgh once told me.

The Mon Valley steel mills employed 100,000 workers at their height. Even as late as in 1979, 28,000 people worked here. Unemployment among Pittsburgh's half a million inhabitants back then was over 13 percent, but it stood at 50 to 100 percent among its steel workers. Between 1981 and 1984 alone, the city lost 120,000 jobs in the manufacturing industry. Residents left the city in droves in search of new jobs. Many of these people belonged to the city's young generation, and most of them are now lost to Pittsburgh forever.

Today, downtown Pittsburgh is a dramatic and uplifting sight, especially when you exit the Fort Pitt Tunnel and see the whole city laid out where the Monongahela and Allegheny Rivers join the Ohio River with some of the finest buildings in America: the HH Richardson's Allegheny Court House, Philip Johnson's and John Burgees' PPG Place in glass, and the August Wilson Center for African American Culture by Allison G. Williams.

There are fine old buildings from the era of the industrial magnates -- Carnegie, Heinz, Mellon, and Frick. It was this "old wealth" that once built Pittsburgh into a fine city with its own symphony, opera and ballet, and the Andy Warhol Museum, honoring its native son. And the city's passionate sports fans have much to cheer. The Penguins have a new hockey arena, the Pirates a new baseball stadium, and the Steelers a new football stadium.

Today, Pittsburgh's recovery and success are rooted in the big business of its universities and hospitals -- biotech, green technology, health care, finance, research, and education. The city is a leader in "green" buildings. Today, the University of Pittsburgh Medical Center's (UPMC) logo can be seen on top of what once was U.S. Steel's 64-story headquarters, and with its 50,000 employees, the University hospital is western Pennsylvania's largest employer.

With just 305,000 inhabitants, Pittsburgh is not one of America's twenty largest cities, but it feels bigger, and it has a position and a history far beyond its size. It's been called "the most livable city" in America. I don't know about that, but it has new residential areas, bicycle paths along the three rivers, and new park areas. There is a strong sense of loyalty and pride among the city's inhabitants, who have found a successful way to transition out of Pittsburgh's crisis and become a thriving post-industrial economy.

*

America's first signs of spring emerge in late February when the professional baseball teams begin spring training in Florida and Arizona. Many Americans flee the winter up north to go to the games and to get up close to their idols before they disappear among the big crowds as the season gets under way in early April.

Then, it's baseball, every day, for six months, with playoffs and the "World Series" in October. And then, the fans wait for spring to come again and a new baseball season...

I have not played much baseball, but I enjoy watching the games, their quiet rhythm, almost boring at times. You have time to relax, talk with neighbor and think about life. In my travels around the America, I always try to go see a baseball game, especially in such historic venues as Wrigley Field in Chicago, Boston's Fenway Park, or where the San Francisco Giants play their home games in the stadium by the San Francisco Bay, with the Bay full of boats whose passengers sometimes throw themselves into the water to get hold of the ball after a home run.

In the summer, it's a special treat to come upon a lit-up baseball field and to see small boys in colorful uniforms playing, their parents and siblings cheering in the bleachers, and to hear the that distinctive crack when the ball hits the bat. Summer in America means baseball. Going to a baseball game is a summer outing to eat ice cream and hot dogs and drink a beer and sit and talk and cheer on your favorite team out there on the field.

Baseball is an intimate part of America and its language is part of the everyday American lexicon. It was a "home run "—that means something was a great success. Now we need to "step up to the plate" -- to get started, take responsibility. He "he hit it out of the park" – he did well. They "play hardball" – it's tough going.

Bill Clinton once said:
"No matter where you go in America, sooner or later there will be a patch of green, a path of dirt, and a home plate. Baseball also teaches us tolerance. It teaches us to play as hard as we can and still be friends when the game is over, to respect our differences, and to be able to lose with dignity as well as win with joy."

When the Nationals, or "Nats" as we call the team, came to Washington, DC in 2005, the capital had not had a baseball team since 1972, when the old Washington Senators left town after years of bad baseball and scarce crowds to seek their fortune in Texas. The Senators became the Rangers.

To be a real big city in America, it must have a baseball team. So the years from 1972 to 2005 had a certain emptiness for Washington residents. Now, we have our home team again and a new stadium, between the Anacostia River and the U.S. Congress. I usually take the subway to the stadium, where a lively district is emerging with new apartment buildings, restaurants, department stores, and supermarkets.

A baseball season is all of 162 games. Half of the games are played at home, so baseball is also big business. But, mostly, it's about joy -- "America's pastime" -- the country's great love. Play ball!

Chapter 9.

THE NINE

The U.S. presidential election on November 7, 2000 was decided by the U.S. Supreme Court after 36 days of intense legal and political battles about the vote count and the ballots in the State of Florida.

Never before had the country's highest judicial body acted in such a blatant political manner as in the case of Bush v. Gore, never before had the Court interfered in such a way in a presidential election, never before, never before ... and, finally, perhaps never before had the Supreme Court's power in the American society been illustrated in such an obvious and clear way.

Jeffrey Toobin, The New Yorker's legal commentator, wrote ten years later:

"Many of the issues before the Supreme Court combine law and politics in a way that are impossible to separate. It is, moreover, unreasonable to expect the Justices to operate in a world hermetically cut off from the gritty motives of Democrats and Republicans. But the least we can expect from these men and women is that at politically charged moments -- indeed, especially at those times -- they apply the same principles that guide them in every day cases. This, ultimately, is the tragedy of Bush v. Gore. The case did not just scar the Court's record; it damaged the Court's honor."

The presidential election of 2000 was the most evenly divided election of modern times. It was decided by just 537 votes in Florida out of a total 101,455,899 votes in the country. In total, the incumbent Vice President Albert Gore received 540,520 more votes than the Republican candidate George W. Bush.

But Gore lost in the Electoral College, which ultimately determines U.S. presidential elections, with 266 electoral votes to Bush's 271.

It takes a minimum of 270 electoral votes to become president. Thus, if Gore had won Florida and its 25 electoral votes, he would have been elected president.

The day after the election, on November 8, the preliminary vote count in Florida showed Bush ahead by 1,784 votes, or less than 0.5 percent of the state's nearly six million cast votes. The tiny margin of victory meant an automatic machine recount, which Bush won again, but this time, by only 327 votes. During the protracted battle that followed about the Florida votes, in what can only be described as a chaotic atmosphere, the Florida Supreme Court, by a vote of 4-3, ordered a recount of all disputed ballots in the whole State. It started at once, but the next day, after an appeal from Bush's lawyers, the U.S. Supreme Court intervened and stopped the recount in a 5 to 4 decision. Bush's lead had by then shrunk to 154 votes. The recount was never resumed.

The Supreme Court majority consisted of five conservative justices, all appointed by Republican presidents and led by Chief Justice William Rehnquist. In their decision, they referred to the U.S. Constitution's fourteenth amendment about "equal protection," i.e. that the recount procedures were not the same across Florida and, therefore, all of the State's inhabitants would not receive equal protection under the Constitution.

In addition, the majority said that there was not sufficient time to conduct a recount, adding that their decision only applied to this specific case, Bush v. Gore, without future precedent. Adding this, the majority of the justices indirectly admitted that they had departed from the basic principle of the Supreme Court, that of establishing constitutional precedents for their actions.

Their argument was not convincing. The Court's four liberal justices argued that the recount ordered by the Florida Supreme Court was completely constitutional and should have been completed, and that the U.S. Supreme Court had no right to interfere in the election in Florida. It was a state issue, not a federal case. The Court's majority acted unwisely, wrote the Court's liberal leader, veteran Associate Justice John Paul Stevens. We may never know with certainty who won in Florida, he continued, but we know who lost -- it was the nation's confidence that the judiciary will impartially ensure that our laws are followed.

What was the Supreme Court's real reason for their actions?

Anthony Lewis, for many years a most respected legal correspondent for the New York Times, recently wrote in the New York Review of Books that he could draw no other conclusion than that the Supreme Court made "a political decision" in Bush v. Gore.

President Bill Clinton later wrote in his memoirs:

"Bush v. Gore will go down in history as one of the worst decisions the Supreme Court ever made."

And Alan Dershowitz, a prominent professor at Harvard Law School, wrote:

"The decision in the Florida election case may be ranked as the single most corrupt decision in Supreme Court history, because it is the only one that I know of where the majority justices decided as they did because of the personal identity and political affiliation of the litigants. This was cheating, and a violation of the judicial oath."

In his book, "Too Close to Call," Toobin wrote that the Supreme Court's decision is doomed to "dishonor." Gore probably would have won in Florida if the vote recount had been allowed to be completed.

According to the book, Justice David Souter, who belonged to the liberal minority, was so shaken after the decision that he thought of resigning. But Antonin Scalia, one of the five in the majority, defended the Court's action by saying that situation in Florida was totally out of control and that the Supreme Court was forced to act. The whole world was laughing at us, France was laughing at us, he said, and responded to critics with -- "get over it."

The liberal journalist Robert Parry described in his book "Neck Deep" Bush's election victory in 2000 as an American "coup d'état." He wrote that never before in history had the Supreme Court used its extraordinary power for partisan political purposes.

The five majority members of the Supreme Court did not see it that way. They saw their role as steering the country out of the deep crisis caused by the election, and they dismissed allegations that they acted for partisan political purposes. According to Parry, Rehnquist said that "the political process in the country has worked, I admit in a fairly unusual way, to avoid a serious crisis."

A dozen years earlier, in June 1987, I had interviewed William Rehnquist. It was a year after President Ronald Reagan had nominated Rehnquist to become Chief Justice, and I had asked him at that time about the risk of the Court's politicization.

"Well, it depends on what you mean by politicization," Rehnquist responded. "If it means that the president would not nominate justices who share his judicial philosophy, then that would go against 200 years of our history. All strong presidents, Andrew Jackson, Abraham Lincoln, Theodore Roosevelt, Franklin Roosevelt, have unhesitatingly attempted to nominate people who reflected their view of how the Supreme Court will function. Meanwhile, the Senate approves appointments and represents other interests. So the system should function."

"But," concluded Rehnquist, "if by politicization you mean adding a bunch of Republicans so that they can vote as the GOP wishes, then, that must not happen. It has never happened and I think it will never happen."

The question is if this is not, in fact, exactly what happened when five of the nine Justices of the U.S. Supreme Court ordered the cancellation of the Florida vote recount and thereby handed victory to George W. Bush.

The Supreme Court is situated next to the Capitol – the U.S. Congress - on Capitol Hill in Washington, DC. It has its own monumental building in white marble. The entrance is dominated by sixteen huge columns in ancient Greek style above which is written, "Equal Justice Under Law."

The Nine in that building preside not only over Washington but over the entire country. They decide whether the country is properly governed and if the President and Congress are acting according to the U.S. Constitution, they decide who gets to vote, to bear arms, pray in schools, have an abortion, burn the American flag, or be executed in America's prisons. The public is allowed to come and listen to the Supreme Court deliberations in the white cathedral designed by architect Cass Gilbert. The building is replete with American history and The Nine are surrounded by an aura of awe and mystery, perhaps in large part because in no other U.S. institution is there so little transparency. The Nine live largely isolated lives, issue few statements and give even fewer interviews.

Over the years, America has focused more and more on what happens in the Supreme Court and among the Justices who decide so much in their lives. Such books have been published as Bob Woodward and Scott Armstrong's The Brethren – Inside the Supreme Court in 1979, and The Nine - Inside the Secret World of the Supreme Court by Jeffrey Toobin from 2007.

News organizations have their Court correspondents, who all try hard to break down the mystique surrounding the Court in order to find out what really is going on behind the walls of the white marble building. At the country's law schools, intense academic research is conducted about the Supreme Court. "Constitutional law" is a leading subject on every curriculum, and there are numerous constitutional experts among the professors who keep writing new academic books about the Court and the Constitution.

In this way, the U.S. Constitution is alive and almost a daily theme in the public debate.

The law, judges, jurists, lawyers, legal academics all play the kind of central role in America that is without parallel in any other Western democracy.

All of America's major issues are – sooner or later – decided by The Nine. The Supreme Court is the conscience of America and its decisions have affected, and will affect, more than perhaps any another institution.

Alexis de Tocqueville wrote in his classic "Democracy in America" from the mid-1800s that the American legal system is the most difficult aspect about America for a foreigner to understand. No other nation has created such a powerful legal system, with the Supreme Court as "the nation's tribunal." A judge in America has great political power, wrote de Tocqueville. In fact, there is hardly a single political issue in America that does not sooner or later become a matter for the judiciary. The reason is that Americans have given their judges the right to base their decisions on the Constitution rather than on the laws. In other words, judges do not allow laws that are contrary to the Constitution, and de Tocqueville concluded:

"The Constitution is the foundation of all authority. The dominant power belongs to it alone."

The Supreme Court is also a passive center of power. It has to wait for the questions and problems to get to the Court through the judicial process, by way of the decisions in the lower courts. And, according to the Constitution, the Supreme Court may only deal with specific cases -- where there is a conflict of interest.

In his book "Gideon's Trumpet," former New York Times Columnist Anthony Lewis described one way this can happen:

In January 1962, the Supreme Court received a letter from an inmate in Florida named Clarence Earl Gideon, who was sentenced to prison for a burglary. He asked The Nine to take up his case. The request was handwritten in pencil. Gideon demanded his conviction to be set aside. He was illegally detained, he wrote, because he could not afford a lawyer before and during his trial and his request for counsel had been denied, although the Supreme Court had ruled in 1942, in Betts v. Brady, that a defendant was not guaranteed legal representation.

The Supreme Court decided to take on Gideon's case, and in Gideon v. Wainwright, the Court sided with Clarence Earl Gideon. A unanimous court declared that Betts v. Brady no longer applied and that all defendants, including the poorest, were entitled to a lawyer.

The immediate result was that 976 inmates in Florida's prisons were released -- they had all been convicted without access to legal representation. Gideon himself was given a new trial where the judgment was "not guilty." After two years in prison, he was a free man. Gideon's triumph shows, wrote Lewis, that even the poorest and the weakest can ask the country's highest legal authority for help and bring about fundamental changes in our country's laws.

Miranda v. Arizona is another example of a fundamental change in the law. Its consequences are on display in American TV shows and movies when a suspect is arrested and may not be interrogated before he/she is informed by the police of the right to counsel. You know how it goes... "You have the right to remain silent, anything said can and will be used against you in a court of law...You have the right to an attorney..."

The case stems from 1963, when Ernest Miranda was arrested on suspicion of robbery, rape and kidnapping. He was never informed of his right to counsel, and after two hours of interrogation he confessed and was eventually sentenced to between 20 and 30 years in prison. Miranda appealed all the way to the Supreme Court, and in 1966, by a vote of 5 to 4, the Court confirmed that Miranda had been unfairly convicted because no lawyer was present during the police questioning. His confession was deemed a violation of the Constitution and he was released. Miranda was later convicted in a new trial and served a five year sentence.

Daily life in America is dominated by lawyers and by legal confrontations in a way that does not exist in Sweden or Europe. When Americans have problems, they go to court. Everyone sues everyone, or threatens to sue everyone, often over the smallest thing, sometimes it's all a bluff.

My wife and I were brutally reminded of that a few years ago, when a cyclist threw himself in front of the car my wife was driving in midtown Manhattan, and then accused her for having and injured him. He was not hit and he was not injured and we thought no more of the matter. A few months later we were sued for five million dollars. This cannot be true, we said to the insurance company. But it was true.

We had by that time moved to San Francisco and my wife flew back and forth on the insurance company's expense so that the company's lawyer could interview her and prepare her defense if it should come to trial. It did. The trial by jury lasted for two full days. My wife continued stubbornly to explain that nothing had happened, that she was innocent, and she refused to admit any liability or agree to any monetary settlement. The man's lawyer gradually lowered his claims, from five million to one million, to one hundred thousand to… a thousand dollars. The judge several times admonished my wife to agree to a settlement, but that would have meant that she admitted guilt and she refused to do that. I am innocent, she repeated, and the jury sided with her in the end. We never believed that man, one of the jurors said afterwards.

So the system worked, but at what price?

An American president has the power and the right to appoint hundreds of federal judges, for life, including to the Supreme Court. The president is free to nominate anyone, with any background or experience. And assuming that his candidate is approved by the Senate, the new judge can remain on the bench for as long as he or she chooses, often until his or her death.

So, the American electorate, by way of who they elect as president, determines the makeup of the judiciary and who sits on the Supreme Court.

This power gives the president the opportunity to make his mark on the country and influence the American society for many years after he has left the White House. But there is no way to plan these appointments for they can only be made when there are vacancies, and federal judges and members of the Supreme Court decide, themselves, when to retire.

Over the years, Democratic presidents have tried to appoint Democratic lawyers, preferably liberals, while Republican presidents have sought to appoint conservative lawyers. This has resulted in moves and counter moves, balance and imbalance, in an increasingly politicized environment. There is a great deal of chance in the appointment process. The president cannot plan and, thus, he can make mistakes, misjudge a candidate.

During the Committee hearings in the Senate in the summer of 2010, after Elena Kagan had been nominated by President Obama to the Supreme Court, Senator Arlen Spector spoke of the ideological struggle and of the reality that every president nominates candidates on the basis of their political ideology. His colleague, Senator Lindsey Graham, one of the few Republicans who eventually voted for Kagan, said that, of course, liberal presidents nominate liberal judges --elections have consequences. Obama's nominee won.

When Ronald Reagan became president in 1981, he and his conservative supporters realized that he would be likely to given the opportunity to appoint several new members of the Supreme Court. This also happened. Sandra Day O'Connor, a Republican from Arizona, became the Court's first female member. Altogether during his eight years in the White House, Reagan appointed three justices and promoted William Rehnquist to Chief Justice. But two of his nominations failed, first Robert Bork and then Donald Ginsburg.

At the third attempt, Reagan nominated a fellow Californian, Anthony Kennedy, who was quickly approved by the Senate by a vote of 97 to 0. Over the years, Kennedy has become the important swing vote on the Court, often deciding which faction, the conservative or the liberal, wins.

With Reagan in the White House and through his appointments, the entire federal judiciary swung to the right, politically. After three years in power, a quarter of Reagan's appointments were millionaires, 98 percent were Republicans, 98 percent were white, and 92 percent were men. By comparison, 5 percent of Jimmy Carter's judicial appointments were millionaires, 20 percent were minorities, 15 percent were women and 90 percent were Democrats.

It has been a central goal of a generation of conservative activists to gain control over the judiciary, and particularly the Supreme Court, Barack Obama wrote in his book "The Audacity of Hope." He saw these activists as "the last bastion of pro-abortion, pro-affirmative action, pro-homosexual, pro-criminal, pro-regulation, anti-religious liberal elitism," while liberals saw the courts as "the only thing standing in the way of a radical effort to roll back civil rights, women's rights, civil liberties, environmental regulation, church/state separation, and the entire legacy of the New Deal."

As senator, Obama voted no to George W. Bush's nominations of both Chief Justice John Roberts and Associate Justice Samuel Alito. Both were eventually approved by the Senate with large majorities.

Sometimes, such as between 1994 and 2005, there were no personnel changes at all at the Court, often because of politically strategic decisions by the Justices themselves. 90-year-old liberal John Paul Stevens, for example, remained so long on the Court because he did not want to give George W. Bush the opportunity to decide who would succeed him. Instead, that honor went to President Obama, thus, ensuring that Stevens' successor also was a liberal jurist. Unlike Stevens, who was healthy when he resigned in spite of his years, many others refused to bow to age or illness.

Hugo Black, 85 years old and 34 years on the Supreme Court, and John Marshall Harlan, 71 years old and 16 years on the Court, were both hospitalized and almost completely blind before they finally resigned. William O. Douglas, appointed by Franklin Delano Roosevelt, also refused to resign despite a long and difficult illness. He eventually stepped down after nearly 37 years on the Court -- longer than anyone else. And when William Rehnquist died in 2005 of cancer, he was still Chief Justice, after having been ill for months and largely unable to do his job.

When I came to America in 1960, Earl Warren, a former Republican governor of California, was Chief Justice of the U.S. Supreme Court. He had been nominated by President Dwight Eisenhower, a Republican, who had the opportunity during his eight years in the White House to nominate an additional four Justices. Later, Eisenhower considered two of them – Earl Warren and Walter Brennan – mistakes. Both turned out to be significantly more liberal than what Eisenhower had anticipated.

President George H. W. Bush had probably never imagined that David Souter, whom he appointed in 1980, would become one of the mainstays of the Supreme Court's liberal faction. And President Nixon had also probably never imagined that his appointment in 1970 of the cautious Minnesota lawyer Harry A. Blackmun would lead to the Supreme Court's landmark decision in 1973, Roe v. Wade that established the right to abortion in America.

Nixon had also, like Reagan, seen the Senate reject two of his nominations to the Court. Both were Southerners and both had little respect in the legal community. The remarkable thing was that Nixon had never even met the two, Clement Haynsworth and G. Harrold Carswell, before he nominated them. That would never happen today.

Ever since 1987, when the Senate refused to approve Reagan's nomination of Robert Bork, the Senate's role of "advise and consent" in Supreme Court nominations has become increasingly important. Bork's openness about his political and legal philosophy, his views on abortion and other sensitive issues, became his downfall, and, in retrospect, his testimony turned out to be the last, frank testimonial before the Senate Judiciary Committee.

Subsequently, both conservative and liberal candidates have become extremely cautious during the hearings and try to say as little as possible about their legal philosophy. Associate Justice Clarence Thomas acknowledged this after his controversial appointment, saying he had deliberately tried to lie low and tell as little about himself as possible during the Senate hearings in the fall of 1991. "If you are yourself, as Bob Bork, you're dead," he said.

This has made the hearings less interesting but also more difficult for the Senators, and the public, to form an opinion about the candidates. Thomas had been nominated in 1991 by President George HW Bush. He was an unknown and inexperienced conservative black lawyer and the Senate approved the appointment with the smallest margin ever for a candidate to the Supreme Court, 52 votes to 48. Thomas succeeded the legendary civil rights lawyer, Associate Justice Thurgood Marshall. Many thought the nomination odd, but Bush needed support from the conservative wing of the Republican Party, and so he chose Thomas, a bona fide conservative, as his nominee.

The Senate hearings in October 1991 were dramatic and developed into a bruising battle, which took a sensational turn when Anita Hill, a female former colleague of Thomas, accused him of sexual harassment.

Hill, a law professor, and, like Thomas, educated at Yale Law School, was an extremely credible witness and Thomas just barely rode out the storm. Hill testified during a full day on October 11, 1991 in a fascinating spectacle that was followed by much of the nation via television. In an opinion poll just after the hearings 47 percent said they believed Thomas, while only 24 percent believed Hill. A year later, the numbers had changed drastically -- 44 percent now believed Hill while only 34 percent found Thomas credible.

Thomas said afterward that the criticism against him did not have anything to do with Anita Hill -- it constituted a political and racial revenge against black conservatives like him. His anger and bitterness are still on display today. Over the years, other women have come forward with similar damning stories about Clarence Thomas and his obsession with sex and pornography, but Thomas is still on the Court after twenty years and has become one of its most dependable conservative members.

The appointment of Thomas, wrote Jane Mayer and Jill Abramson in their 1994 book, "Strange Justice, The Selling of Clarence Thomas," was a clear example that "the end justified the means." Thomas, himself, launched a long and intensive campaign among American conservative groups to be appointed to the Supreme Court. The book provides a frightening insight into the politicization of appointments to the Supreme Court. The White House at the time spared nothing and no one to secure Thomas' approval in the Senate. It was political war.

Is the system democratic? Curiously, the appointment process to the Supreme Court is very little discussed. Why are the appointments for life, for example? One could imagine a time limit of ten to fifteen years, an age limit of 75 years, or something similar.

In the autumn of 2011, some 30 legal scholars and former judges proposed that new Supreme Court Justices be appointed every two years, with 18 years as a maximum term.

During the Republican primary election campaign of 2011 and 2012, the Republican presidential candidate, Texas governor Rich Perry, called the system of lifetime-appointed Justices "undemocratic" and he proposed a constitutional amendment to give every president the opportunity to replace two justices per four-year term and create a regular nomination procedure. Liberals like Hendrik Hertzberg, a political commentator in The New Yorker, endorsed Perry's proposal. The Supreme Court really needs to become more democratic, he wrote.

It was in June 1986 that President Ronald Reagan promoted William Rehnquist to Chief Justice of the U.S. Supreme Court. The news came as a complete surprise although the 61-year-old Rehnquist had served as an Associate Justice on the Court since 1971. He had previously served as Assistant Attorney General in the Nixon administration and worked in Arizona where he belonged to the Barry Goldwater wing of the Republican Party. Rehnquist would succeed the 77-year-old Warren Burger who resigned. The promotion of Rehnquist gave Reagan the opportunity to appoint a new Associate Justice and he chose Antonin Scalia, another conservative jurist, just 50 years old.

During his 15 years on the Court, Rehnquist became something of its conservative conscience. His promotion to Chief Justice came shortly after he had voted against a woman's right to abortion. With the nominations of Rehnquist and Scalia, the Court took a marked step to the right, something the Senate clearly realized, for the battle over Rehnquist's nomination was fierce. In the end, fully 33 of the Senate's 100 members voted "no," including then leading moderate Republicans, Charles Mathias, of Maryland, and Lowell Weicker, of Connecticut.

Never before had so many voted against such a nomination, and never before had such a controversial jurist as the 61-year-old Swedish-American William Rehnquist been selected to lead one of the most powerful institutions in America.

Sweden's ambassador in Washington, Wilhelm Wachtmeister, was for a few years in the 1980s the Dean of the diplomatic corps in the U.S. capital. At an evening at his residence on Nebraska Avenue of music and dance, "Ville," as he was called and known for his extensive contacts, had three members of the Supreme Court as guests, Rehnquist, Sandra Day O'Connor, and Anthony Kennedy. Rehnquist, who was newly appointed, had not given any interviews since taking over as Chief Justice. His grandfather's name was Anderson and his grandmother's name was Törnberg. The two Swedish immigrants had met in Chicago and married.

An interview? Why do not give it a try? A colleague from Swedish Radio and I approached Rehnquist and asked.

"Well, maybe," said Rehnquist. "Write me a note and we'll see..."

We did, and in June 1987, the interview took place.

"I guess my Swedish roots are the reason for this exception," explained William Rehnquist with a smile at the beginning a nearly hour-long conversation in his office at the Supreme Court. He did not know much about Sweden, he conceded willingly, nor about his Swedish ancestors. He knew that his grandfather had taken the name Rehnquist because there were so many Andersons on the boat across the Atlantic, and that his grandfather and his two brothers had parted ways in Chicago. His grandfather went north to Milwaukee where Rehnquist was born and grew up. His father did not know any Swedish because nobody was allowed to speak Swedish at home. That was common in Swedish immigrant families...one should become American.

But he knew that Sweden does not have a constitutional court. The advantage of the Supreme Court in the United States, explained Rehnquist, is that if you have a written constitution the provisions are best enforced by a court that is used to interpreting what Constitution says on various issues. This allows the courts in the United States to be powerful in an almost political sense, though I do not mean politically partisan but, rather, it gives a sense of how the U.S. is governed.

Did he see any disadvantages with the American legal system?

"The risk is that a very small group of judges act like an oligarchy. But because the president nominates judges and the Senate approves them there are ways to prevent any tendencies that the Supreme Court becomes anti-majority institution. "

William Rehnquist was quite tall, slightly bent, and with thin hair. He was dressed in gray trousers, a blue jacket, a brown and white striped shirt and a blue tie. He spoke slowly and thoughtfully throughout the interview and gave the impression of being very serious. But his face lit up every so often with a large smile and he showed occasional flashes of fine humor and a hearty laugh. He was informal and he has a reputation for being a great practical joker.

Rehnquist was considered, even by many of his opponents, a brilliant jurist with a sharp intellect, but many also questioned his integrity, and Senators accused him during the debate of insensitivity towards minorities and women. Rehnquist is too extreme, said Ted Kennedy. A brilliant legal intellect serving racism and injustice is neither a virtue nor a qualification to become Chief Justice.

In the interview that day in June 1987, Rehnquist said that he saw the U.S. Constitution as an outstanding document that lays out how power is shared and balanced in the United States between the executive (the President), the legislative (Congress) and the judiciary (Courts). He called the participants in the Constitutional Convention in Philadelphia in the summer of 1787 for an unusually capable group of people, who did not, however, regard themselves as perfect.

"Consequently, they allowed for the Constitution to be amended and that has led to the Constitution's adaptation to societal changes over the years," said Rehnquist.

It protects the judiciary and the judges who cannot be removed. I do not need to fear, he said, that something may happen to me because of how I have voted in different cases. He also fully supported the president's the right to appoint Supreme Court members. It has worked well in the past, he said, and what are the options anyway?

When I asked Rehnquist to select some historical rulings by the Court, he described the case of Marbury v. Madison from 1803 as the cornerstone of the entire American legal system. It determined the Supreme Court's sovereignty and the right to determine whether the executive and the legislature had adhered to the Constitution in their decisions. He cited the Dred Scott case of 1857, which held that blacks could not be U.S. citizens and that Congress could not prohibit slavery in the territories outside the then U.S. borders. A few years later, in 1861, the American Civil War broke out over slavery's continued existence. And he mentioned Plessy v. Ferguson, which at the end of the 1800s ruled that separate schools for blacks and whites were legal, but he added that in 1954, in Brown v. Board of Education, the Supreme Court reversed itself when it unanimously declared that racial segregation in America's schools was unconstitutional.

"The Supreme Court makes important decisions, but very few of these issues are settled once and for all," said Rehnquist, and when asked which area has been particularly affected by the Supreme Court over the years, he answered: civil liberties.

"The Supreme Court has always intensely wanted to protect the freedom of the press, religious freedom, and the rights of defendants in trials."

He said, the Supreme Court has always wanted to protect citizens' rights by prohibiting discrimination of various kinds. He said he also believed in moderation and that the Court should act as a brake on society. Its primary mission, he believed, is to ensure that the Constitution is followed.

Many years after my interview with Rehnquist, the Court stated in a notable case that freedom of expression applies even if the message is one of hatred. The case was between a grieving father and a church, whose members demonstrated at the funeral of the father's son with hateful placards proclaiming that "God hates fags" and "Thank God for dead soldiers "- all as part of their crusade against homosexuals in America. The placards reflected the church's belief that God is punishing America because the country tolerates homosexuality.

Words can cause great pain, said Chief Justice John Roberts, but we cannot react to pain by punishing the speaker. Freedom of speech protects even hurtful words so that public debate is not stifled.

About the same time that I interviewed Rehnquist, a bitter political battle in California continued about Rose Bird, Chief Justice of California's Supreme Court. In 1977, at 41 years of age, she became the first female judge of the court. Ever since then, she has lived with controversy, and in the end, in November 1986, after eight attempts, did California's voters succeed in voting her out of office.

Rose Bird's appointment to Chief Justice by then Democratic governor Jerry Brown was a sensation and caused a backlash among the state's conservatives. Bird was a woman, she was young, she was a liberal, and she had never served before as a judge, although she had a solid legal education and among other things was the first female law professor at Stanford University. The appointment was approved by a deeply split legal commission and by California's voters, but with only a 52 percent majority - the thinnest margin of victory ever for a judge in California's history.

In a book from 1983, "Framed - The New Right Attack on Chief Justice Rose Bird and the Courts," journalism professor Betty Medsger painted a dark picture of how the right wing in California, with branches in Ronald Reagan's White House, had long pursued a deliberate and carefully planned campaign to unseat Rose Bird.

"I have no greater desire to think about the past," said Rose Bird during an interview with me in her office in the courthouse in San Francisco in the fall of 1983. "There is no point. I want to look ahead, but I think there is a group, a very small group in this country, that would like to take over the judiciary. It believes that the judiciary should be more responsive to their points of view. This is about the changes in our society in recent years and the recognition of the rights of our minorities."

She said that this group, whose attacks have been more purposeful in California than in other States, believes that courts have been too liberal in terms of individual rights and freedoms. They would like to the courts to limit these rights rather than expand them.

Is there justice in America today?

"I guess there is some measure of justice, but a democratic system requires constant supervision. I believe that it is still important who you are in this society. Race still matters. We try to be conscious of this, but if we are to be honest, racism is still our biggest problem."

Rose Bird did not agree at all with those who spoke of the power of the judiciary and of the courts as the country's most powerful institutions, not at all.

"They are the weakest link in the American political system, and they are not more powerful than the respect they receive from those who hold political power. No, the courts are very fragile, but they have the important task of being the protector of the individual. If courts are weakened so are also the individual's rights and freedoms."

She also saw a danger in the fact that the courts are often handed tasks that belong to the executive or the legislature, for example the abortion issue, and making the courts decide life begins and ends. The Courts' expanded tasks are a consequence of a certain stagnation in the executive and legislative power -- they have become prisoners of various interest groups, Rose Bird said. No one wants to offend anyone and so the courts have to take over.

"Our party system has broken down. The political parties have become redundant and the individual is at the mercy of interest groups. It has also become too expensive to try to get elected to an office in this country. We must find a way for people to engage in politics without having to sell their souls," Rose Bird said.

The death penalty had at that time long been a particularly thorny issue in California. At the time of the interview, 141 waited on death row for a final decision. Rose Bird did not want to say where she stood on the death penalty, but it was clear from her many decisions that she was an opponent.

During her ten-year tenure, Rose Bird never approved a lower court's death penalty judgment. She voted "no" in all 61 cases that reached the California Supreme Court. But she was not alone. In over 55 of these cases she had the Supreme Court's majority with her when the death sentences were overturned in favor of new trials or a life sentence without the possibility of parole.

Her opposition to the death penalty was to be the main reason she was attacked so hard from the right.

Rose Bird's struggles to remain Chief Justice of the California Supreme Court ended in the election of 1986 after the most obvious political campaign ever against a U.S. federal judge. Along with Rose Bird, California's voters also voted out two other liberal judges on the State's Supreme Court, Cruz Reynoso and Joseph Grodin. All three were opposed to the death penalty. Nothing like this had ever happened since the right of the voters to approve judiciary appointments had been introduced in California 50 years earlier.

For Rose Bird, it was all a battle for the judiciary's independence.

"You're wrong, "she said just before the election in November 1986 in a speech directed at the Republican governor George Deukmejian, "when you try to dismiss judges because they do not meet your requirements, because you have not appointed them, because you do not control them. You do not understand in a fundamental way how our society works, what the law says and what constitutes a constitutional government."

After her resignation, Rose Bird stayed active but away from the limelight. She died in 1999 of breast cancer, 63 years old.

Her fate was repeated in 2010 in the State of Iowa, where a unanimous Supreme Court had legalized same-sex marriage. The judgment resulted in that three of the justices were thrown out by the voters in the election of 2010. It was the first time such a thing had happened in Iowa and it was a frightening message, wrote USA Today:

"They are not corrupt or incompetent. They are not even politicians. They're Supreme Court Justices, and the circumstances of their eviction should be deeply troubling to anyone who believes in the rule of law. The judges' sin was that they did their jobs."

By the end of his first term, President Barack Obama had nominated two Supreme Court Justices, Sonya Sotomayor and Elena Kagan, both prominent liberal female jurists. Three on the Court are now women, more than ever before, but Obama has not managed to do anything about the conservative majority with John Roberts as Chief Justice. And he may never get the chance, if none of the four other conservative justices -- Samuel Alito, Antonin Scalia, Clarence Thomas, and, the sometimes wavering, Anthony Kennedy -- resign or somehow is forced to resign. Sotomayor and Kagan succeeded liberals David Souter and John Paul Stevens – and the liberals are still in the minority.

The Court has become more political, seemingly split into two political blocks -- five appointed by Republican presidents versus four appointed by Democratic presidents. The era of the big, unanimous decisions seems to be something of the past, such decisions as the 1954 Brown v. Board of Education or the 1973 decision to order President Nixon to release the White House tape recordings in connection with the Watergate scandal.

But the Court has not only become more political. It has also taken a major step to right, exemplified in the 2010 decision in Citizen United v. Federal Election Commission, when the Court's five conservative Justices gave the green light to unlimited campaign contributions from individuals and private companies. The decision has become so controversial that The Nine might very well take up the issue again, especially if the liberals recapture the majority on the Court.

In June 2012, the Supreme Court issued a decision that the whole country had waited for – its judgment on whether President Obama's major health care reform was constitutional. The judgment was preceded by heated debate and wild guesses on how The Nine would vote. In the end, all predictions proved wrong. Chief Justice John Roberts sensationally sided with the four liberals and, in a 5 to 4 ruling, the Supreme Court declared the reform constitutional. In the weeks after the decision, there was much speculation about the reason for Roberts's vote.

It is possible that he simply did not want to lead a Court which had voted down Obama's biggest reform as president, a reform that had been passed in full accordance with all rules of the majority in Congress. A "no" verdict would have further eroded the Court's already tarnished reputation -- less than half of all Americans say they approve of its work. At the same time, no one believes that Roberts' common cause with the four liberals signifies a long-term change in the Court's conservative orientation. As long as the current nine justices remain on the Court, there will be no ideological change.

The Court's decision constituted new proof of the uniqueness of the American system -- where the biggest issues for the American society are determined by The Nine on the Supreme Court. And once again it can be said that the United States has the court the country and its citizens deserve.

Whoever becomes president is determined by voters, and the president then decides, as vacancies arise, who becomes a member of the Supreme Court. For many Americans, there is no more important task for a president, and for many Americans there is no more important reason to vote. The fact that The Nine, as now with John Roberts, not always vote as predicted and in accordance with their political ideologies, is also part of the Supreme Court's mystique and of its unique role in America.

Chapter 10.

WAR, WAR, WAR…

It was a memorial that no one wanted about a war that everyone sought to forget.
Such was the mood when the Vietnam Memorial opened in November 1982, on the National Mall in the middle of Washington, DC next to monuments honoring the giants of American history, George Washington and Abraham Lincoln. The new memorial quickly became the most visited monument in the American capital, with over two million visitors in the first year alone, and now, 30 years later, with over three million visitors a year.
The memorial's popularity is has been an important part of the healing process from America's hitherto longest and most hated war, and for restoring the honor of the men who fought and died there but who had once returned home in shame to a nation that wanted to forget them. The memorial's history is as controversial as the war's, or perhaps just because of it. It grew out of an idea that no one at first put much faith in, an idea proposed by Vietnam veteran Joe Scruggs in the book "To Heal a Nation."
The Vietnam Memorial consists of two black stone walls below ground level. They run 75 yards straight out from the center towards the Washington Monument in one direction and the Lincoln Memorial in the other direction. It is surrounded by trees in such a way that one must get quite close before it suddenly becomes visible.

In its simplicity, the Vietnam Memorial is my favorite monument on the National Mall, where, unfortunately, war monuments abound, commemorating the Korean War, World War II, and soon, surely, the two most recent wars, in Iraq and Afghanistan. That is, if there is room, for it's beginning to get crowded on the Mall.

The atmosphere at the Vietnam Memorial is solemn and quiet, despite all the visitors. The two long black walls are inscribed with the names of the 58,022 dead and missing in Vietnam, from July 1959 until April 30, 1975, when Saigon fell and America left Vietnam. Flowers, mostly roses and carnations, are continuously placed on the ground at the foot of the walls, usually close by the name of a fallen brother, husband, father, cousin ... Some cry, while others prefer a moment of solitude and quiet. Many of the visitors are among the more than two million Americans who served some time in Vietnam. Some of them visit the memorial time and again, others less often. But sooner or later, they all seem to come here.

Over the years, the Vietnam Memorial has become one of America's most famous monuments, created by Maya Lin, then a young architectural student at Yale University. Her unusual and abstract idea was controversial and for a long time it seemed that it would never be realized. But, today, her influence is seen in the similar dark stone memorials throughout America. Her idea and design have somehow become synonymous with war and death and sacrifice for America in the many wars that followed Vietnam, almost without interruption, since my first years in California in the '60s: Lebanon, Grenada, the Gulf War, Somalia, Bosnia, Serbia, Afghanistan, Iraq, and Libya. Every president went to war, except Jimmy Carter, president from 1977 to 1981.

The civilian and military casualties ran into the millions -- two million in Vietnam; 700,000 in Iraq; 100,000 in Afghanistan. And millions of refugees in Iraq alone.

A militaristic America? A warlike America?

Professor Coit Blacker, director of the Freeman Spogli Institute for International Studies at Stanford University, said in an interview in February 2012 that, yes, American foreign policy has developed in a "militaristic" direction since the mid 90's. The Obama administration has tried to adapt to this by relying less on conventional forces, but it shows no signs of abandoning the direction of this policy.

"Part of this has to do with the availability of our forces and their quality," said Blacker, "but it also has to do with certain impatience when we face difficult problems, without clean and straight forward diplomatic solutions. We have a tendency not to ask the hard questions before we send in our troops, and we seem to try to convince ourselves that this time it will be different. Unfortunately, there is no evidence of this in our history."

The United States is still, by far, the world's largest military power -- really without comparison, without competition. Although the world in 2010 spent 1,630 billion dollars on the military, according to SIPRI (Stockholm International Peace Research Institute), the increase from the previous year was only 1.3 percent -- much slower than the 5.1 percent increase from 2001 to 2009. The U.S. accounts for almost all of this increase, or 19.6 of 20.6 billion dollars in total, and over 42 percent of the world's total military spending, while the figures for China are 7.3 percent, Russia 3.6, Britain 3.7, and France 3.6 percent. The U.S. military budget amounts to 4.8 percent of GDP (Gross Domestic Product,) which is more than twice as much as in China, Britain and France. In Europe, total military spending amounts to 1.6 percent of GDP.

In the coming years, the Pentagon's budgets will contain heavy cuts totaling 259 billion dollars in the first five years and nearly 500 billion dollars over the next ten years. New initiatives in Asia, a further move away from Europe, and fewer soldiers are planned. It will no longer be possible for the U.S. military, as in Iraq and Afghanistan, to wage two wars at the same time. The 570,000 soldiers in the army will be reduced to 520,000. Before Iraq and Afghanistan, the figure was 480,000 soldiers. All figures are considerably lower than at the end of the Cold War, when the U.S. army had nearly 900,000 soldiers.

It seems to me that during my years in America, the military has come to play an increasing large role. There is a kind of reverence for the military, especially for the regular troops, and to criticize them is almost taboo. The military is also highly present in everyday life, perhaps more than in any other Western democracy.

President Eisenhower spoke in his farewell address as president in 1960 of the dangers of the "military-industrial complex," warnings that have become reality today. The military employs millions of Americans, who depend on it for their careers and their families' livelihood, either on bases around America but also in Germany, Okinawa, or on any of the over 600 military installations the U.S. has around the world -- 54,000 soldiers in Germany, 39,000 in Japan, 10,800 in Italy, 9,300 in the UK. The total costs are upwards of two billion dollars a year.

In addition, there are countless industries related to the military and weapons manufacturing, plus all the interest groups and lobbyists all of which make up a giant network, and all of which are interested in maintaining and further expanding America's military might.

The benefits of a military career are many, especially for all those young men and women who cannot find jobs or security elsewhere. They are taken care of on a base somewhere, everything from wages, food and shelter, schooling, health insurance to medical care, and then, in the end, they are able to retire after 20 years on almost full pay with continued health care and health insurance. It is quite understandable that so many turn to the military, despite the dangers and risks if they are ordered to go to war.

So I can understand my cousin – grandson of our Swedish-born grandfather - who signed up and joined the navy after college and who had a good career sailing the world's oceans. He eventually became a captain, lived well with his family in a San Diego suburb and is now collecting a good pension after nearly 30 years of service plus a salary as an employee in one of the thousands of companies across America that do business with the U.S. military.

And I can understand my other cousin's son, who is married with three sons, and who has only a high school education. He also chose the military, an option that looks pretty good in today's weak U.S. economy. For him, the Marine Corps meant training, a good salary, security, housing, healthcare, but it also meant two nearly year-long periods of service in Iraq, and a third in Afghanistan- - all with the family far away in a townhouse on a base in California.

It has not always been like this, and it was especially not like this during the Vietnam War, when the mood was quite anti-militarist. The war, back then, touched everyone, because America still had the draft. All of us young men at the time carried a draft card in our wallet in the back pocket, unlike today's youth. When America ended the draft and created a professional military, it changed America and Americans' attitudes to their soldiers.

Over the years, they have become hailed as "heroes" -- all of them – and they have been universally celebrated. No sporting or other public takes place these days without a tribute to "the heroes" – complete with flags, the national anthem, salutes, applause, cheers.

The big question is whether or not the end of the draft and the advent of a corps of professional soldiers made America more ready to go to war.

What is certainly true is that the wars in Iraq or Afghanistan have not touched America in the same way as Vietnam did. There are no peace marches or student protests. There are no campaigns to help rebuild Iraq or Afghanistan, no charity, no open doors for refugees those countries to come to America. It is as if the wars are so far away that they seem unreal, with average Americans unaffected. Sure, many have died, far too many, but the wars and the deaths have never felt like a sacrifice for the rest of the country, for all those who do not have a son or daughter, father or mother, fighting in a distant land. They have voluntarily chosen this life, seems to be the overriding message.

Every now and then we are reminded of the victims when newspapers or TV news program show the photos of those who have died. In February 2012, for example, the Washington Post printed a full page of photos of the latest victims in Afghanistan, a total of 42 soldiers, most of them from America's small towns: Apache Junction, Arizona; New London, Connecticut; Hickory, North Carolina; Checotah, Oklahoma; Red Broiling Springs, Tennessee – from recruits as young as 19 years old to tanned sergeants at the age of 44. Weariness with war is increasingly being felt in America, according to the polls.

In March 2012, 60 per cent of respondents in an ABC/Washington Post poll answered that the war in Afghanistan has not been worth the deaths and sacrifices, and a majority, 54 percent, said the U.S. should withdraw all troops, even before the Afghan forces can assume responsibility themselves.

In the book "The Icarus Syndrome," Peter Beinart wrote about three unnecessary wars: World War I, Vietnam, and Iraq. They were disasters, founded on ideas that were rooted in progressivism, liberal anti-communism and neo-conservatism, all of which, in turn, were rooted in hubris of various kinds, and, in Iraq's case, to dominate through force.

One of these wars, the Vietnam War, changed American history and is still a great influence on America's foreign and security policy, columnist William Pfaff wrote in the New York Review of Books in December 2010 and added that what happened after 9/11 is proof of that. The struggle against Marxism-Leninism during the Cold War may have been turned into a fight against militant Islam, but America has the same role as then, that of the universal peacemaker.

And the domino theory lives on, according to Pfaff, the theory to which President Eisenhower referred after France's major defeat at Dien Bien Phu, in Vietnam, in 1954, that put an end to France's colonial role in Southeast Asia. The "Domino theory," wrote Pfaff, explained "why we were in Vietnam." It was not the reason the U.S. got involved in Vietnam, but it explains why America remained there for so long, and it came to influence both George W. Bush's and Barack Obama's policies towards Afghanistan.

In my interview, professor Blacker at Stanford University said he did not think that Vietnam plays a particularly large role anymore among today's foreign policy makers.

Barack Obama was 14 years old when Saigon fell in 1975, and for everyone on his foreign policy team, with the exception of Hillary Clinton, Vietnam is a "fading memory."

"No, Iraq plays a much bigger role," said Blacker. "Iraq, which started as a war of liberation but became a decade-long occupation of Iraq with enormous costs both for them and for us. This was a 'war of choice' – and wars should not start that way. The consequence has been that the American people have a harder time accepting facts when there is great uncertainty, which explains why we did not take the lead in Libya. The strategy towards Libya was a direct result of what had happened in Iraq."

"After 9/11, Bush had no choice in Afghanistan," Blacker continued, "but I don't think that anyone could imagine that we would still be there, ten years later. Here, the comparison between Vietnam and Afghanistan is apt -- no one, in 1965, thought we would be in Vietnam ten years later."

Blacker's Stanford colleague, democracy expert Larry Diamond who served in 2004 as an adviser in the Coalition Authority in Iraq, replied when I asked him about Iraq that the invasion "was a mistake." It was not in the U.S. interest to overthrow Sadam Hussein, said Diamond, who in 2005 came out with the book "Squandered Victory: The American Occupation and the Bungled Effort to Bring Democracy to Iraq."

"Of course," said Diamond, "it is morally preferable that Hussein is gone, but the way in which it happened is unfortunate and it has meant significant costs to the U.S., both economically and militarily. Moreover, once we invaded we committed huge mistakes in the beginning because of arrogance, ignorance, isolation, and ineptitude. Today, we are still facing important, but unanswered questions: can Iraq's security be maintained without the presence of American troops and the country can develop into a real democracy?"

"On the other hand," he continued, "the invasion of Afghanistan was necessary, but we cannot stay there forever. No, I believe more in a kind of compromise solution to reduce our presence and reduce our costs while ensuring that the country does not collapse."

And in five or ten years, what will Iraq and Afghanistan look like?

"I don't know, but I am more optimistic about Iraq than about Afghanistan. Iraq will not collapse, but I'm not sure that won't happen in Afghanistan."

The United States left Iraq at the end 2012, and the question now is how and when will the U.S. leave Afghanistan? The war is becoming ever more unpopular. Only 31 percent said in a survey in the spring of 2011 that Afghanistan was "worth fighting for." In the spring of 2012, greater impatience and an even greater fatigue were evident. According to Gallup, half of the respondents said the United States should quickly withdraw its troops from Afghanistan; a quarter of them felt America should stick to the timetable and pull out in 2014; and 21 percent said the U.S. should stay in Afghanistan as long as it takes. Still, 59 percent of respondents felt it was the right decision to attack Afghanistan after 9/11. The decade-long war against terrorism has left its marks -- America is tired of war -- and the Arab Spring has brought new crises and new demands on the United States.

There used to be an unspoken convention in U.S. foreign policy, and, above all, when America went to war: that "politics stops at the water's edge," meaning that Republicans and Democrats supported the president, no matter what. That is no longer true. Party politics has seriously inserted itself into foreign policy, as witnessed time and again in recent years, most recently over the multinational operation against Libya.

President Obama's Libya intervention was criticized by Republicans for tardiness, even though the then Secretary of Defense Robert Gates and the military leadership, well aware the strained resources, were not even were willing to deliver weapons and training to the Libyan rebels. And on a matter of U.S. ground forces in Libya, Gates replied, "not so long I have this job." In a much-publicized speech at West Point, the army officer school, in February 2011, Gates had also said that -- the U.S. military must evolve with changes in the world. In one piece of the speech, he even said that any Secretary of Defense who recommends that the president send a large American fighting force to Asia, the Middle East or Africa, should have his head examined.

Eventually, the U.S. intervened in Libya. America, again, went to war, but this time it ended with a quick success. It was a different kind of war, not the usual American action with the United States in the lead role, but a European-led, multilateral action, something that neither the politicians in Washington nor the American public were used to. No president before Obama had relied on the international community to such a degree. And it was a success that involved no American ground troops. The skeptics never thought this possible for they just did not believe that the Europeans could carry this off.

In a broader perspective, and as pro-democracy movements have taken hold in the Arab world, a new Obama Doctrine emerged. Professor Blacker of Stanford University mentioned three things that have characterized Obama's foreign policy:
• an extensive, but mostly invisible, fight against terrorism;
• attention to the broader Middle East -- from Pakistan to Israel; and
• the Chinese challenge.

Russia is no longer a major threat to the United States, said Blacker, although there is significant anti-Americanism in Russia today and although the Russians are deeply skeptical of the U.S. role in the world. His statement seems to have been confirmed in a recent poll by the Pew Research Center, where only two percent of respondents, compared to 93 percent in 1980 and 32 percent in 1990, identified Russia as America's greatest enemy.

"And the war on terrorism is going well," Blacker continued, "although the situation in the Middle East is full of uncertainty, and I am much more pessimistic about the Middle East's and Pakistan's future than about the Chinese challenge, even though the U.S. has not been challenged in a similar way since Soviet days in the 70s."

"But I don't believe in a new superpower game, that China is aiming to become the 21st century's new Soviet Union. I see no Cold War relationship with China. We must try to convince the Chinese that the current world order is in their interest. But the world will not in the long run tolerate to be flooded by cheap Chinese products. China must develop its own domestic economy. I think the Chinese want to change -- they don't want to go the same way as Russia or Egypt."

President Obama's years in the White House have been marked by constant foreign policy crises, and in the winter of 2012 the war drums in America began to rumble once again as Iran's nuclear program and the civil war in Syria took increasingly serious dimensions and as the pressure from Israel to take military action against Iran increased. At the same time, the conflict between Israel and Palestine continues to fester after four years with Obama in the White House. A peace settlement seems as distant as ever. Obama's cool personal relationship with hawkish Israeli Prime Minister Netanyahu has not favored any peace efforts.

Obama's statement about the seemingly obvious fact that peace between Israel and the Palestinians must be based on 1967 borders, before the Six Day War of that year, resulted in a tense summit between Obama and Netanyahu in the White House in May 2011.

The Republicans tried for many years to exploit the frozen Israeli-Palestinian peace efforts and capture as many Jewish, and traditionally Democratic, voters as possible. They did not succeed in the 2012 presidential election.

The truth is that Israel under Netanyahu has shown very little interest in any peace negotiations. In fact, wrote the New York Times' Tom Friedman in May 2011, that Netanyahu has so far avoided trying to reach a settlement with the Palestinians. Now, in Obama's fifth year in the White House, his new Secretary of State, John Kerry, has launched a new strong peace effort, such as not seen before during the Obama presidency.

Obama, in contrast to many previous Democratic presidents and presidential candidates, is politically strong on foreign policy. He can point to a range of successes during his presidency that make it extremely difficult for the Republicans to criticize him in a credible way. Foremost among these successes has been the war against the international terrorism led by al Qaeda.

Obama was successful at the one thing that George W. Bush had failed to do for seven years: to capture/kill al Qaeda's leader Osama bin Laden. In announcing bin Laden's death, Obama declared that "justice has been served," he also said that bin Laden's death did not mean the end of the fight against terrorism. We must continue to be vigilant, he said, and he stressed that this is not a war against Islam but a war against al Qaeda.

It is a secret war without virtually any transparency. Since Obama became president, at least 1,300 people have been killed in such attacks in Pakistan alone, according to press reports. But the attacks have not led to a broader debate, and opinion polls in the spring of 2012 showed a solid support among the American public for Obama's war on terrorism. 70 percent of the respondents in an ABC/Washington Post survey supported the decision to keep the Guantanamo prison open, and 83 percent supported the drone attacks.

Former Assistant Attorney General in the Bush Administration, Jack L. Goldsmith, wrote in the New York Times that the attacks were justified because the United States is at war against terrorism. Andrew Sullivan on his blog, The Dish, was of a similar opinion:

"My own position is that we are at war, and that avowed enemies and traitors in active warfare against the U.S. cannot suddenly invoke legal protections from a society they have decided to help destroy."
But many are concerned.

"There is in general no justification for these attacks (on American citizens)," said Karen Greenberg, director of the Center on National Security at Fordham University Law School, to me in an interview. And the journalist Glenn Greenwald wrote that it now seems ok to murder U.S. citizens without formal charges, prosecution or trial. He called the drone attack and the killing of Anwar al-Awlaki, the American born al Qaeda leader in Yemen, illegal.

Among those concerned is the mighty voice of the New York Times. In a lead editorial in March 2012, the newspaper stated that the Obama administration had not explained why drone attacks against U.S. citizens are not subject to prior judicial review and the paper characterized Holder's policy on this issue as "disturbing."

The administration, the editorial said, should seek a go-ahead from a court before killing an American citizen, and the administration should publish the legal memoranda on which these attacks are justified. It concluded:

"We cannot understand why President Obama would want to follow President Bush's terrible example to withhold important information from the public."

In a speech in Chicago in March 2012, Attorney General Eric Holder tried to justify the drone attacks, even against American al Qaeda members. They constitute an "imminent terrorist threat," his argument went, but they probably cannot be caught alive. The president needs no authorization by any federal court before he orders such an attack, said Holder. This is no "assassination." That would be illegal. The United States is in an armed conflict, and we have the right to take action against the enemy in accordance with international law.

President Obama has also been criticized for another issue that occasionally pops up in the American foreign policy debate. It is rooted in the Constitution and in the balance of power between the president and Congress, and it is renewed with each new war. It concerns the War Powers Act, which was enacted after the dubious so-called Tonkin Resolution in Congress that gave President Lyndon Johnson the go-ahead to bomb North Vietnam. The War Powers Act aimed to curtail presidential power when it came to war and stated that the president would need Congressional authorization to do so. President Bush never sought such permission before he attacked Afghanistan and Iraq and neither did Obama before the attacks on Libya.

Presidential power is one of the mysteries of the American political system, Thomas Powers wrote in an article in the New York Review of Books.

But Bruce Ackerman, professor of law at Yale University, went further and argued in an article in Foreign Policy that Obama was now breaking new ground in building an "imperial presidency," where the president acts increasingly independently from Congress. Not even Bush went so far, concluded Ackerman.

Obama also met with harsh criticism from liberal academics and journalists for his broken election promise to close the prison at Guantanamo Bay as soon as he became president. It has not happened and it still looks like it will not happen. In fact, Obama has had to beat a full retreat on the issue. There are still 166 detainees at Guantanamo. Congress has rejected all attempts to close the prison, move the detainees to civilian prisons on the U.S. mainland, and initiate charges against the accused terrorists in civilian courts. Even observers, who are usually supportive of Obama, have been deeply critical.

Obama's decision is "cowardly, stupid, and tragically wrong," wrote Dahlia Lithwick at Slate, and she called the decision to a "capitulation." Amy Davidson agreed in an article in the New Yorker entitled, "Fear, Shame, and Guantanamo Bay."

The new guidelines mean that some 50 of the 166 who are still deemed to pose a security threat, will continue to be held captive indefinitely, without trial, although their cases will be more regularly looked at than before. Others will face military tribunals, which are to re-start after a long break.

Since 9/11, nearly 800 detainees have been sent to the Guantánamo Detention Center, but the prison at Guantanamo Bay is no longer at the center of the American political debate. In America today, other issues have overtaken it.

The foreign policy debate in the United States was dominated for decades by communism and the fear of communism. Being "soft" on communism was considered almost a crime, and Republicans frequently wielded such charges, particularly at election time.

Today, with communism defeated and the Cold War over, president Obama is instead accused of being a "European socialist" – sort of the current term for being soft on communism. I am for the Constitution, Newt Gingrich has said, while Obama is for "European socialism."

But the question that then follows is: if Europe is not free, why are we still members of NATO, and why have the Republicans not advocated that we break with our European allies, asked Harold Meyerson in his column in the Washington Post in February 2012. Is Europe our friend or foe? The truth is, he continued, that Europe was America's loyal ally in the fight against the Soviet Union and now, most recently, in Libya.

For Andrew Sullivan, the British-born, conservative, Washington-based journalist and Obama sympathizer, the domestic political balance in the debate on U.S. foreign policy has shifted. He wrote on his popular blog "The Dish" that the Republicans have weakened on national security. Bush started a war in Afghanistan, he wrote; but he followed that with a completely unjust war in Iraq that was a disaster; he allowed the al Qaeda leadership to flee to Tora Bora; his torture program destroyed our moral standing in the world. Obama put an end to torture and conducted a real war, not an ideological spectacle. Obama is now about to win the war that Bush lost.

Much of today's foreign policy debate in the United States is about the country's continued leadership role in the world, at a time when China and India are fast becoming serious rivals to America. One recognizes that the U.S. is no longer the undisputed leader after the collapse of the Soviet Union, but Robert Kagan, a neoconservative foreign policy expert, argues that America's alleged decline is a myth and that it applies more to the country's deep economic crisis in late 2008 than to geopolitical shifts in the world.

Let us not forget, Kagan wrote in the Wall Street Journal in February 2012, that even if China's economy will soon become the world's largest, the country is far from being the world's richest. China is still relatively poor compared to the U.S., Germany and Japan. Their per capita GDP is 40,000 dollars while China's is 4,000 dollars -- on a par with Angola's, Algeria's and Belize's. And if all predictions hold, China's per capita GDP will by 2030 still only be half as large as the United States', or on the same level as Greece and Slovenia today.

President Obama did not agree with talk of the United States being in decline. On the contrary, he said, in his 2012 State of the Union address, "America is back:"

"The renewal of American leadership can be felt across the globe, renewed alliances, a commitment to nuclear nonproliferation, an effective counterterrorism strategy, a stronger presence in Asia... Anyone who tells you otherwise, anyone who tells you that that America is in decline, or that our influence has waned, does not know what they are talking about."

But with Obama, there is a different kind of American leadership. It was described by a close adviser of Obama, quoted in a New Yorker article in May 2011 by Ryan Lizza, as "leading from behind."

Although the United States continues to be the world's only "indispensable" nation when it comes to tackling major international problems in the world, the adviser said, Obama believes in multilateralism. The U.S. cannot do everything on its own. Coalitions are necessary and the U.S. needs allies. The adviser summed up:

"It's so at odds with the John Wayne expectation for what America is in the world, but it's necessary for shepherding us through this phase."

Foreign policy expert Walter Russell Mead, professor at Bard College and author of "Special Providence," he wrote about four historical traditions in American foreign policy, named after the four "giants" in the country's history: Alexander Hamilton, the nation's first Secretary of the Treasury, and the former presidents Woodrow Wilson, Thomas Jefferson and Andrew Jackson.

Hamilton's tradition advocates a strong government and a strong military that can drive a realistic global policy whose main purpose is to promote American business and economic interests abroad; in Wilson's tradition, democracy and human rights play a central role; for Jefferson's tradition holds that it is important to cut down on U.S. obligations abroad and reduce the national security state as much as possible; and the Jackson tradition harbors deep skepticism towards the previous three and great support of military strength, honor, and bravery.

Of America's modern presidents, George H W Bush can be said to belong to the Hamilton tradition; Bill Clinton, is somewhere between Hamilton and Wilson; George W. Bush, is a mixture of Jackson and Wilson; and Obama, who before he became president was a leading opponent of the Iraq war, comes from the old Jeffersonian wing of the Democratic Party, whose strategic goal is to reduce America's costs and risks abroad, and limit the country's foreign obligations as much as possible.

But Obama's policy also includes aspects of the Wilsonian tradition with its emphasis on democracy and human rights.

According to Russell Mead, Obama believes that the United States can best spread democracy and work for peace if it sets a good example on democracy at home and conducts a moderate foreign policy. He wants a peaceful world so he can concentrate on necessary domestic reforms at home. In accordance with the Jeffersonian tradition, Obama also believes that war is something extremely serious and should be started only as a last resort.

This has led to much criticism, not the least in the winter and summer of 2012, in connection with the increasingly bloody civil war in Syria. But Obama has once again underlined how serious it is to go to war. That is not something one does casually. This caution and restraint, according to Russell Mead, is the foundation of the Jeffersonian tradition, and it is a vision that feels necessary in today's America.

It has been almost four decades since America's humiliating defeat in Vietnam in 1975 and the world has changed dramatically since then. The Soviet Union has collapsed. China and India are the potential new rivals to American leadership in the world. As in Vietnam, it will be difficult to "win" in Afghanistan and a retreat is now underway. The challenge is to find a solution that avoids Vietnam-style humiliation but also prevents Afghanistan's complete collapse and reversion to Taliban rule and becoming a base for al Qaeda again. In the Middle East, the "Arab Spring" has created an entirely new political situation, which in turn has led to the need for a new U.S. policy with many new demands on its diplomacy.

"If I look ahead over the next decade, U.S. power relative to the rest of the world will be reduced," said professor Blacker in my interview. "There will not be any new superpower, but our ability to influence what happens in the world will diminish, because our economy will be smaller in relative terms compared to today. Moreover, the American people are tired of what it sees as foreign policy adventures. So I anticipate a reduced American role in the world, no retreat or collapse, but simply a diminished role for America abroad."

For the American public, this is not of primary concern. In the last major opinion poll by the Pew Research Center in early 2012, only 9 percent of the respondents said that Obama should focus on foreign policy. It is the lowest figure in 15 years. The truth is that for this vast country of over 300 million people, the outside world simply plays a minor role. In the middle of the vast American continent, in states like Nebraska, Iowa, and Kansas, in America's "Heartland," the world beyond this country's borders often feels very far away.

Chapter 11.

AT THE EDGE OF THE ABYSS

Perhaps no other American president in modern times, with the exception of Franklin Delano Roosevelt in 1933, entered the White House in times as bleak as Barack Obama did in January 2009.

He arrived with high hopes and dreams of change, of a new start for a nation that had put its best foot forward by electing its first African-American president. But as Obama entered the White House, the U.S. economy faced its biggest decline since the 1930s and the Great Depression. The crisis that met the new president had begun already during President George W. Bush's final year in the White House. America stood at the edge of the abyss, teetering on total economic collapse. 800,000 jobs were lost every month. A new depression seemed likely.

For Jacob S. Hacker and Paul Pierson, authors of the book "Winner-Take-All Politics," the first ten years of the 21st Century has essentially been a lost decade, economically. During this time, the country has only slowly and laboriously crawled up onto safer ground, away from the collapses of the real estate and stock markets and the car industry, away from unemployment and growing inequality, away from political paralysis in Congress, the war in Iraq, the debt ceiling crisis, budget deficits, yes, and away from an the kind of economic plunge not seen since the Great Depression. It was so dire that in August 2011 the rating agency Standard & Poor's downgraded the U.S. credit rating.

There is a serious imbalance between expenditures and revenues in the U.S. economy. According to FactCheck, the country's spending is at its highest percentage since World War II and incomes are at their lowest in over 60 years. This means that spending represents 24 percent of the gross domestic product (GDP). Of that, 20 percent goes to Social Security, 13 percent to health care for the elderly (Medicare,) and 8 percent to health care for the poor (Medicaid), while 20 percent goes to defense. Foreign aid accounts for only 0.9 percent of total federal spending. Federal revenues have fallen to 15 percent of GDP.

These facts have resulted in a budget deficit of 10 percent of GDP, the biggest since 1945. Tax cuts and America's wars in Iraq and Afghanistan are the reasons for the deficit. Individual tax revenues have fallen drastically after George W. Bush's tax cuts -- from 10 percent of GDP to 6 percent.

So, without doubt, Obama inherited America's deep economic problems. What has he done to solve them as president? Not a lot, a little, or almost nothing, said 52 percent of the respondents in an opinion poll on the third anniversary of Obama's presidency. By Obama's fifth year in the White House, the country still faced strong headwinds, bleak economic times, and unemployment still unacceptably high.

Still, Obama has accomplished a great deal, much more than Americans generally believe: health care reform, a massive economic stimulus package; Wall Street reforms; the end of the Iraq war, the killing of Osama bin Laden; the rescue of the automotive industry from bankruptcy and the introduction of incentives for more environmentally friendly cars; ending the so-called "don't ask, don't tell" policy so that gays can now openly serve in the military; an end to the torture of terrorism suspects; the reform of the student loan system; the START agreement with Russia on nuclear weapons; stricter rules for hazardous coal plants.

The stimulus package of nearly 800 billion dollars is estimated to have contributed between 1 and 3.5 million new jobs and to have increased GDP by between 1 and 4.5 percent. The automotive industry has seen a reversal in its fortunes from just a few years ago when it was on the verge of total collapse. President George W. Bush handed out over 17 billions of dollars in aid to General Motors and Chrysler in his last months in the White House – because, he said later, he did not want to see unemployment increase to 20 percent, and Obama added some 60 billion dollars in return for a commitment to radical changes in how the car companies were run and what sort of cars they produced.

In 2011, General Motors passed Japanese Toyota to become once again the largest car company in the world with 9 million vehicles sold annually and with a record profit of 7.6 billion dollars. Chrysler also returned to profitability and repaid its entire debt of 6 billion dollars to U.S. taxpayers six years ahead of schedule. Around 100,000 jobs were rescued in all.

Yes, wrote Kevin Drum in the liberal magazine Mother Jones, Obama can be placed up there alongside the most successful presidents ever, but he has failed to change the political culture in Washington; he was too naive and relied too much on Republican good will. That turned out to be a mistake. Still, Drum continued, Obama has accomplished more for the progressive cause than Clinton, Carter, Kennedy or Truman, and almost as much as Lyndon Johnson, if you exclude the disappointment in Obama's national security policy that has continued to allow the U.S. to kill American citizens suspected of terrorist activities, that has kept the Guantanamo Bay prison open, and that he has continued to apply the Patriot Act.

"For an actual, existing human being, that's pretty damn good," wrote Drum.

With the historic health care reform, "The Patient Protection and Affordable Care Act," which the president pushed through Congress with no support from the Republicans, Obama succeeded where no other president before him had had success. The Republicans voted "no" just as they had to all proposals from the Obama administration. Quite apart from philosophical differences, there was a deep and overwhelming Republican reluctance during his first four years to give Obama anything that could help him win re-election in November 2012.

The U.S. is the only Western democracy without the kind of universal health insurance that was introduced in the United Kingdom as early as 1945, in Canada in 1966, and in Australia in 1974, to give just three examples. The issue has been debated for decades in the U.S., but all previous reform attempts, often denounced as un-American, socialist, even communist, had failed with the exception when president Lyndon Johnson succeeded in creating Medicare in 1965. Though it closely resembles universal health insurance systems in most European countries, Medicare is only for those who are 65 years and older. "Medicare for all" – for all age groups, for all Americans -- has become a slogan often heard in America as the best solution for a health care system which leaves 50 million people uninsured, and which today, by far, is the most expensive health care in the world. Only then would America have universal health coverage, as in all of Europe.

One often hears that the United States has the best health care in the world. But, according to the World Health Organization (WHO) the U.S. ranks only 37th in the world. France was ranked number one. In addition, America's health care system is increasingly expensive: it consumed 12 percent of GDP in 1990, 17 percent in 2010, and, according to new surveys, it will be 25 percent of GDP in 2025.

By comparison, Sweden's health care spending for 2005 was 9 percent of GDP, according to OECD statistics.

Sooner or later, everyone, regardless of whether they have insurance or not, needs health care. An average family in America today now has to pay an additional 1,000 dollars a year in higher insurance premiums to cover the health care costs of those who without health insurance. It is estimated that the health care for the uninsured costs 40 billion dollars every year.

Many supporters of universal health care insurance argue that health is a human rights issue, not a privilege. Former Washington Post reporter T.R. Reid compared the world's health care systems in his book "The Healing of America," which came out before Obama's health care reform, and concluded that universal health insurance would eliminate basic inequities in today's America. It would also reduce costs. Americans' belief that the private sector can do this best is wrong, Reid wrote. All the evidence from around the world points to the contrary.

"But we ignore the foreign models because of our 'exceptionalism,' because we believe that America has nothing to learn from the outside world," wrote Reid.

The last attempt of major health care reform failed in 1994, when Bill Clinton was president, and when Hillary Clinton led those efforts. The failure was of historic proportions, wrote John F. Harris, in his book "The Survivor." The proposal was too big, 1,342 pages, and too complicated, and it never received the political support needed, not even from Democrats.

After the failure, the Democrats felt too burned on the issue to take it up again. It can be said that 18 years were lost before Obama took up the issue again and crowned it with success in March 2010, when he signed The Affordable Care Act into law.

It has been widely dubbed "Obamacare," a derogative name that eventually was eventually adopted by the President himself. Whatever the name, his health care reform is his greatest achievement as president.

The law differs very little from the health care reform put in place in the state of Massachusetts in 2007, during the term of Governor Mitt Romney. Romney's reform became the model for Obama's reform. Both contain so-called individual mandates, which have become so controversial. These mandates force everyone who does not have insurance through their job or through Medicare/Medicaid to buy insurance in order to bring down the overall costs and make the system fairer.

In Massachusetts, those who fail to buy insurance can be fined up to 1,200 dollars per year. Obama's reform also contains financial penalties. Despite this, when Romney ran for president in 2012, he stubbornly denied any similarities between his Massachusetts reform and the president's. Instead, he promised to repeal Obamacare if he became president.

In Massachusetts, the reform has produced immediate and positive results. Today, almost 100 percent are insured. In an article in The New Yorker, Dr. Atul Gawande, who practices in Massachusetts, described what he saw as the biggest change as a result of the reform: that none of his patients had had to ask about the costs of the treatment he recommended, and no one had told him that he/she had to postpone cancer surgery until they had found a new job and obtained health insurance.

In America, health insurance is tied to employment, to a job. A good and permanent job means "benefits," especially health insurance and retirement savings. But it also means that if you lose your job, quit, change jobs or get fired, you lose your health insurance. Not having a job is not only a hardship, it can also be very expensive if you get sick.

There are few things that Americans worry more about than the costs if, and when, they get sick. It's estimated that 20,000 Americans die every year because they cannot afford to go to the doctor. Many hundreds of thousands go bankrupt because of medical and hospital expenses. This is a constant concern, a constant dinner-table conversation, one which does not exist in Europe.

No other issue, except maybe for parents worrying that they will not be able to afford to pay for their children's increasingly expensive college education, is discussed so frequently and so passionately. The cost of higher education is another crucial difference between life in America and Europe.

When my wife lost her job a few years ago, her temporary, transitional insurance cost more than 400 dollars a month, for several months. And when one of my sons was home on summer break from college one year, he was the victim of a dog attack and spent several days at Georgetown University Hospital. He had no insurance, which was my fault, because I had forgotten that his college health insurance was not valid during the summer holidays. Bills from Georgetown rolled in for a long time, from different doctors and from various departments, and amounted eventually to many thousands of dollars. I learned the lesson that so many in America had learned before me.

And now, that both my wife and I are over 65 and have Medicare, we can breathe a sigh of relief. It gives us good protection and a sense of security that is so often hard to find in America.

Two years after president Obama had signed his health care proposal into law, a large poll by the Pew Research Center stated that 47 percent supported the law, while 45 percent disliked it. A year earlier, 41 percent supported the law, while 48 percent opposed it.

A slight majority, 53 percent, responded that Congress should either extend the law or simply leave it as it is. The individual mandates remain extremely unpopular -- 56 percent opposed them.

Views on the new health care law differ markedly between Democrats and Republicans. While 76 percent of Democrats support the law, 84 percent of Republicans oppose it. 83 percent of Republicans oppose the individual mandates, while 66 percent of Democrats do. And 44 percent of Independents support the new law while 60 percent disapprove of the individual mandates.

All these figures should be taken with a grain of salt, since the polls also reveal that the American public does not really understand, or know, in detail what the law contains and what its consequences are. In a New York Times/CBS survey in conjunction with the Supreme Court's deliberation on the law, 48 percent responded that they did not understand the law. No wonder then that 47 percent said they disliked the law and only 36 percent supported it. 16 percent gave no answer at all.

The Republican opposition to Obamacare, and particularly to the individual mandates, is hard to understand if it is put in a historical context. The whole idea of individual mandates was a conservative idea that originated in the late 1980s at the Heritage Foundation, a conservative Washington think tank. The argument was that an individual mandate was necessary to maximize participation and to ensure that everyone had insurance that, at a minimum, covered accidents or catastrophic illnesses.

When President Clinton was fighting for his health care reform the question of individual mandates played a prominent role. Then Republican Senate leader Robert Dole gave his support to a Republican proposal, backed by over 20 Senators, which included an individual mandate.

Today, no Republican wants to acknowledge or admit this. The Heritage Foundation stated publicly that it had "committed a mistake" in its past support for the individual mandate. It was a full retreat, in other words, underscoring just how politically toxic the whole issue had become.

The health care reform will not completely enter until next year, but parts of it have been implemented and proven to be popular, and they have resulted in:
- over three billion dollars in lower drug costs for five million retirees;
- tax breaks for small businesses seeking health insurance for their employees;
- 2.5 million children will now be able to stay insured longer, until the age of 26, under their parents' health insurance;
- 54 million more Americans are getting preventive care; no child any longer be denied health insurance because they are already sick – a so called "pre-existing condition."

In my home state of Maryland, which has 5.8 million inhabitants, nearly half a million women have received expanded insurance coverage for preventative mammograms; over 500,000 seniors and people with different disabilities have already received free preventive care; and over 50,000 youth under 26 are now protected through their parents' insurance.

At the end of March 2012, the Obama health care reform law reached the Supreme Court for consideration after 26 States had sued the Obama administration, claiming that individual mandates, the core of the new health care reform, were unconstitutional. This legal battle was basically about the distribution of power in the U.S. political system, about the balance of power between the federal government and the States, and about how far congressional authority extended.

It was an historic constitutional confrontation that created huge attention and endless speculation about how The Nine would come down on the reform. Congress' Commerce Clause gives extensive powers to the Congress, but opponents to the health care law argued that it is unconstitutional to force someone to buy something, in this case health insurance.

The Supreme Court's decision in late June 2012, on the Court's last day before the summer holidays, constituted a historic victory for President Obama, as the Court pronounced the entire health care reform law consistent with the Constitution. The victory came with slimmest possible majority, 5 votes to 4, and only thanks to the totally surprising support of conservative Chief Justice John Roberts. He had been appointed by George W. Bush, an appointment that Barack Obama, then a Senator, voted against.

In what was an totally unexpected ideological and political switch, Roberts voted with the Court's four liberal Justices to uphold the law, while Associate Justice Anthony Kennedy, who usually plays the role of the swing vote, this time joined the other three "'no" votes from the Court's most conservative trio, Samuel Alito, Antonin Scalia and Clarence Thomas.

In its decision, the Court upheld the individual mandates that required everyone to buy health insurance or pay a fine. The mandates are compatible with the Constitution because they can be regarded as a tax, and Congress has the right to levy new taxes. While the Democrats cheered, the Republicans, who had expected a "no" from the Court, were deeply disappointed, and promised a continued fight.

Since then, in vote after vote, the Republican majority in the House of Representatives has shown its displeasure with Obamacare and voted over 40 times to repeal the law, or parts of it, without offering any alternative plan.

The votes have been purely symbolic and politically completely meaningless, since the Senate, controlled by the Democrats, has no intention to vote on, or even debate, the issue.

President Obama was pleased about the Court's verdict, but he was cautious in his comments:

"The Supreme Court has reaffirmed a fundamental principle that here in America - in the wealthiest nation on Earth – no illness or accident should lead to any family's financial ruin. I know there will be a lot of discussion today about the politics of all this, about who won and who lost. That's how these things tend to be viewed here in Washington. But that discussion completely misses the point. Whatever the politics, today's decision was a victory for people all over this country whose lives will be more secure because of this law and the Supreme Court's decision to uphold it. "

The Court's verdict a few months before the November 2012 election was a major setback for Obama's Republican opponent, Mitt Romney. However, Romney maintained that his first act as president would be to kill Obamacare despite its many similarities with his own successful reform in Massachusetts. Should he win in November, he promised to introduce a totally new system rooted in the States and in the private insurance industry. He lost. The Supreme Court's decision no doubt strengthened Obama's bid for re-election since a "no" would have meant a huge political and prestige loss for Obama and the Democrats. But the verdict is primarily a victory for America, the only Western democracy without universal health insurance.

Obamacare does not mean that the United States will now have health insurance for all its citizens. It will insure 30 million of the almost 50 million people now without any insurance and represents a major step towards universal health coverage for all Americans.

At the end of Obama's first four years as president, many seemed to have already forgotten the Bush years, when repeated and irresponsible tax cuts, mainly for the wealthiest, turned the large budget surpluses after Bill Clinton's eight White House into huge deficits, and when criminal behavior on Wall Street led to the collapse of the real estate market and a deep financial crisis.

The mood in America was grim. The summer of 2011 had been marked by an unrelenting political battle over the U.S. debt ceiling, usually a routine decision by Congress. Good friends here in Washington -- journalist colleagues, lawyers, lobbyists, all passionately interested in politics and social issues -- were deeply concerned. Not since World War II had the jobs figures been so bad - zero new jobs according to the statistics; unemployment remained 9.1 per cent, which meant that 14 million were unemployed, with another 9 million who had to settle for part-time jobs, while over 6 million had given up and stopped looking for a new job.

Most of my friends, like the majority of people who live in the Washington Metro area, are Democrats, often liberal Democrats, and they had given their overwhelming support to Barack Obama in 2008. They still liked him, but they were worried, and they were disappointed in him and his leadership, or lack of leadership. They wanted him to be strong, strike hard, fight, and stop giving in to the Republicans and their demands. They had no interest in compromise. Why would the Republicans contribute to strengthening Obama's chances to be re-elected?

Republican Senate leader Mitch McConnell had early on declared that his primary political goal was to ensure that Obama was not re-elected, and Rush Limbaugh spoke loudly and often on his radio program about his hopes that Obama would fail.

My friends were uncertain. They did not really know where the president stood, but they said that Obama must now understand that it was futile to try to work with Republicans and particularly the Tea party movement, whose goal was to prevent Obama's re-election at any cost. But they did not know if Obama had it in him to fight. Jimmy Carter's name came up. In 1980, Carter was defeated by Ronald Reagan and became one of the few presidents in recent decades not to win re-election. Obama -- a new Jimmy Carter? It was a question that they barely dared to ask.

In the summer of 2011, the debt ceiling was raised and the country avoided a financial disaster. But the victory would turn out to be short-sighted. The compromise in Congress did not come about until the Tea party movement had held the country hostage for a considerable time in what can only be described as extortion aimed at forcing concessions on president Obama and the Democrats.

This was "war on America," in the words of New York Times columnist Joe Nocera, and the end result deeply disappointed progressives in the Democratic Party. They saw themselves as losers since the agreement did not contribute to any new jobs and lacked measures to reduce economic and income inequalities.

It was not the "balanced solution" that the president had demanded; it contained no revenue enhancement, no tax increases, not even on the wealthiest. But Obama and the Democrats managed to eliminate the debt ceiling from the public debate before the November elections.

"A Tea Party triumph," wrote conservative Wall Street Journal in an editorial while liberal New York Times called the agreement "a terrible deal." The Democrats won virtually nothing except to avoid bankruptcy and the paper's influential columnist Paul Krugman felt that the president had capitulated.

Obama said afterwards that America had chosen a divided government in the 2010 elections, but not a dysfunctional government. Still, he did not exactly make a victory lap. He had lost many Democrats, 95 in total, or exactly half of the Democrats in the House of Representatives, among them the Blacks, the Hispanics, and many in the progressive group, who voted no to the deal. So did half a dozen progressive members of the Senate. And over 80 over the most conservative Republican Senators and House members also voted no, because the budget cuts were not sufficiently deep.

After the deal on the debt ceiling, Washington and the country seemed to want to put the debt crisis behind them as quickly as possible. It was about time. This had been an artificial crisis that wasted months of valuable time. Never before had an increase in the debt ceiling had been used for such obvious partisan purposes. With the debt settlement behind him, Obama could now concentrate on efforts to revive the weak economy and create new jobs.

The big losers in the debt ceiling negotiations were the politicians in Washington, especially Congress, which had become a laughing stock, according to National Journal's Charlie Cook, one of the country's best-informed political commentators.

"Right now, we are at a very, very low point, the worst I've seen since I moved to Washington in September 1972. Never in my memory have both parties and both ends of Pennsylvania Avenue appeared as dysfunctional as they do today. The stakes are so high and the performance is so utterly disappointing."

In the opinion polls, Obama received record low support, 40 percent, but confidence in Congress was even lower – only 11 percent. At the end of 2011, Congress was said to have had the worst year of everyone in the capital, according to one of the Washington Post's political bloggers.

By this time, the fiasco of the twelve-member bipartisan Super Committee was a reality. Under the terms of the debt ceiling deal, the committee was tasked to come to an agreement before November 23 about an additional 1,200 billion dollars in savings over the next ten years. The twelve negotiated under the threat that automatic budget cuts – so-called sequestration – would go into effect in early 2013 if they failed. The spending cuts would affect the whole range of important programs, including the military and the tax cuts introduced by President George W. Bush in 2001 and 2003 that were due to expire, which would mean that the tax rates would return to the pre-tax cut levels.

The Super Committee never reached any agreement. It failed, utterly, and its failure underscored once again how poisonous the political situation in Washington had become and how paralyzed Congress was.

The new Republican majority in the House of Representatives after the mid-term elections in 2010, got most of the blame for Congress' poor ratings. There were 63 new Republican members most of whom were members of the Tea Party movement. At the end of 2012, they went too far, pushed too hard, when their effort to end a payroll tax holiday resulted in a humiliating defeat. The prominent Republican columnist Charles Krauthammer in the Washington Post called the push "kamikaze politics" and the Wall Street Journal said it was a "fiscal fiasco."

In July 2011, Nate Silver, the man behind the New York Times' splendid political statistics blog "FiveThirtyEight" explained why the Republican Party so opposed to any compromise on the debt ceiling, budget and taxes. Entitled "Why the Republicans Resist Compromise," Silver wrote that the Republican Party is today more dependent on conservative voters than in any election since 1984.

Fully 67 percent of those who last year voted for Republican candidates to the House of Representatives called themselves conservative, compared with 58 percent two years earlier and 48 percent a decade ago. Terms like 'Republicans' and 'conservative' are becoming increasingly synonymous – there are steadily fewer non-conservatives who vote Republican and steadily fewer Republicans who are not conservative.

The fierce partisan struggle that characterizes America today can be seen daily in Congress. It has its origins in the big Republican election victory in 2010, but also in the fact that the Republicans failed to win a majority in the Senate. The end result was that power in Washington was divided into three parts, a Democrat in the White House, a Democratic majority in the Senate, and Republican control of the House of Representatives -- just as the Founding Fathers had envisioned.

They did not want a strong central government in the new America that emerged in the late 1700s, a United States that came about after a revolution and after the strong, almost autonomous colonies finally came together and agreed to unite in a new country.

The word "sabotage" popped up in the American political debate. It referred to the fact that, so far, the Republican Party has said "no" to just about every Democratic proposal, earning its nickname the "Party of No." It is as if "in the national interest" no longer mattered, or even existed. The New York Times columnist Paul Krugman wrote about "pure blackmail" from the Republicans, and for the commentator Michael Tomasky at the Daily Beast, it had become obvious that the economic recovery would benefit Obama, and that, therefore, the Republicans preferred to sabotage the economy:

"Today's GOP is about ideological maximalism on all fronts ... They cannot negotiate, because negotiating means accepting something you don't like, which the noise machine will not permit. And worse, because the noise machine wants Obama to fail and is so powerful, Republican office-holders inevitably arrive at that point too."

Where is the Republican Party heading, wondered a worried David Brooks, the New York Times' wise Republican columnist, around the time of the debt ceiling negotiations. Responsible Republicans, he counseled, must now take control of the party to reach a settlement, otherwise the independent voters would conclude that Republican fanaticism led to the failure, that the Republicans are not fit to govern, and they would be right. But:

"We can have no confidence that the Republicans will seize this opportunity. That's because the Republican Party may no longer be a normal party ... The members of this movement do not accept the logic of compromise. The members of this movement have no sense of moral decency ... The members of this movement have no economic theory worthy of its name."

This picture of today's Republican Party was further illustrated in the spring of 2012 when the book "It's Even Worse than It Looks" laid the blame for the political crisis squarely on the Republicans. Written by two highly respected and independent political observers, Thomas E. Mann of the Brookings Institution and Norman E. Ornstein of the American Enterprise Institute, their conclusion landed like a bomb in the debate:

"In our past writings, we have criticized bothering parties when we believed it was warranted. Today, however, we have no choice but to acknowledge that the core of the problem lies with the Republican Party."

"The GOP, they continued, "has become an insurgent outlier in American politics. It is ideologically extreme; scornful of compromise; unmoved by Conventional understanding of facts, evidence and science; and dismissive of the legitimacy of its political opposition. When one party moves this far from the mainstream, it makes it nearly impossible for the political system to deal constructively with the country's challenges."

The fact that the Republican Party is becoming increasingly conservative could perhaps not have been better illustrated than when the respected, moderate Republican senator Richard Lugar lost to a Tea Party sympathizer in the Republican primary election in Indiana in the spring of 2012. Moderate Republican senators are becoming fewer and fewer.

David Kennedy, professor of history at Stanford University, drew an historical parallel with today's partisan battles in my interview with him. He pointed out that president Herbert Hoover, who was no fool, according to Kennedy, tried in the early 30's through a series of measures to boost the economy and get out of the deep recession. But the Congressional Democratic majority gave him no support, about which Hoover later bitterly complained in his memoirs.

Michael Barone drew another historic parallel in the 2012 edition of "The Almanac of American Politics" between today's Congress and the Congress that Democratic president Harry Truman came to call the "Do Nothing Congress" in the years 1946-48. Its Republican majority acted completely contrary to Truman's wishes and directives but then lost badly in the 1948 elections. Truman, in a huge upset won, and the Democrats took back control of Congress.

However, there is no need to go as far back as to Hoover and Truman to find parallels with today's battle between Obama and Congress.

In his book on Bill Clinton, "The Survivor," John F. Harris wrote that Clinton spoke about a new type of Republican, different from those of the Eisenhower and Nixon years. They are against everything we stand for, Clinton said. Republicans have become an opposition party that just says, "no, no, no, no, no, no, no, no "... his 'no' was heard nine times in a memorable speech in Boston in March 1994.

The Congressional Republicans in the 1990s hated Clinton, just as today's Republicans hate Obama.

The Tea party movement, which won such support in the mid-term elections in 2010, was born from this hatred of Obama. The Republicans won seven new seats in the Senate and 63 new seats in the House of Representatives, the majority of which went to Tea party sympathizers. It was the biggest change since 1932, when 101 Republicans lost their seats in the House of Representatives. It is the biggest new political force during Obama's first three years in the White House, much bigger and more important than the Occupy Wall Street Movement, which went up like the sun, but down like a pancake. Its protests against inequality in America today received a lot of attention at first, but it has by now largely disappeared from the political debate. In contrast to the Tea Party movement's negativism, the Occupy movement had a positive message. But it lacked a leader and a central political message.

The Tea party movement got its name from the so-called Boston Tea Party in 1773, when American patriots dumped English tea in the Boston harbor in protest against new tariffs. Today's movement got its name from a frustrated CNBC reporter named Rick Santelli, who one morning in February 2009 invited Obama to a tea party in Chicago. From that point on, the movement spread rapidly to all parts of America.

Tea Party members are angry, they dislike taxes, they do not like Obama's health care reform, and they hate Obama, who, they insist, was not born in America and who should not be allowed to be president.

The movement's center today is not Boston, but the South, and journalist Michael Lind claimed in an article on Salon.com in the fall of 2011 that there is a connection between the Tea party movement and the far right in the South, which, ever since the Civil War, has sought to hold America back and hold American democracy hostage. The Tea party movement has further cemented the South as the Republican Party's stronghold.

Tea party supporters are against almost everything except freedom and individualism, and they have been supported by the demagogic news channel Fox News, according to Mark Lilla, professor at Columbia University in New York, who wrote in 2010 in the New York Review of Books:

"An angry group of Americans wants to be freer still - free from government agencies that protect their health, wealth, and well-being; free from problems and policies too difficult to understand; free from parties and coalitions; free from experts who think they know better than they do; free from politicians who don't talk or look like they do (and Barack Obama certainly doesn't). They want to say what they have to say without fear of contradiction, and then hear someone on television tell them they're right. They want to be people without rules - and, who knows, they may succeed."

It's not like with Ronald Reagan, admittedly also a conservative, wrote Lilla. Reagan governed on the basis of ideas from leading conservative intellectuals like Milton Friedman and Irving Kristol.

No, Lilla continued:

"Today's conservatives prefer the company of anti-intellectuals, who know how to exploit non-intellectuals, as Sarah Palin does so masterfully. The dumbing-down they have long lamented in our schools they are now bringing to our politics, and they will pull everyone and everything along with them."

When the Republican primary election campaign got going in earnest in the summer of 2011, many were called: Mitt Romney, Michele Bachmann, Herman Cain, Ron Paul, Jon Huntsman, Newt Gingrich, Rick Santorum, and Rick Perry. No one said a bad word about the Tea party movement. The field was weak, unusually and obviously weak. None of the heavyweights, such governors and former governors as Chris Christie, Jeb Bush, Haley Barbour, Mitch Daniels, were candidates. Sarah Palin long kept her supporters guessing, but, in the end, she also decided not to run. 44 percent of the voters, according to a survey by Pew Research, were "unimpressed" with the candidates, while only 12 percent had something positive to say about them. The rest didn't know.

One reason that the heavyweights decided not to run was, of course, that a primary election campaign is always dominated by the most dedicated and most conservative voters in the Republican Party, in this case the Tea party movement, the Christian Right, and the Libertarians. Consequently, those representing the more moderate Republican establishment faced difficult odds. Another reason for not running was, most likely, that they were unsure if they had a real chance to defeat president Obama, despite the weak economy.

During the fall of 2011, growing unease and uncertainty were noticeable in the Republican Party. No panic, but unrest in the ranks.

A president, approved by only 43 percent of voters and in the midst of a deep economic crisis with an unemployment rate of over 8 per cent, should be vulnerable and the Republicans should have a good chance to win. But the Republican voters had yet to decide whether they were going to follow their hearts or their minds, as political observer Stuart Rothenberg wrote in his newsletter:

"The question is whether there are enough true believers to nominate someone other than Romney, thereby putting up a weaker general election candidate against Obama. In other words, is this 1964, when Republicans listened to their heart over their head? That year, of course, President Lyndon Johnson looked unbeatable, so the Republican nomination did not have the value it is likely to have next year ... Barry Goldwater's famous 1964 campaign slogan was, 'In your heart, you know he's right.' He went on to lose 44 states. Often, in politics, the head is a better guide than the heart."

The Republican voters' lack of enthusiasm and commitment was clearly visible in the low voter turnout during the primary election campaign. In fact, voter participation was often so low that many of the election results should be taken with a large grain of salt.

In Maine's nomination meetings, for example, with a population of 1.3 million, a total of 6,135 people voted, only two percent of the State's registered Republicans. In Nevada, a total of 12,000 fewer people voted than in 2008; in Minnesota 15,000 fewer; in Colorado 5,000 fewer; and in Missouri less than half compared to 2008. The Republican voters' indifference and lukewarm attitude towards the party's candidates did not bode well for the coming big clash in November's general election, no matter who was to lead the battle against Obama.

In March 2012, Obama had the upper hand in the polls against all the four remaining Republican candidates. In a large study by the Pew Research Center Obama led over Romney by 54 percent to 42 and over Santorum by 57 percent to 39. Obama's support among American women voters was especially worth paying attention to, for it was 20 per cent higher than for Romney, and 26 percent greater than for Santorum. Over 50 percent in the survey gave Obama their approval, which was the highest in almost a year, and when the respondents were asked to predict the election results, 59 percent responded that Obama would beat Romney, and 68 percent said he would defeat Santorum.

At the end of March 2012, Romney led the Republican battle for electoral votes, and with the primary election in Texas at the end of May, he had captured the necessary 1,144 electoral votes to win the nomination at the Republican Party convention in Tampa, Florida in late summer.

By this time, it was possible to speak of two Obamas – one before the debt ceiling crisis of the summer of 2011, and another after it. It was as if Obama had had enough of the political paralysis in Washington, as if he thought that he had now extended his hand long enough without anyone grabbing it on the other end. Obama seemed in a way liberated, and the more forceful Obama who had had such electoral success in 2008 returned.

His supporters asked why he had waited so long, and why he had not better used the opportunity when the Democrats controlled the White House and both houses of Congress. One explanation is that Obama really had only three and a half months with the necessary 60 votes in the Senate to overcome Republican filibusters, or the threats of filibusters, to prevent the Senate from even voting on new bills.

The period was so short because of Senator Ted Kennedy's illness and death and the subsequent upset victory by Republican Scott Brown in the Senate election in Massachusetts to fill Kennedy's seat. The Democrats' filibuster-proof majority disappeared, and, suddenly, it was much harder for Obama and the Democrats to get anything through the Senate.

The filibuster is an old tactic, although not written into the Constitution. For many years it was seen as a last resort, for decades is was used less than once a year, and only in exceptional circumstances, for example by Senators from the old South to prevent new civil rights laws.

This changed during the Clinton years, when, what might be called the "permanent filibuster" was launched by a new and aggressive Republican Party led by Newt Gingrich, Tom DeLay and Trent Lott. Today, the filibuster, or often just the threat of a filibuster, is a regularly-used tactic in the Senate. In 2009, the Republicans used it on 80 percent of the new bills proposed by the Obama Administration, which makes simple majority rule almost impossible, which, in turn, makes it much more difficult to govern. The result is that very little gets done in Congress.

The new and more forceful Obama was evident as he gave a big speech in 2011 in Osawatomie, Kansas, about equality and justice. The speech launched a new offensive. Here was the Obama we elected in 2008, wrote Robert Reich, professor of economics and former member of President Clinton's cabinet, on his blog. Finally, wrote Michael Tomasky at the Daily Beast. Obama has found his voice, wrote John Cassidy in The New Yorker.

The populist speech became the foundation for Obama's re-election campaign.

It was a speech about the growing economic inequality, the struggling middle class, and about economic justice. We have not seen this level of economic inequality since the Depression and it hurts us all, said Obama. It is wrong and it is contrary to everything we believe:

"I believe that this country succeeds when everyone gets a fair shot, when everyone does their fair share, when everyone plays by the same rules. These are not Democratic values or Republican values. These are not 1 percent or 99 percent values. They're American values, and we have to reclaim them."

The president made clear he intended to fight. But the U.S. economy in the early summer of 2012 promised no major improvements on the horizon. The unemployment rate refused to drop below 8 percent and millions of Americans constantly found their hopes for a new job dashed and facing the frightening prospect of unending unemployment and expiring unemployment benefits. Only Ronald Reagan in 1984 has been re-elected since the days of Franklin D. Roosevelt with an unemployment rate of more than 7.2 percent. When Obama became president in January 2009, unemployment was 7.8 percent. That's almost exactly where it stood at the time of the 2012 campaign.

Still, in the end, Barack Obama was re-elected. His victory was not quite as overwhelming as four years ago, when Obama beat John McCain by 10 million votes and captured 365 electoral votes to McCain's 173. But it was a solid, even sweeping, victory, and, for me, it reaffirmed my faith of an inclusive America.

It had been an awfully long and emotionally draining election campaign. Most were just happy that it was over and at least 61 million voters were happy about the outcome.

Clearly, the voters chose the man they trusted to continue to lead them in these difficult economic times, while Mitt Romney, a man who would not release his tax returns, who never explained why he invested millions in tax havens in the Cayman Islands and in Switzerland, who had disregarded 47 percent of the electorate, and who denied his own moderate record as governor of Massachusetts -- supportive of a woman's right to choose and implementer of his own sweeping health care reform -- failed to gain their trust.

The bruising Republican primary campaign forced Romney steadily further to the right, and by the time he had captured the nomination, it was too late to change in a credible way. The result was that the planned "etch-a-sketch" strategy in the last month of the campaign, when the "severely conservative" Romney was supposed to return to being a moderate, never worked. By then, the Obama campaign had already defined him for the voters.

Obama's victory pointed the way to the country's future politics. He won among the African-Americans (93 percent), Hispanics (71 percent), and Asians (73 percent), among women (53 percent) and among working women with children under 18 (62 percent), among gays and lesbians (76 percent), among those between 18 and 29 (60 percent) and those between 30 and 44 (52 percent), among those in big cities (69 percent), among Jewish voters (69 percent) and Catholics (52 percent), among those without a high school diploma (64 percent) and among those with a post-graduate degree (62 percent,) and among those earning less than 50,000 dollars (56 percent).

Romney won among men (52 percent), among those above 45 years of age, among white voters (59 percent) among those with incomes above 50,000 dollars per year, in the small towns (56 percent), in rural America (61 percent), and among the protestant voters, including the white born-again or evangelical Christians (78 percent).

The Obama coalition lost only two of the so-called battleground states he had won in 2008: Indiana, traditionally Republican, and North Carolina, in the South. He conquered the rest: Nevada, Colorado, Iowa, Wisconsin, Ohio, New Hampshire, Virginia, and Florida. In the end, he captured 332 electoral votes against 206 for Mitt Romney – many more than the 270 needed to win.

The conclusion of the 2008 and 2012 presidential elections makes for a somber message for the Republicans: it is no longer possible for them to win the presidency with support only from America's white voters. There are simply no longer enough of them. This trend will continue, even strengthen, in the coming years as America's population changes.

This is the big future dilemma for the Republican Party. It needs to change, but will it be able to do so? A year after the 2012 elections there are no signs that it will.

Chapter 12.

WHICH AMERICA?

"I am a stranger here in a strange land, but I know this is where I belong."
"Red River Shore" by Bob Dylan

Everyone thinks they know America, wrote Tony Judt, the Anglo-American historian, in his fine book, "The Memory Chalet," published shortly after his death in 2010.

Judt came to the United States in 1975 and thought he knew everything about America: Bing Crosby and Hopalong Cassidy, Kojak and Elvis, and he had read Steinbeck and Fitzgerald. He found an America that was at the same time both intensely familiar and completely unknown. But he had, he wrote, no idea what Memphis or Detroit or Southern California looked like, and he had no idea how large and varied America was.

Over the years, he added, he was "seduced."

So was I. But my view of America during my many years in this country has also turned into disappointment, even bitterness, with a country I like it so much and which could be so good, but which can sometimes be such a crushing disappointment. The question is: Which is America? Which America are we talking about? There are so many Americas, which, of course, is an important reason why it is so interesting and so fascinating but also why it is so frustrating and so difficult to understand.

The American dream is everywhere; it's part of the daily debate. It's a cliché, of course, a myth, but it lives within people who want it to be there and who seek it. It was a dream for me as a young man, like all immigrants in all times.

It's synonymous with optimism and faith in the future, but it has now also come to mean something more ordinary, like having a job, taking care of one's family, owning a car or two and a house in the suburbs.

For many, as for me, Barack Obama's election victory in 2008 renewed my faith in the American dream, and his re-election strengthened that faith -- the feeling that something good and important had taken place, something more positive than maybe anything else since my first days in California.

Romantic? Of course, wrote historian Bernard DeVoto once:

"Sure you are romantic about American history ... It is the most romantic of all histories. It began as a myth and has developed through three centuries of fairy stories ... Ours is a story made with the impossible, it is by chaos out of dream, it began as a dream and has continued as a dream."

The dream about America is not dead. Just listen to president Obama, whose own career can be seen as a genuine example of the American dream. This is how he described it when he visited Ireland in 2011, where he has distant relatives on his mother's side:

"Standing there in Moneygall, I could not help but think how heartbreaking it must have been for that great-great-great grandfather of mine, and so many others, to part - to watch [the] Donegal coasts and Dingle cliffs recede, to leave behind all they knew in hopes that something better lay over the horizon. And as they worked and struggled and sacrificed and sometimes experienced great discrimination, to build that better life for the next generation, they passed on that faith to their children and to their children's children - an inheritance that their great-great-great grandchildren like me still carry with them. We call it the American dream."

Obama has returned to the American dream many times, including in his State of the Union in 2011:

"We do big things. From the earliest days of our founding, America has been the story of ordinary people who dare to dream. That's how we win the future."

The American dream -- "you have to be asleep to believe it," the late comedian George Carlin said once, perhaps in view of the fact that every statistic today shows the United States becoming an increasingly unequal society. The number of Americans below the poverty line: 46.2 million; the number of Americans without health insurance: 49.9 million; the percentage of Americans in deep poverty, with an income of less than 5,569 dollars a year: 6.7 percent; the number of pensioners who would live in poverty if they did not have social security: 14 million; the percentage of children in poverty: 22 percent.

The growing inequality in America is creating tension and the talk of "class war" is heard more often in the public arena. The billionaire Warren Buffett put it this way: yes, we have a class war, and my class won! But Buffett also thinks that he and his rich friends pay too little in taxes. Even his secretary, he said, pays more tax than he does, 28 percent on her salary against his 15 percent on his capital gains. Obama paid 26 percent tax on an income of $ 1.7 million last year, which is infinitely lower than what he would have paid before the series of tax cuts of the Reagan and George W. Bush years. Today, the maximum federal tax is 35 percent. It used be much higher, over 70 percent before the Reagan era began in 1981.

Countless statistics and other evidence paint a picture of an unequal America that is becoming more unequal every year.

In 2010, income increases of 288 billion dollars went to the richest one percent of the U.S. population, those who, on average, earn over a million dollars a year. In addition, 37 percent of those 288 billion dollars went to 0.01 percent of the population, to the richest of the rich, to those who earned more than 23 million dollars annually. The incomes of the remaining 99 percent went up by an average of just 80 dollars per person that year.

In their book "Winner-Take-All Politics," Jacob S. Hacker and Paul Pierson from Yale University and the University of California at Berkeley, argue that this trend is the consequence of the policies pushed by Washington politicians for years, beginning in 1980 –" a thirty-year war." The policies have increasingly favored America's high earners, not least the country's business leaders. While a company director in the United States in 1965 on average earned 24 times more than a typical worker, that director earned 300 times more than a typical worker in 2007. That same year, the average annual director's salary was more than 12 million dollars in the 350 largest firms in America.

Examples of banking executives pay in 2011 include: JP Morgan's Jamie Dimon: 23 million dollars; Goldman Sachs' Lloyd Blankfein: 16 million; Citigroup's Vikram Pandi: 15 million. Incomes for hedge fund managers have increased even more, from an average of 30 million dollars in 2002 for the 25 biggest funds to 100 million dollars in 2004 and 130 million in 2005. And by 2007, the average income of the same 24 leading fund managers had increased to 360 million dollars annually.

That year, according to Hacker and Pierson, each head of the five leading hedge funds earned over a billion dollars.

"How," they asked, "in a country governed by majority rule, a country born of a revolt against persistent differences in power and opportunity, could policy and government so favor such a narrow group, for so long, with so little response?"

The growing inequality in America has negatively impacted the country's social mobility, they also wrote:

"The American dream portrays the United States as a classless society where anyone can rise to the top, regardless of family background. Yet, there is more intergenerational mobility in Australia, Sweden, Norway, Finland, Germany, Spain, France, and Canada."

Today, America's inequality can be compared to developing countries such as the Ivory Coast and Jamaica. The talk of class war stems from the reality that the richest one percent of the U.S. population owns 84 percent of the country's wealth, while the poorest 40 percent own 0.3 percent. The median salary for a full-time employee has increased from 1972 to 2010 by just 165 dollars per year, or by 3.17 dollars a week. Since 2010, an additional 2.6 million people have fallen below the poverty line and more Americans now live in poverty than in 52 years. It takes an income of below 22,000 dollars per year for a family of four to fall below the poverty line.

The inequality in America can also be illustrated by members of Congress. The average annual income in 1984 for a member of the House of Representatives was 280,000 dollars. That had risen to 725,000 dollars in 2009. During that same period, the median income for an average American family decreased from 20,600 to 20,500 dollars. It is a system "of the one percent, by the one percent, and for the one percent," wrote Joseph Stiglitz, Nobel Laureate in economics.

Many Americans seem unaware of this. They believe that America is much more equal than it actually is, according to a recent study, "Building a Better America," by two academics at Duke and Harvard Universities. Over 7,000 people participated in a study in which participants were shown unidentified diagrams that reflected income distribution and they were asked which diagram they thought reflected the United States. Almost all, 92 percent, picked the Swedish model of income distribution. In other words, without knowing it, they wanted America to be Sweden, with more equality and better income distribution.

Not only is America not like Europe, it's becoming less and less so as the years pass. America is more conservative, more religious, more individualistic and much more hostile to the government. It's not "big money" that Americans dislike, it's "big government."

"We love our country but we have never liked the government," Colorado College professor Thomas Cronin once said.

Adam Gopnik wrote in The New Yorker in September 2011 that there is a reason why America does not have beautiful new airports and fast trains like the Japanese and the French. It's because a substantial number of Americans see such things as symbols of the dreaded state – the government in Washington:

"We don't have a better infrastructure or decent elementary education exactly because many people are willing to sacrifice the movement between our cities, or better-informed children, in support of their belief that the government should always be given as little money as possible."

The great storyteller Garrison Keillor, was unusually serious in an article in the New York Times a couple of years ago about the Republican "big lie" that dates back to St. Ronald's years (Ronald Reagan's presidency) and which contends that the government is an inefficient swamp. Regardless of what the Democrats do, they are accused of being socialists and backing big government, he said.

So, Keillor suggested, extend Medicare to everyone and let's be socialists and do exactly what we did with socialist Social Security – that's "big government" and it works pretty well. Mr. Obama, he concluded, don't worry about party politics, do what's right!

At the same time, Americans demand more of their government than anyone else in the world, wrote Washington Post's Anne Applebaum in 2010. Applebaum, who has reported from abroad for many years, wrote that Americans do not only want their government to keep the peace and ensure that everyone has equal opportunities, but they also want it to avoid every accident or they want to be fully compensated if an accident occurs. And if the price of their home falls, or someone tries to blow up an aircraft in the air, or when an oil derrick in the Gulf of Mexico explodes, then it's the White House's fault.

It has come to a point where Americans see the president as the source of all problems and the solution to all problems, wrote the Cato Institute's Gene Healy recently in his book "The Cult of the Presidency." This trend has been observed for many years and it has, of course, made the job of president increasingly impossible. The concept of "the good government" does not exist in America, it never really has. Americans protest at every attempt to extend the power of the government, whether on health insurance or gun control.

That's socialism, they cry, and it leads to higher taxes, or restricting our freedom, and we don't want that. There is no collective agenda in America and there is never any talk of solidarity.

The Tea party movement and the born-again Christians, who do not belong to the country's best paid, have an innate hostility against the government, combined with opposition to abortion, gun control, same-sex marriage, and they place great importance on their conservative social values. They often share this individualism, this hostility to the state, with many of America's blue collar workers, although, of course, no one in America talks of proletarians or a working class. The result is that these groups actually vote against their own economic interests when they support an increasingly conservative Republican Party, which many times lately has shown its hostility to these workers.

Just look at what happened recently in Wisconsin and Ohio, where newly-elected Republican governors, Scott Walker and John Kasich, led intensive anti-union campaigns to reduce the unions' power and influence by abolishing collective bargaining for public employees.

Ultimately, the purpose was political: to weaken the Democratic Party's base. That America is not Europe could not have been illustrated any better, for this could never have taken place in Europe.

A fierce political battle ensued when the union movement in both states fought back. It was more than a fight for survival for the American labor movement; it became a battle about America's democracy. It went on for over a year and mobilized all of Wisconsin's political forces. In 1959, Wisconsin had been the first state to introduce collective bargaining for public employees, so a steep union tradition was threatened, and Wisconsin became during this period the epicenter of the fierce ideological struggle that today characterizes American politics.

The battles in Wisconsin and Ohio took different forms. In Wisconsin, voters went to the polls in June 2012 to decide whether to unseat Governor Walker in a special "recall election." They failed. In Ohio, Governor Kasich's new law was reversed in a referendum.

The recall election in Wisconsin became one of the most expensive state elections ever, with over 60 million dollars spent. Millions of dollars in contributions rolled in from all over the country, especially to governor Walker. Two thirds of the 30 million dollars in campaign contributions came from wealthy conservative donors outside of Wisconsin. The victory meant that the conservatives' attempts to kill off the American labor movement are now likely to increase in intensity. The trade union movement lost an important battle in Wisconsin, and its future is now even gloomier.

Jonathan Chait wrote on his blog in New York Magazine:

"Walker's win will certainly provide a blueprint for fellow Republicans. When they gain a majority, they can quickly move to not just wrest concessions from the public sector unions but completely destroy them, which in turn eliminates one of the strongest sources of political organization for the Democratic Party. And whatever backlash develops, it's probably not enough to outweigh the political benefit. Walker has pioneered a tactic that will likely become a staple of Republican governance."

Trade unions have played an important role in America over the years -- to push for a 40-hour work week, holidays, pensions, health care, but in recent decades, especially since President Reagan's years in the White House, they have stood under almost constant attack. The result is that union membership in the private sector has steadily decreased, from 25 percent in the 1970s to 7 percent today. In the public sector, unions have coped better with membership figures of around 36 percent.

It is precisely these public employees who were targeted by Walker and Kasich in their attempts at "union busting." Ultimately, this is also a struggle for political power in America, and it will go on.

As the American union movement's membership has declined in the private sector, the decline has been accompanied by a significant increase in economic inequality. Political leaders have contributed to this development with a lack of support for the country's trade unions, according to Hacker and Pierson in their book "Winner-Take-All Politics." The declining membership numbers, they believe, are major contributor to the growing economic inequality in America.

"It has created a political and economic vacuum that has proven deadly to those seeking to redress winner-take-all inequality and friendly to those seeking to promote and consolidate it."

The fact that the Republican Party has become the white middle class/working-class party is not only illogical, it's sad. How could it have come to this? It's the result of the tax revolts in the 70s and of President Reagan's victory in 1980, sweeping in with the message that the federal government in Washington, DC was the problem, not the solution, for America and its future. America's workers identified with that message and abandoned the Democratic Party in large numbers. In the South, this flight also had racial undertones dating back to the time when the region's Democrats switched parties to protest against Lyndon Johnson's mid 60s civil rights and voting rights reforms.

White voters in the South have not yet returned to the Democratic Party. The South is now a Republican Party stronghold and is expected to remain so for the foreseeable future.

When it comes to struggles over social values, the abortion battle is in a class of its own, both in terms of its bitterness and its length. It plays a prominent role in every election campaign -- "pro-choice" = right to abortions = Democrats; "pro-life" = ban on abortions = Republicans.

The right to abortion was established by the Supreme Court in Roe v. Wade, in 1973, but many opponents hope the Court's conservative majority will re-consider. For Slate magazine's excellent legal writer Dahlia Lithwick, Roe v. Wade is already dead. In reality, it is no longer the law of the land, even if no one says so out loud. She points to hundreds of new laws and regulations out in the States restricting the right to abortion. All of them are illegal. But the abortion opponents ignore this and win, victory after victory.

The striking fact about the abortion debate and the Conservatives' support for a total ban is that the groups that ordinarily most strongly oppose the government and government involvement in their lives, now want the government – the state -- to ban abortion. Suddenly, their obsession with individual rights and freedoms, for which they fight so hard, no longer applies. Suddenly, the government is the solution in their efforts to deny women the right to an abortion and the freedom to decide what happens to their own bodies.

Abortion opponents argue that abortion is murder and the most conservative among them believe that abortion should never be permitted, not even in cases of rape, incest or when a woman's life is in danger. But the same conservatives see no problem with the state executing people for serious crimes ever since the Supreme Court in 1977 gave the go-ahead for executions to resume after a years-long moratorium.

Since then, 1,267 people have been executed in the United States, 477 of them in Texas alone. 3,251 prisoners are currently on death row awaiting execution. The death penalty is allowed in 33 American states. China, Iran and Saud Arabia execute more people, but among western democracies America is in a class of its own.

Can this be said better than by Robert Scheer, liberal journalist on the blog "Truthdig?"

"There is something stunningly disgraceful about the company we (the U.S.) keep on this issue ... Execution is a means of summarily ending the pursuit of justice rather than advancing it."

America is also in a class of its own when it comes to the number of murders and the number of inmates in its jails. America's murder rate is more than twice as high as Europe's, or five per 100,000 people per year, compared to two in Europe. There are 2.3 million inmates in America's prisons, almost one per 100,000 inhabitants, the highest in the world, and four times more than the world average.

The right to bear arms is guaranteed by the Constitution's Second Amendment, where it says, "A well-organized militia, being necessary to the security of a free State, the right of the people to keep and bear Arms, shall not be infringed."

But, according to Harvard Professor Jill Lepore in a big article in The New Yorker in April 2012, many gun laws have been introduced over the years, even as long ago as in Kentucky and Louisiana in 1813, which forbade anyone to carry a "concealed" weapon. Even one of today's most powerful lobby groups, the National Rifle Association (NRA), founded in 1871, supported many of these laws, among them the major gun law, the National Firearms Act from 1934.

The assassination of President John F. Kennedy in 1963 fundamentally changed the gun debate, according to Lepore. It became part of the "rights revolution" -- the right to bear arms, including hidden weapons – as part of every American's fundamental rights and freedoms. No longer did this have anything to do with the right to form an armed militia or with general defense. The Second Amendment began to be reinterpreted. With the Reagan victory in 1980, the first president the NRA ever endorsed, gun rights became part of the broad, conservative, anti-government message.

Since then, the NRA has repeatedly demonstrated its power, most recently in the so-called "Stand Your Ground" laws that was enacted in Florida in 2005, and is now the law in two dozen states. This law, strongly backed by the NRA, gives a person the right to use deadly force against another person "in self-defense," if he or she feels threatened in their home, in their garden, or even their car.

The law attracted enormous attention in the spring of 2012, when Trayvon Martin, a black, unarmed 17-year old was shot to death by an armed Neighborhood Watch volunteer in a residential area in Florida. It took a month for the volunteer, George Zimmerman, to be arrested and charged with the second degree murder. A jury eventually found him not guilty.

Critics call the law "Shoot First" and want it abolished. Prosecutors in Florida agree –it is widely abused, they say, including by gang members, who use it to justify shooting rival gang members. New York City Mayor Michael Bloomberg is a leading spokesman for stricter gun laws:

"These laws have not made our country safer; they have made us less safe…all Americans already have a right to defend themselves with commensurate force."

"These 'Shoot First' laws," he continued, "have nothing to do with that or with the exercise of Second Amendment rights. Instead, they justify civilian gunplay and invite vigilante justice and retribution with disastrous results."

There are no indications that America's weapons culture is about to undergo major changes. In recent decades, the right to carry weapons, including concealed weapons, has become almost absolute. Several Supreme Court opinions have contributed to this.

It has been a little over 30 years since Ronald Reagan was gunned as he left a hotel in Washington. He was seriously injured, but survived, and he was re-elected and remained U.S. president for eight years. But Jim Brady, Reagan's press spokesman, who also injured in the assassination attempt, was never able to work again. He and his wife Sarah became the country's leading advocates for stricter gun laws in America. And they had some success. After many years of struggle and contentious debate, Congress voted for the Brady Handgun Violence Prevention Act.

I met Jim and Sarah Brady in the late 80's. Brady, who had been paralyzed and suffered speech difficulties, displayed his famous fighting spirit and humor and said, "You must play with the cards you have in hand, and I try to do that as best I can."

Since the Reagan and Brady tragedy, there have been so many more: Columbine, Blacksburg, Tucson, and, most recently, in December 2012, at the Sandy Hook Elementary School in Newtown, Connecticut. During these years not much has happened regarding gun control. Armed Americans continue to shoot and kill some 100,000 people across the nation every year.

A gloomy Sarah Brady wrote recently in the Washington Post that she understands those who think nothing ever changes about gun control in America.

But she struggles on, despite a strange silence from President Obama during his entire first term, a silence that was not broken until the Newtown tragedy. Then, finally, he launched an all-out effort for stricter gun control.

"We can't tolerate this anymore. These tragedies must end. And to end them, we must change," Obama declared and promised something he had not previously promised during his four years in the White House:

"In the coming weeks, I will use whatever power this office holds to engage my fellow citizens — from law enforcement to mental health professionals to parents and educators — in an effort aimed at preventing more tragedies like this. Because what choice do we have? We can't accept events like this as routine. Are we really prepared to say that we're powerless in the face of such carnage, that the politics are too hard? Are we prepared to say that such violence visited on our children year after year after year is somehow the price of our freedom?"

It was a valiant effort, but in the end, the gun lobby once more proved too strong. Nothing happened, no new gun laws were enacted. It was a bitter defeat for all those who are for sensible gun laws in America.

America's population, now 313 million, is undergoing major changes, and as those changes happen, the country is changing, too. Between 2000 and 2010, Hispanics and Asians increased by far the fastest of all population groups, each by 43 percent. The country is becoming more and more bilingual. Where I live just outside Washington, DC, Spanish can be heard everywhere, and many shops communicate in two languages. In other parts of America, especially along the border with Mexico, Spanish is spoken almost exclusively.

America's white population is still the largest and it makes up two thirds of the population. But it is growing the slowest and is already a minority in Texas, California, New Mexico and Hawaii. In the spring of 2012, it was officially reported that fewer than half of all children born in the previous year were white.

The new figures were seen as a demographics milestone. Hispanics now amount to 50.5 million people, and that does not include the 11 million illegal immigrants, mainly Hispanics. Hispanics now account for 16 percent of America's population, surpassing the African-Americans, the country's former largest minority, who now number 42 million. There are more Mexican immigrants than immigrants from any other country in America' history, although new figures suggest that 1.4 million -- mostly illegal immigrants -- have returned to Mexico in the past five years. It is impossible to say whether this trend, which mainly stems from the U.S. economic crisis, will continue.

The Asian population amounts to 14.7 million. As America's ethnic groups go through these major shifts, customs and traditions are changing rapidly. This is particularly evident in the increase of interracial marriages, which were banned throughout the South as late as 1967. In 1980, three percent of all marriages were multi-ethnic. Today, the figure is over eight percent.

The question is who will benefit politically from these ethnic shifts. Today, the answer is the Democrats, who have the overwhelming support of the Hispanics. The Republican Party is a predominantly white party, and if that does not change, its future is bleak. To survive long-term, the party needs to rethink its strategy and attract new voters from the major ethnic groups.

No such recalibration could be seen during the Republican primary election campaign -- quite the opposite. The Republican presidential candidates' hostility to immigration reform and to America's 11 million illegal immigrants led to an overwhelming support for Obama among the large ethnic voting groups: 93 percent of the African-Americans, 71 percent of the Hispanics, and 73 percent of the Asians.

Centuries ago, Alexis de Tocqueville wrote that nothing is more annoying in the daily contact with the Americans than their patriotism -- "the last refuge of the scoundrel," as Tony Judt wrote. American patriotism is still annoying to outsiders. Americans often know little about the outside world, but they still do not want to hear criticism about their own country and its political system.

I was reminded of that again, recently. Given the political paralysis in Washington, maybe, I thought, the parliamentary system did not look so bad. Just look at Canada! I recently watched on C-Span a debate in the Canadian Parliament, both in English and French, which was followed by a vote of no confidence. The conservative government fell by 156 votes to 145 about the next year's budget. The very next day, Prime Minister Stephen Harper handed in his resignation and Parliament was dissolved. An election followed three weeks later. So quick, so efficient. I envied the Canadians. This stands in stark contrast to the never-ending U.S. election campaigns which come at a cost of billions of dollars.

Elections in America have become an industry, which is growing every year, and on which more and more are economically dependent: TV stations, election experts, campaign advisers, advertising people, hotels, car rental agencies, airlines, journalists, polling institutes. I am afraid that for those who seek real change to this system, it's only a pipe dream.

Every time I am in New York, I am astounded by how millions of New Yorkers live together and do so in a mostly friendly and caring way. Every day in New York, people make compromises and show consideration for one other in a way that the politicians in Washington and the loud talking heads on cable TV never do. On the subway, in the shops, restaurants, and on the sidewalks, you always hear a friendly "excuse me" or "pardon me". And, often, "Have a nice day!" I love it.

Jon Stewart, the comedian who is at the same time a serious observer of American politics, came to Washington a few years ago and held a big, public meeting with Stephen Colbert, another extraordinarily funny and politically-focused comedian on television's Comedy Central. The National Mall was packed as several hundred thousand people gathered in the warm and festive afternoon. Stewart talked about the importance of getting along, of tolerance and unity, about the importance of being considerate and having respect for one another in order to get anything done, especially here in Washington, where the knives are drawn. And he showed a video of New Yorkers in rush hour, driving separately one by one, each taking his or her turn, into the darkness of the tunnel under the Hudson River to New Jersey on the other side. He used the video clip to illustrate how cooperation works even though no one in those cars knew each other or asked what the other did or thought. In those cars, Stewart said, are all of us who live in America:

"These cars - that's a schoolteacher who probably thinks his taxes are too high. He's going to work. There's another car -- a woman with two small kids who cannot really think about anything else right now. The lady's in the NRA and she loves Oprah. There's another car -- an investment banker, gay, also likes Oprah. Another car's a Latino carpenter. Another car -- a fundamentalist vacuum salesman, an atheist obstetrician, a Mormon Jay-Z fan. But this is us."

"Every one of the cars that you see," Stewart continued, "is filled with individuals of strong belief and principles they hold dear – often principles and beliefs in direct opposition to their fellow travelers. And yet these millions of cars must somehow find a way to squeeze one by one into a mile-long 30-foot wide tunnel carved underneath a mighty river... And they do it. Concession-by-concession. You go. Then I'll go. You go. Then I'll go. You go. Then I'll go. Oh, my God, is that an NRA sticker on your car? Is that an Obama sticker on your car? Well, that's OK -- you go and then I'll go."

In California, where I first arrived and where I have returned many times to visit and to study and to work, the dream and pride and promise of the Golden State, dating all the way back to the 1849 gold rush, has been crushed. The roads, once the state's pride, can't handle all the cars.

Commuters commute ever longer distances, often many hours in each direction, and for the most part, by themselves, one in each car. Public transport is still substandard, particularly rail services. Schools that once were among the best in the country are now ranked among the last. Crime is a problem. The prisons are so full that the Supreme Court ordered the state to cut drastically its prison population.

In 1945, after World War II and until 1960, polls showed that Californians were enthusiastic about their home state and its future. But negativism slowly crept in, including doubts and complaints about taxes. People found they could no longer afford to live the Californian dream, which was behind the tax revolt of 1978, officially known as Proposition 13, in which the majority of California's population voted to freeze property taxes at 1975 levels. Proposition 13 also regulated future tax increases for both private and commercial properties.

The referendum's outcome has cost California billions of dollars in lost tax revenues, a shortfall which has mainly affected the school system and from which it has still not recovered. Besides the schools, lost tax revenues have also negatively affected other public investments, which had been the foundation for the state's successes: universities, parks, roads, canals and water systems, the magnificent California coast, and all its splendid nature. In Forbes magazine's list today, Stockton, is America's most miserable city, followed by Miami, Florida with three other inland California cities coming in third to fifth place: Merced, Modesto, and Sacramento. Stockton's eventually went bankrupt, at the time the largest city in America ever to do so. That "honor" befell Detroit this year.

Karen Greenberg at Fordham University Law School Center on National Security is pessimistic when she thinks of today's America and what the future may bring for this country. We were not ready for a world without borders, she said when I interviewed her, we were not ready for the 21st Century. We have always fought against the global community as an equal partner, but how do we reconcile our "exceptionalism" with our determination to dominate the world?

"Yes, I am sad. Leadership becomes more and more difficult. Obama's intentions were good. Conservatism in America? Sure, we are a conservative country, but to be conservative and violate the Constitution are two completely different things. What happened to the Republicans? What happened to the Eisenhower Republicans?"

The debate about if President Obama was born in the United States is one of the saddest, and, for the country and the president, a most humiliating debate. The "birther" discussion, with its serious racist undertones, should never have taken place and should never have received the attention it did.

But powerful conservative political interests, as well as strong commercial interests on Fox News and other conservative TV- and radio stations, exploited it and they did not want to let it go.

The whole matter should really have been ignored, commented law professor Sherrilyn Ifill, who is black, in a television interview. It had, she said, nothing to do with where Obama was born, it had to do with his race. Would Obama have been subjected to these humiliating questions from Donald Trump, Sarah Palin, Michele Bachmann and the whole bunch of other "birthers" if his father had not been an African from Kenya?

Many former presidential candidates, including Mitt Romney and Donald Trump, and presidents like Thomas Jefferson and Andrew Jackson had one or even both parents who were born abroad. And Obama's opponent in 2008, John McCain, was born on a U.S. military base in Panama - is that America? A reasonable question, for it has to do with whether McCain was actually born in America and, thus, eligible to become president. But there was no discussion about McCain – why?

"Sure, Obama is fighting against racism," said Stanford professor Clayborne Carson in my interview. "Just look at the weak support he received in the South, in the Bible Belt, among the white voters there -- less than five percent, less than ten percent in many precincts. No, the election of Obama has not meant a turning point for race relations in America."

When Obama finally requested that his full birth certificate from Hawaii be released after three years in the White House, it was intended to put an end to this sad debate. He had been forced to do so by the "birther" movement, forced to prove that he was as much an American as any other and that he met the American Constitution's conditions that a president must be born in the United States.

The certificate said that Barack Hussein Obama II was born in Honolulu, Hawaii on August 4, 1961, and that his mother's name was Stanley Ann Durham and his fathers, Barack Hussein Obama.

He said that he now hoped that this debate was over. That has happened, apart from a few minor efforts to keep the issue alive. And it was really no issue in the 2012 presidential election. Still, the debate had been unprecedented debate in modern American politics, and, perhaps, its saddest legacy.

The political system in America is built on power sharing and checks and balances. The result, someone once said, is that it's hard to get things done, but it's easy to put a stop to them. The system invites, and yes, demands compromises, if it is to work. But it does not work when the two political parties are ever more rigid ideologically and ever more reluctant to compromise or negotiate. Political polarization characterizes Washington today, and in this "balkanized" political system, it is only in moments of real danger that meaningful reforms can come about, as The New Yorker's John Cassidy once wrote.

But the politicians in Washington apparently see no such threat today, even though the economy is verging on a new depression. America's democracy is in trouble. How can we have confidence in a system that allows itself to be bought and sold in a way that the Supreme Court's decision in Citizens United now allows.

Since that decision, there have been millions of dollars in new donations from men like Harold Clark Simmons, the 80-year-old billionaire in Texas, who donated over 18 million dollars to defeat President Obama. He has of course the right to say, as he did to the Wall Street Journal recently, that it does not matter who among the Republican candidates wins, they would all be a better president than the socialist Obama, America's most dangerous man.

But for America's wealthiest to have such leverage in this country's democracy is most depressing. There must be a better system.

And how can we have confidence in a political system in the face of the dumbing down that was on display during the Republican primary election campaign in 2012? Is it really enough to be a manager of a pizza chain to become president in the U.S.? And why are demagogic television and radio voices like Rush Limbaugh and Glenn Beck taken seriously?

This political dumbing-down is the legacy of Sarah Palin, wrote Richard Cohen in the Washington Post. After Sarah Palin, it seems to have become a badge of honor to be ignorant -- vote for me, I know nothing and I hate the same things you do! Experience, knowledge, to have accomplished something, it is as if that has come to mean very little or nothing at all.

The low voter turnout in American elections has long been a fact, but it is a problem that does not seem to come closer to a solution. About 40 percent of America's eligible voters never vote. In the Presidential election in 2008, turnout was 61.6 percent while only 40.9 percent participated in the 2010 mid-term election. In 2008, Obama captured almost 70 million votes. In 2010, the Republicans in the House of Representatives received a total of 30 million votes. How can the Republicans argue, which they do, that they have a national mandate behind them, wondered political scientist Andrew Hacker recently in an article in the New York Review of Books.

Ahead of the 2012 elections, there was an intense battle about the right to vote and about voting procedures, a battle that resulted from proposals in many states where Republicans ruled. In 15 States, new voting rules were proposed and in some States implemented.

The main requirement of these new rules is that voters must to have an ID card with a photo in order to vote. Show a photo ID to vote – it seems reasonable, one would think seem.
But the problem is that many Americans, particularly lower-income Americans, do not have such photo IDs, it's often complicated to get them, they cost money and many cannot afford them, so these eligible voters will essentially be disenfranchised.

Keeping such voters from voting would benefit the Republicans, because most of them tend to vote for the Democrats. The Obama administration has sued several states, which had to back down, and the battle over these new voting laws did not have a large effect on the 2012 election.

In the second decade of the "War on Terror," America is still under threat and often on high alert. To put an end to this war, wrote David Cole, a law professor at Georgetown University in 2011 in an article in the New York Review of Books, Obama must resolve the future of the prison at Guantanamo Bay. Cole added that if the president wants to build on Osama bin Laden's death, he has come to some kind of official closing in the torture debate.

"Our collective reluctance to deal with our past threatens to undermine our core values," wrote Cole, whose views met with little sympathy among the Republican presidential candidates. With the exception of Ron Paul and Jon Huntsman, all of them expressed their support for "enhanced interrogation techniques," including water boarding of captured terrorist suspects.

Which America?

I don't know, and maybe I have come to know less and less during my years in America. The American dream is not credible anymore and neither is American "exceptionalism."

America has problems, economic problems, political problems, social problems, but major and necessary decisions are not made to resolve them for they require compromises, and in this era of ideological strife and political paralysis, compromise is a dirty word.

It's difficult to see how even the constant and famous, or perhaps infamous, American optimism can take the country forward. Still, in spite of chaotic governance, it is the broad and exciting public debate, the readiness for new ideas, the energy, that give hope for the future.

In the White House, America has a president who might have been politically naïve and inexperienced, but who is also a man of intelligence and integrity. His first term was free of scandals, and he represented a new and steadily more diverse America. He sought to bring about change with a new constructive tone in Washington, a new way to conduct politics. He sought compromise across party lines and unity among citizens -- but he failed – and he has been deeply disappointed by the strength of contradictions in American politics, by the unwillingness to compromise, even when it came to the national interest of the United States.

Still, his victory in November of 2012 was a victory for what is best in America -- tolerance, optimism, diversity, and openness. A loss would have meant a step back, a retreat, and it would have encouraged a change to a more selfish and cynical policy, which unfortunately also is part of today's America, and its disregard for the poor and the minorities.

"Oh, America, sweet America" ... Ray Charles sang in his beautiful rendition of "America the Beautiful," a song that, in my mind, ought to be the American national anthem. Yes, "sweet America," what should I do with you?

The legendary Swiss-born photographer Robert Frank once said when he arrived in America for the first time in 1947, "I felt as if the door had opened - and you were free." But Frank added, "how lonely it can be in America, what a hard country it is."

Which America?

Yes, America is a land of dreams, but it's no dreamland. Still, I am a citizen now, and America is my home.

THE AUTHOR

Klas Bergman, born and raised in Stockholm, Sweden, has spent most of his adult life abroad, primarily in the United States ever since his student days in California in the 1960s. He is a graduate of Stanford University where he also spent a year as a Professional Journalism Fellow.

A veteran journalist, Bergman has reported from many parts of the world, Western and Eastern Europe, North Africa and the Middle East, Central America, Canada, and the United States, primarily for the Swedish daily Dagens Nyheter and the Christian Science Monitor.

He is the author of two previous books. The first, published in Sweden in 1981 and called "Tredje bordet från höger" (The Third Table from the Right), was the result of his years as a foreign correspondent in the Balkans and Eastern Europe. In the fall of 2012, his second book, "Amerika – drömmarnas land" was published, also in Sweden. Land of Dreams: A Reporter's Journey from Sweden to America is the revised and updated English version of this book.

Klas Bergman lives in Silver Spring Maryland, just outside Washington DC, where he writes a blog, mostly on politics, called "Random notes on America," and is at work on a new book.

BIBLIOGRAPHY

Alter, Jonathan. The Promise – President Obama, Year One, New York, 2010.
Ben-Veniste, Richard. The Emperor's New Clothes – Exposing the Truth from Watergate to 9/11, New York, 2009.
Bernstein, Carl & Woodward, Bob. All the President's Men, New York, 1974.
Cannon, Lou. Reagan, New York, 1982.
Cannon, Lou & Cannon, Carl M. Reagan's Disciple – George W. Bush's Troubled Quest for a Presidential Legacy, New York, 2008.
Carson, Clayborne. In Struggle – SNCC and the Black Awakening of the 1960s, Cambridge, MA 1981.
Cole, David. The Torture Memos – Rationalizing the Unthinkable, New York, 2009.
Conaway, James. The Kingdom in the Country, Boston, 1987.
Dickenson, Mollie. Thumbs Up, New York, 1987.
Drew, Elizabeth. Politics and Money – The New Road to Corruption, New York, 1983.
Dylan, Bob. Chronicles – Volume One, New York, 2004.
Frazier, Ian. Great Plains, New York, 1989.
Garreau, Joel. The Nine Nations of North America, New York, 1982.
Hacker, Jacob S. & Pierson, Paul. Winner-Take-All Politics, New York 2010.
Hagstrom, Jerry & Peirce, Neal R. The Book of America, New York, 1983.
Halberstam, David. The Making of a Quagmire – America and Vietnam During the Kennedy Era, New York, 1965.
Halberstam, David. The Children, New York 1999.
Harris, David. Dreams Die Hard – Three Men's Journeys through the Sixties, New York, 1982.

Harris, John F. The Survivor – Bill Clinton in the White House, New York, 2005.

Heileman, John & Halperin, Mark. Game Change – The Race of a Lifetime, New York, 2010.

Ifill, Gwen. The Breakthrough – Politics and Race in the Age of Obama, New York, 2009.

Ivins, Molly. Shrub – The Short but Happy Life of George W. Bush, New York, 2000.

Judt, Tony. The Memory Chalet, New York, 2010.

Kerouac, Jack. On the Road, New York, 1957.

Kesey, Ken. One Flew Over the Cuckoo's Nest, New York, 1962.

Least Heat Moon, William. Blue Highways – A Journey into America, New York, 1982.

Lewis, Anthony. Gideon's Trumpet, New York, 1964.

Lewis, Michael. The Big Short, New York, 2010.

Lichtblau, Eric. Bush's Law – The Remaking of American Justice, New York, 2008.

Lukas, J. Anthony. Common Ground – A Turbulent Decade in the Lives of Three American Families, New York, 1985.

Lyman, Richard W. Stanford in Turmoil – Campus Unrest 1966-1972, Stanford, CA 2009.

MacPherson, Myra. Long time Passing – Vietnam and the Haunted Generation, New York, 1984.

Mann, James. Rise of the Vulcans – The History of Bush's War Cabinet, New York, 2004.

Mann, Thomas E. & Ornstein, Norman J. It's Even Worse Than It Looks – How the American Constitutional System Collided With the New Politics of Extremism, New York, 2012.

Mayer, Jane & McManus, Doyle. Landslide –The Unmaking of the President 1984-1988, Boston, MA 1988.

Mayer, Jane & Abramson, Jill. Strange Justice – The Selling of Clarence Thomas, New York, 1994.

Mayer, Jane. The Dark Side – The Inside Story of How the War on Terror turned into a War on American Ideals, New York, 2008.
Medsger, Betty. Framed – The New Right Attack on Chief Justice Rose Bird and the Courts, New York, 1983.
Nelson Limerick, Patricia, The Legacy of Conquest – The Unbroken Past of the American West, New York, 1987.
Obama, Barrack. Dreams from My Father, New York, 1995.
Obama, Barrack. The Audacity of Hope, New York, 2006.
Palmer, John L. & Sawhill, Isabel V. The Reagan Record, Washington, DC, 1984.
Palmer, John L. (Editor) Perspectives on the Reagan Years, Washington, DC, 1986.
Phillips, Kevin. The Politics of Rich and Poor – Wealth and the American Electorate in the Reagan Aftermath, New York, 1990.
Reid, T.R. The Healing of America, New York, 2009.
Reisner, Marc. Cadillac Desert – The American West and Its Disappearing Water, New York, 1986.
Remnick, David. The Bridge – The Life and Rise of Barack Obama, New York, 2010.
Roberts, Gene & Klibanoff, Hank. The Race Beat – The Press, the Civil Rights Struggle, and the Awakening of a Nation, New York, 2007.
Stegner, Wallace. The American West as Living Space, Ann Arbor, MI, 1987.
Stegner, Wallace. American Places, Moscow, Idaho, 1983.
Thompson, Hunter S. Fear and Loathing in Las Vegas, New York, 1971.
Thompson, Hunter S. Fear and Loathing on the Campaign Trail '72, New York, 1973.
de Tocqueville, Alexis. Democracy in America, New York, 1969.
Parry, Robert. Secrecy & Privilege – Rise of the Bush Dynasty from Watergate to Iraq, Arlington, VA, 2004.

Parry, Robert. Neck Deep – The Disastrous Presidency of George W. Bush, Arlington, VA, 2007.
Schrag, Peter. Paradise Lost – California's Experience, America's Future, Berkeley, CA, 1998.
Toobin, Jeffrey. A Vast Conspiracy, New York, 1999.
Toobin, Jeffrey. Too Close to Call – The Thirty-Six-Day Battle to Decide the 2000 Election, New York 2001.
Toobin, Jeffrey. The Nine – Inside The Secret World of the Supreme Court, New York, 2007.
Viorst, Milton. Fire in the Streets – America in the 1960s, New York, 1979.
Wills, Garry. Reagan's America – Innocents at Home, New York, 1987.
Wolfe, Tom. The Electric Kool-Aid Acid Test, New York 1968.
Woodward, Bob & Armstrong, Scott. The Brethren – Inside the Supreme Court, New York, 1979.

Made in the USA
San Bernardino, CA
19 December 2014